Sustainable Innovation

Michele Visciola

Sustainable Innovation

Thinking as Behavioral Scientists, Acting as Designers

Springer

Michele Visciola
Experientia
Zurich, Switzerland

ISBN 978-3-031-18750-6 ISBN 978-3-031-18751-3 (eBook)
https://doi.org/10.1007/978-3-031-18751-3

This Springer imprint is published by the registered company Springer Nature Switzerland AG
The registered company address is: Gewerbestrasse 11, 6330 Cham, Switzerland

To Daphne and future generations who will have to manage, with creativity and critical thinking, many of the challenges our generation was not able to overcome.

Acknowledgments

This book collects many years of my consulting and teaching activity. It is always nice to think of friends, collaborators, and colleagues who over the years have stimulated reflections, observations, and practices. If I look back at the last 20 years, I should mention hundreds of people who have marked my action as consultant and professor. Some colleagues and collaborators are expressly mentioned in my book. My gratitude goes unconditionally to all those who have collaborated in a stable way or only in the limited context of some of Experientia's projects. Their active and critical participation has been able to guarantee recurring success and full independence of thought and interpretation in the different roles played by all of us while thinking as behavioral scientists and acting as designers.

Testimonial

Guido Palazzo Professor of Business Ethics at HEC Lausanne, University of Lausanne.

"The ecological crisis is accelerating, and our societies need to profoundly change. While in the past, it was often naively assumed that such a change would simply result from technological innovations, we now understand that the ecological transition requires a holistic perspective. The success of sustainable innovations depends on a thorough analysis of the cognitive (both psychological and cultural) conditions in which they are embedded. Michele Visciola's book provides the cognitive toolbox for the design of impactful sustainable innovations."

Don Norman Distinguished Professor and Founding Director (Retired) Design Lab, University of California, San Diego USA.

"Michele Visciola's book provides a deep, informative analysis of the many factors that go into people's behavioral and thinking processes.

The book builds upon the work of the numerous scholars who have examined the issues to provide a coherent summary of the theoretical implications, but then the narrative goes further to show how the ideas can be put into practice to produce changes in everyday behavior and thought through sustainable innovation programs. To help people to change their behavior and thought patterns is one of the most difficult components of all innovation endeavors. But these are necessary if we are to move from today's complex difficulties to produce a more stable, livable, and sustainable world.

Furthermore, the book shows how behavioral science can improve the activities and actions of designers, elaborating the idea that design and behavioral sciences can be better integrated to address innovation challenges.

The book combines both fluid and enjoyable discussions on innovation and change in behavior and cultures as well as sections that are deeply packed arguments and examples to focus on.

Because the book goes deeply into the open advancements of scientific work, the deep substantive discussions that result require careful study, reflection, and discussion. Those who spend the necessary effort will be amply rewarded."

Elizabeth Churchill - Executive Vice President of the Association of Computing Machinery (ACM); Director of User Experience at Google.

Key to our future is sustainability. Drawing on the work of many scholars and many examples from his own experience with research programs over many years, Michele Visciola showcases how we can change the way we think about the design of behavioral change to move toward sustainable ecosystemic, sociotechnical systems.

Rather than focusing on technological solutionism, Visciola shows how we need to design ecosystems of context-sensitive, collective behavioral change through thoughtfully designed prevention and intervention programs.

In our thinking, we need to move from classic models of "technological readiness" to models of "sustainable innovation readiness" at the individual (cognitive), social (participatory), and cultural (policy) levels.

We need to chart and measure impact from many angles over time and foster personal and community awareness and engagement for change. From pixels to policies, an integrated approach to designing behavior change that addresses sustainability is possible.

Contents

About the Author

Michele Visciola is president and cofounder of Experientia (www.experientia.com). Over the course of his career, he has directed project teams on prominent topics, anticipating trends, and developing new research languages, in numerous sectors such as: economics of services for small landowners (Kenya, 2013); services for the elderly masterplan (Singapore, 2013–2014); personal finance management and design of digital aids to facilitate savings (Europe, 2015); behavioral economics for investments and savings in the retail bank (Italy, 2016); fossil energy footprint reduction to zero (Europe 2013–ongoing); patient-centered service models to facilitate behavior change and lifestyles improvement (Switzerland and Europe 2017–ongoing). Michele has more than 10 years of teaching experience divided between Politecnico di Milano ("Digital culture for designers") and Bicocca University Milan ("Evolution of user research methods"). He has written several scientific publications, articles, and books; was part of the core team that founded World Usability Day. He is Master and Professor of the DeTao Academy in behavioral design and modeling.

Part I
A Common Ground for Sustainable and Responsible Innovation

Abstract Innovation without sustainability leaves out large swathes of population or generates maladaptive or misappropriate behaviors. Normally, the human factor accounts for 40–50% of technological innovation being a success or a failure. Technology and business models can address Agenda 2030s cultural and behavioral challenges if they successfully involve the citizenry and people affected by the challenge, improving literacy, skills, and cooperation. Economic goals through sustainable innovation (SI) should also include the *intention* to modify behavior and culture, considering welcome consequences and avoiding or limiting unwanted ones. Innovative solutions will be sustainable if they can retain individual and group differences while offering greater benefits for the common good. If designers and life, human, and social behavioral scientists work together, they can add value, offering process and method creativity, promoting behavioral changes to the advantage of sustainable models in all fields. A new paradigm recognizing professional consultants as SI agents can then flourish.

We need to know what we share to become aware of how we differ. I have always been mesmerized by the variety of human knowledge, something I discovered when I had just turned 13 and had recently become aware that education does not begin and end with set schoolbooks. The Head of the Classics High School I attended gathered books and magazines for the school library following his own rhyme and reason, and occasionally needed someone to help him tidy the largest room of the building that he had understandably reserved to the purpose.

One afternoon after school while I was volunteering my services at the library, he regaled all of his "assistant librarians," including me, with one of his favorite stories. According to his published and rightly highly commended research, at the time the sole Region of Apulia (the "heel" of the Boot of Italy) claimed at least 84 regional spoken languages or dialects. There were derivations and references to at least four major ethnolinguistic groups: Latin, Greek, Arabic, and Franco-Provençal. His book included 84 versions of the Parable of the Prodigal Son,[1] one for each of Apulia's

[1] Melillo [1].

dialects, with a description of the method used and the phonetics for each dialect (see Fig. 1). The Headmaster also delighted in highlighting some differences among the various dialects of Daunia—the school district. He then asked all the youngsters within range to tell him where they were from so he could get to know them and identified commonalities. He took the opportunity to tell us to continue using our dialects at home, but to acquire the subtleties of the Italian language at school. In fact, our Headmaster was not only a brilliant original scholar of dialects and linguistic varieties but was also knowledgeable about his students' linguistic habits and aware of the difficulties and commitment required for us to adapt to our new context.

It took me years to appreciate the more general meaning of his extracurricular lesson: each context and situation requires adequate semantic codes and representations to relate to. At a certain point I understood that seamless communication in the family was the result of shared experience with the same people, daily routines, the memories, and meanings, all of which reduced the effort required to exchange and communicate. Were we to remain in the same context throughout, we would remain anchored to our daily routines and linguistic patterns and probably would not need new words and expressions unless we experienced unknown or unfamiliar events. In time, contexts change as well as the opportunities to learn, and as the reasons required to understand what is changing around us increase, we need to know how to foresee changes that affect the world we had become used to/acquainted with.

Evolutionary biologists refer to this adaptation as *multilevel selection* to indicate the specific pressure due to diverse environmental and social events offering the conditions to learn about and adapt to. As a result, an individual has better chances of

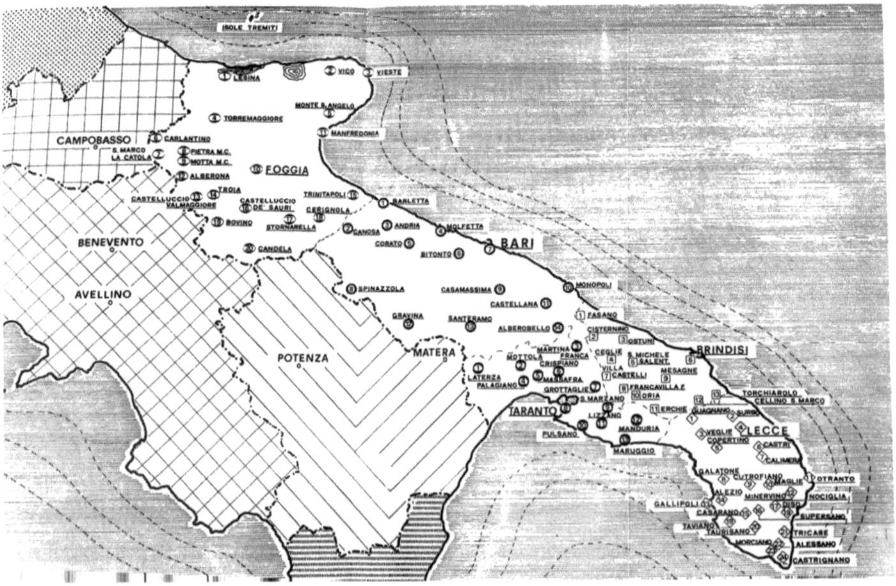

Fig. 1 Map of Apulia with its 84 dialects by area

surviving and reproducing in their environment, and the group becomes stronger, thus increasing its chances of survival, even when this is to the disadvantage of a single member. By sharing the same language, one enters a closer relation with others, developing implied and expressed cultural norms that make it possible to establish closer cooperation: intragroup ties become stronger as does group identity increasing the group's chances of survival. A biologist would say, the same individual adapts to selection pressure by absorbing the differences in context, cultural norms, and using their mother tongue at home and in their birthplace, while using a standard language—be it from their native country or from another—when working or living.

The above figure could be described otherwise if seen through the eyes of scholars from Life Sciences or Humanities: a cultural anthropologist would highlight "*cultural group selection*" where group culture develops on the basis of cultural traits. Absorbing the words and languages of other ethnic groups gives an advantage over the others, such as the preferential access to goods and commodities with distant peoples; a behavioral-evolutionary scholar, for instance a cognitive evolutionist, would highlight *cognitive automatisms or lock-ins*, automatic processes that no longer require controlled processes. As a result, the effort to adapt to selective pressure progressively decreases.

A social psychologist would analyze the level of self-efficacy attained thanks to language skills, thus increasing the ability to adapt. This enables a person to better control their environment and more successfully overcome the tests natural and social pressure present throughout their lives.

A methodology expert would focus on the empirical evidence debating why there is such a *large number of languages and dialects* in a relatively small strip of land. Such an expert would pick up on the fact that the selected text is well known both in literature and in painting, which means it is accessible to everyone. Lastly, the expert would also observe that the empirical evidence—that is, the 84 versions of the Parable—would pass all the experiential knowledge tests required to substantiate the study.

I could detail adding references to this short story to increase its level and strength of analysis so that we could infer the range of human knowledge. Probably some of you have already identified other central issues or found inspiration to develop a theme-based study using specialist tools or methods. Each facet highlighted by the story is rich in details and corresponds to specific areas of knowledge worthy of being funded in its early stages or in its further developments.

The availability or access to such a range of knowledge and methodological contributions holds great promise in dealing with the complex challenges we will have to address in the coming 10 years. In fact, we are slowly moving into a post-COVID era. The pandemic is and was dangerously strong and adds to the great challenges already on the agenda of the *Homo sapiens*'s emergency that have to be overcome not to perish: threatening climate change, the unstoppable increase in inequality, racism, and gender issues, the decline of a welfare state that maybe no longer be able to cope with the steep growth in chronic diseases and assisted elderly. As we shall see in the next chapters, when faced with such challenges, new solutions can be found and strategies outlined to overhaul our cultures and change our behaviors. Life and Human Sciences have been called to the front line to shape policies as well as the choices of the Green New Deal (GND) Agenda, the UN Sustainable Development Goals (SDG) and the strategies to meet the social challenges by 2030.

We have to shed specialist remits, acknowledging that a wide range of instruments will be effective only if and when we learn how to use and make them available by pooling specialist knowledge.

The urgency and the seriousness of these challenges call for us to develop new alliances, new interdisciplinary arenas, and a sort of lingua franca to bridge the gap and extend cooperation beyond our limited gazes. *Think like a scientist and act like a designer*!—the motto of this book. Specifically, I suggest the analytical skills of Life and Human Sciences should be implemented using the good designer's ability to synthesize. In other words, we need to piece knowledge, methods, techniques, and practices together as if the cogs of a wheel to be turned and use them appropriately and at the right times.

As we shall see in the chapters ahead, it is an alliance of disciplines, knowledge, and practices focusing on change and the evolution of behavior. *Modeling* is at the center of these techniques, highlighting the different ways to develop desirable, accessible, tailored sustainable strategies and processes of change. The challenges ahead are best expressed by the term "*sustainable innovations*," a definition I am suggesting to distinguish it from the term "*sustainable development*" that the previously mentioned (sustainability) agendas use: *green economy* and *Sustainable Economic Development Goals* (SEDGs). SEDGs speak to the economic, social, and environmental aspects of national development, promoting inclusion, developing growth goals compatible with defending the environment and common goods for future generations.

Public and private organizations' yearly Profit and Loss Balances are now completed by Corporate Social Responsibility (CSR) Reports that consider the social impact of the organization's economic activities to meet the UN Sustainable Development Goals (SDGs). Companies or organizations that subscribe to these goals are not only profit oriented but also consider the well-being and the quality of life of their staff and of the clients who use their products and services. It certainly is a commendable approach and is a beacon for any organization considering the ethical implications of their actions.

I also believe in highlighting the importance of *sustainable innovations* as a critical incitement for organizations not to underestimate the necessary commitment by the *whole* company (system). In fact, while *sustainable development* can be attained gradually by standardization, *sustainable innovation* (SI) requires the pace of change to become faster than it has been in the past 20 years of this century. Breaking away from the past, we have to clearly pursue a holistic approach to streamline while also holding onto complexity. Disciplines of change can be allied or converge, assuming the constant pressure to change each and every biological organism has, from cells to economic organizations.

However, innovation without sustainability leaves out large swathes of population or generates maladaptive or misappropriate behaviors. Normally, the human factor accounts for 40–50% of the chances of technological innovation being a success or a failure. Technology and business models can address Agenda 2030s cultural and behavioral challenges if they are successful in involving the citizenry and people affected by the challenge, improving literacy, skills, and cooperation. Economic goals through SI should also include the *intention* to modify behavior and culture, considering welcome consequences but above all how can we avoid or limit the unwanted outcomes.

"*Ecological validity*"—as it is called in Humanities—is the main force driving the convergence of the disciplines of change, which is the ability to develop general principles applicable on a large scale using small scale experiments and tests. We should not oversimplify by just referring to scale, which was the hallmark of innovation actions and developments right up to the postindustrial era that ended last century with first signs of what we now call digital economy. Cultural diversity has to be considered in developing innovative and sustainable solutions, so they may be accepted and prove adequate at the various levels of development in our societies. Innovative solutions will be sustainable if and when they are able to retain individual and group differences while offering greater benefits for the common good.

If designers and life, human, and social behavioral scientists work together, they can add value. This will make process and method creativity available, promote behavioral changes to the advantage of sustainable models in all fields. Our professional ethics will also have to advance likewise not to burden others with the responsibility of our actions: a new paradigm recognizing professional consultants as agents of sustainable innovation can then flourish.

Fortunately, we can build on preexisting foundations. The paradigm of human-centered design and its more recent offshoots, such as *behavioral* and *service design*, enshrine key reference systems. Furthermore, the public administration (civil service) *behavioral insight team* contributing to define changing behavior policies, such as the spread of collective *nudging* into the private, financial, and well-being spheres, is important additional points of reference. However, this is not enough, and we have to move further. A systematic change calls for a new alliance of Design, Social and Life Sciences, and Humanities, striving to a common goal. What roots do the disciplines of change share? and which are useful in outlining a common strategy for sustainable innovation? What knowledge skills should we pool to rise to the challenge of sustainable innovation? What can we do jointly to develop sustainable development models?

These are the themes I will discuss in the chapters and paragraphs that follow. I hope expert readers will find new topics or facets to address. Any reader new to this topic will have the opportunity to develop an opinion and appreciate up-to-date knowledge on how to meet innovation challenges. Lastly, a knowledgeable reader can further develop themes and skills underlying their professional expertise.

Reference

1. Melillo, M. (1980). *I pronomi dei dialetti di Puglia, nelle versioni della parabola del figliuol prodigo*. Università degli Studi di Bari.

Chapter 1
Understanding Behavior for Sustainable Innovations

Nearly 150 years ago, Wilhelm Wundt established the first laboratory of experimental psychology, marking the handover of research on human brain properties and functions from philosophy and medicine to psychophysiology.[1] Establishing the center was an act of great courage and determination. It was soon to become the late nineteenth century's most dynamic and creative research laboratory in Europe. It immediately attracted young researchers from the United States, coming to learn the new experimental discipline leading to the drive to the new utopian construction of a new civilization. The New World proved swifter and shrewder in finding applications for the new science previously limited to laboratory settings. Stanley Hall and Edward Titchener applied the new technique to education and training, James Cattell to work.

Hugo Münsterberg was a German who moved to the United States when William James invited him to lead the first laboratory of experimental psychology in Harvard. He applied the technique to the industrial/organizational sphere as well as being a journalist and developing poster and billboard for railway timetables or underground maps now a designer's purview. His experimental studies highlighted how colors, spacing, and typeface could affect attention and ability to remember. Nor should Walter Dill Scott be forgotten either: he studied in Leipzig with Wundt and, on returning to the Northwestern University in Chicago, became the director of the first experimental psychology laboratory. WD Scott was also one of the first to observe suggestibility in people and prone to acting on a not entirely rational manner. The techniques he developed to inform and convey visual and audio contents

[1] Wilhelm Wundt founded the first physiological psychology laboratory and the experimental psychology in Leipzig. Wundt's initial work was based on reviewing the work of his physiology teachers—including von Helmholtz and Müller: as a result, he based the paradigm of experimental research in psychology on introspection or systemic observation of what happens to our senses when they are subjected to stimulating experiences.

M. Visciola, *Sustainable Innovation*,
https://doi.org/10.1007/978-3-031-18751-3_1

are considered the basis of pre-digital advertising informing techniques such as AIDA (Attention, Interest, Desire, Action).

Although these techniques have been greatly criticized by cognitivists who currently dominate the world scene in Science Academia, there were other great American psychologists who successfully focused on analysis and behavioral change: John B. Watson and B. Frederic Skinner. The former was the founder of the Behaviorist School, a reaction to the introspective approach imported from Europe in experimental psychology. He strongly believed that behavior could be totally explained as a response to sensorial stimuli: just like a child's sudden crying is a natural reaction to fear caused by a sudden noise, salivation and appetite in adults are a reaction to something they see or the smell of a tasty dish. The aim of behaviorists' studies was limited exclusively to what could be observed in behavioral responses to environmental stimuli without dwelling on introspection.[2] Unlike early theories, Skinner's radical behaviorism included all the stimulus and response relationships in emotions and cognition. They also linked the analysis of cognitive properties to the same variables which determine or control behavior. All behavior was seen the result of a sequence of conditioning and reinforcement that create antecedents (reinforcements) able to discriminate and led to the avoidance of (punishment) other stimuli from the environment. Operant conditioning is a technique that led to a number of applications many of which still used today, for instance, in cognitive-behavioral therapy in correcting phobic psychopathologies. It is best known for its applications to social engineering, the so-called ASA (*applied behavioral analysis*, aka *behavioral engineering*) used to facilitate change of socially unacceptable behavior and to change (organizational behavioral management).[3]

The behavioral scientists mentioned so far shared the will to improve the people's living conditions, and the applications they developed were intended for social purposes and widely shared by democratic cultures. Empathy for humans' endeavors is part and parcel of experimental research: it is the thread that still links human and social sciences to their applications and the drive to further innovation and progress.

To this day, it is debatable whether these twentieth-century scientists wanted to manipulate behavior for commercial reasons or to favor the few with the knowledge of the weakness of human rationality—a topic extensively discussed in the later chapters. However, the challenges we now have as designers and behavior scientists no longer allow for the old rhetoric on other people's responsibility for the application of experimental research results. Nor can we use the alibi of the independence of those who pursued pure knowledge. Scientists and designers alike are equally responsible of what they plan or design and can foresee or imagine the impact or effect of their work, despite useful fine lines of distinction and detailed specifications. I refer readers to later chapters for an argument on this issue: the professional ethics of the agents of change is discussed in Part II.

---

[2] Watson [1]; Watson and Rayner [2]

[3] See Skinner [3].

Simultaneously with the emergence of electronic technologies, around the engineering schools where the first prototypes of digital computers were developed, the first nucleus of experimental psychologists dedicated to the study and understanding of cognitive processes was also born. These pioneers determined the prevalence of cognitivism over behaviorism and also were successful in other areas of application. Joseph Licklider's is one of the most ambitious, important stories with the greatest impact but also scarcely known. He was a psychophysiologist specialized in psychoacoustics at the MIT Lincoln Laboratory and first director of the Office of Information Processing Technique and Behavioral Sciences (IPTO) at US Department of Defense DARPA (Advanced Research Projects Agency). In this position, Licklider created and led a program which strongly accelerated the vision emerging among the main developers of digital computers: Vannevar Bush, Norbert Wiener, Claude Shannon, and John von Neumann. The idea was that computers were not only tools for enhanced computing or calculation, but that they could become human cognitive prostheses, repairing human errors, becoming the timeless repositories of data, information, and books, and could consult them faster than any expert librarian or documentalist and gifted with extreme flexibility. Licklider took the lead when he convinced ARPA general management of his theory of an interactive machine, an idea briefly illustrated in an essay entitled "Man-computer Symbiosis" that can be considered the first, inaugural scientific article of human-computer interaction or interaction design.[4] Unlike other researchers with a technical and engineering background, Licklider used a language that distanced any notion of comparing a computer to the human mind. Although he expressed an opinion that computers would soon be able to compute faster than a human mind, he believed the role of machine was to support the cognitive abilities of humans where speed and stability are required. Furthermore, he thought computers would favor cooperation and communication processes in interpersonal relations. These were premises for a great innovation process, with clear intentions, especially as far as applications and the possibility of changing work-related behavior. They also saw them as a chance to increase decision-making, creativity, communication, and cooperation skills. IPTO budgets were tenfold the large research budgets of the time, and their mandate was "*think big* and *do it fast*."

Licklider believed that the subsequent 10 years would see the basis for efficient computer-aided cooperation in most professions. He called it the Intergalactic Computer Network, a remote cooperation among computers through the phone line, and believed it would succeed only if the digital machine were highly interactive and available to all. By increasing the cooperation network and user numbers, it would have been simpler to improve the system and invent and circulate new ideas. The idea was described in an article[5] written with Robert Taylor, a psychologist who was also one of his closest collaborators who later succeeded him in his position at ARPA. Basically, they suggested that resources shared via computer would have

[4] Licklider [4]

[5] Licklider and Taylor [5].

enhanced creativity and problem-solving, some of it as group solving as well as enabling dynamic decision-making with an immediate appreciation of results.

The idea of a human-computer symbiosis (where mind meets machine) and of a computer being a communication rather than a computational machine as well as that of a computer-backed collaborative network were not just visions of the future: cooperation among networks of excellence among IPTO research centers and laboratories were being reported and made public. Centers included MIT; the three main Californian Universities—Berkeley, Santa Barbara, and Los Angeles—the Stanford Research Institute (SRI); Carnegie-Mellon; the University of Utah; and then recent companies such as Digital (DEC), the Rand Corporation, and the System Development Corporation. One of the experiments with the human-computer system was designed by Doug Engelbart[6] and his group at the SRI Augmentation Research Center. A number of researchers convened to discuss projects underway in a room specially equipped with an interactive system. According to the experimental protocol, researchers spent fruitful time in front of the screen consulting and looking at graphs and texts rather than spending time in conference to solve misunderstandings. According to Licklider and Taylor, the exchange of information and the creation of new mind schemata and patterns were at the core of computer-facilitated cooperation. "*By far the most numerous, most sophisticated, and most important models are those that reside in men's mind.*" Mental models develop in a person's brain by processing images and data stored in their memory. Since these models are personal and private, they have to be externalized for others to perceive, discuss, and share them. Communication is a constructive not a passive mechanism: by externalizing mental models, actions can be agreed on and coordinated, thus enhancing cooperation between the designer community and the collective control on the environment. The authors stated that if computer and communication technologies could be made accessible to individuals, they had the potential to become the most powerful cooperation tool ever invented leading to new habits and work patterns and models.

Cooperation would become more fluid and dynamic, totally different from the one using previously available technologies. New technologies would imply the ability to share information, to switch from a macro to a detailed level of information analysis, to assemble and deconstruct thought models, to cut and paste data and information to comment texts written by others, or to jointly write a text and the like. Furthermore, the possibility of working remotely, even outside one's normal workplace, would increase the use and usefulness of the means, exponentially increasing the creative collaborative potential. As mentioned, it was the most comprehensive ever program implemented after several pilot schemes under controlled conditions, and it was to change office work behavior and cooperation.

We can conclude that the objectives aimed at transforming user community tools and technologies have been fully attained. Licklider's network of excellence tested

[6] Doug Engelbart is known for having invented the computer mouse; however, he also developed the idea of a digital workstation with all the associated peripherals that is still the same as the one we use in computer workstations to this day.

all the parts that now make up computer and network technology: from the mouse to graphic displays, from writing software to sharing worksheets and hypertext, to package transmission to the definition of the two protocols currently governing the Internet, that is, TCP, the *Transmission Control Protocol*, and the *Internet Protocol*, IP. I see it as a wonderful multi-disciplinary cooperation program which started as experimental research and managed to remain as such only so long as guidelines and aims were shared, that is to say till the design of the first browser by CERN many years later. Hypertext technology was initially only possible inside a computer, but when it became possible *among* networked computers, the invention of browsers completed the ARPAnet vision, especially the possibility of extending remote cooperation to most non-technology literate users.

Browsers marked the end of public research institutions playing a role both in Europe and in the United States in developing work transformation programs and communities communicating with digital technologies. Subsequent digital transformations and above all the research for new business models laid the foundations of what we now call digital economy. However, in opening these other spaces to generate a new economy and value, the application potential of the US Government or of the European-funded patents, up to Horizon 2020, went to the private sector distorting the inspiration and vision of digital technologies and their applications. There was a lack of regulatory capacity to prevent the rise of global monopolies, the misuse of personal data, spreading of fake news, and manipulating intentions. Major corrective measures will have to be implemented in the next 10 years for all of this to reconnect to sustainable development leading to a digital economy. I will return to these matters in Part IV.

1.1 Cognitive Engineering and Emotional Engagement

Donald Norman is one of the most prominent experimental psychologists who focused on the applications that would change and improve people's living conditions. His work has proved especially popular among the younger digital economy professionals and interaction designers. In his best seller *The Psychology of Everyday Things,*[7] Norman illustrates some of the basic principles developed following experimental research on perception, attention, and knowledge representation. His remit covers the design of everyday objects, from doors to tea pots, to highly engineered products such as cars and computers. His work has been especially effective in showing the *power of affordance*, i.e., well-designed built environments for which humans need no special instructions, nor do they have to learn how to behave. Just as nature presents *Homo sapiens* with environmental conditions that do not require constructive categories, likewise the built environment should offer complementary elements to favor control and easy flow.

---

[7] Norman, D. *The Psychology of Everyday Things*, 1988, also Norman [6]

The notion of *affordance* comes from James Gibson, a psychologist who developed the ecological approach to visual perception. Such an approach implies a complementary nature between humans and nature and a co-evolution: "The affordances of the environment are what it offers the animal, what it provides or furnishes, either for good or ill. The verb to afford is found in the dictionary, the noun affordance is not. I have made it up. I mean by it something that refers to both the environment and the animal in a way that no existing term does. It implies the complementarity of the animal and the environment".[8] Norman focuses on *invitations to action* that objects designed by humans have. The *gulf of execution* is defined as the distance between the intention to act and its execution. Human objects or artifacts with an invitation to action suited to human motor and cognitive perceptions have a small gulf of execution and therefore do not require a major mental effort nor special attention. In contrast, objects that require instructions must be learnt. Norman continues in his convincing narrative stating how the need to use an object for its purposes and aims does not depend on how simple or complex its function is, which means frustration and a sense of inadequacy may arise. For instance, a door bar with *pull* or *push* is the wrong invitation or affordance: in fact, a panic door bar does not require the indication *push* just like a knob does not requires *pull.* Even a more complex product follows the above-described principle of affordance.

According to the principles of the engineering usability or cognitive ergonomics, as it was referred to in the 1980s, a good designer will breakdown complex actions into simpler ones, turning invisibles into visibles and offering a clear mapping of the layout of commands, sequencing of actions, size, and surface spaciality. The constraints that we come across in our everyday lives, that is, physical, logical, semantic, and cultural constraints, will also be used. Lastly, it will send feedback at the end of the action. In another two subsequent tests, Don Norman[9] added to this work offering a personal and original approach on how psychology can inform good design and specifically how to equip designers with human-environment-artifacts interaction so that they can do things in the best possible way. The model is based on a key notion of cognitive science that *Homo sapiens* is extremely capable of developing a good representation of the outside world, though there are limits to it. George Miller, Licklider's proto-cognitivist colleague at MIT, and much later research on glial cell mechanisms proved our short-term memory has limited capacity.

Furthermore, we find it difficult to solve complex problems in our minds: we make mistakes and do not always realize we have made them in time to avoid them which limits our decision-making processes. Our brain has developed unique abilities to overcome these limitations, using information drawn from the environment as well as creating aids (prostheses) or external cognitive artifacts in the environment and developed heuristic methods to reduce uncertainty in analyzing information and decision-making processes. Norman's model on how the brain works

[8] Gibson [7].

[9] Norman [8, 9].

outlines an environment like the cognitive models of human information processing and is based on three levels: *visceral, behavioral*, and *reflective*. Usability engineers mainly use the behavioral level; designed centered approaches focus on the visceral level. Thus, with one swift move, Norman introduced an important part of cognitive research on emotion into the knowledge sphere of designers. In fact, emotions play a key role in how we understand the world and influence our perception of reality. Later in the chapter, I discuss how emotions underlie automatic processes and can also easily mislead us with the weight of the attribute to information or by orienting the representations we use in our decision-making processes.

Good design will smooth out interaction and also play a major role in attracting, seducing, and convincing. Distinctive interaction design practice uses the combination between engineering, usability, and design according to the model *wow-show-flow*, to best describe the three ingredients of human experience: attraction (*wow*), seduction (*show*), and interaction (*flow*).

A good designer will have to be aware of the need to:

(a) Attract the user's limited attention applying appropriate engagement and onboarding strategies.
(b) Convince the user by showing that the artifact answers expectations.
(c) Attain objectives with a degree of ease and control[10].

Designers make the action flow in the environment thanks to functional and cognitive prostheses that facilitate people's lives by adapting to a complex task. This approach holds true both in physical and analog environments by designing products that have actual substance (materiality) and tangibility. It also works in digital environments where well-designed graphic commands and functions invite to action and do not require a specific learning curve. Don Norman's work is ideally connected to the vision developed by Licklider's group and his network of excellence. Licklider found the right approach to steer digital design culture toward greater inclusiveness, thus contributing to the development of sustainable innovation models. According to a human-centered design approach, usability engineering and good design play an important role in facilitating the acquisition of perceptive-motor routines that easily become habits requiring a low cognitive involvement.

This important facet of digital innovation must be analyzed in more detail: cognitive automatisms are one of the foundations of behavioral science (discussed more in depth in Part II). Applications in all fields of design, marketing, and engineering use perceptive-motor automatisms and the acquisitions of these automatisms. When successful, all this impacts on business strategies. In other words, if we wish to understand how we can generate sustainable innovation, we have to focus on the formation of automatisms, preferences, and choices. As you will see below, the power and strength of behavioral automatisms also play a major role in the development of new design ethics aimed at the evolution of models of sustainable life. The

[10]The relationship and similitude between this model and the AIDA's to explain the persuasion mechanisms of advertising are remarkable.

basis of the digital innovation paradigm will have to be reviewed for behavior designers and systemic change agents like us, to legitimately aspire to collective action with a major social impact.

1.2 Cognitive Automatism

As creatures of habit, we try not to waste our mental resources in our daily lives, and this is why our brains have learnt to develop *automatic processes*, automatisms, or mental routines to minimize or avoid the loss of energy in exchanges in familiar environments. In the course of our lives, we are subjected to situations which require us to make decisions without always knowing the consequences they will have on our future. In the course of evolution, we have had to learn how to limit mistakes both to stay on our chosen path and more so to avoid irreparable consequences.

We have been endowed with behavior that is mostly based on perceptive-motor routines that enable us to act swiftly in our environment and to use cognitive resources sparingly in our daily lives.

We are able to do many things at the same time, as long as we can maintain a balance between aims and associated risks. For instance, if we are seasoned drivers and love to chat in the car, we can drive with our usual level of safety and at the same time pursue a challenging conversation and possibly also listen in to background music. However, if the traffic suddenly becomes heavier or the road is rougher, the conversation will have to be reduced or even stopped to avoid an accident. In that situation our perceptive-motor automatisms become less effective, and we need to re-establish control on driving. Current experimental research is focusing on this extremely important mechanism, that is, shifting between automatic and attention-controlled processes. In fact, automatic processes are the dorsal attention network that connects feelings with thought.

In the 1970s, Shiffrin and Schneider, two Chicago researchers,[11] started a series of experiments studying the mechanisms of attention and memory, what is known as the theory of *automatic and controlled processing*. It is also one of the most advanced expressions of the so-called dual process theory.[12] Accordingly, automatic processes are fast because our senses are able to receive information from the environment acting in a slightly mismatched parallel time relation. The model has been validated by recent neurophysiological research. Results show that the areas of the brain that process sense-generated information analyze exteroceptive, proprioceptive, and enteroceptive information in parallel and pass processed information to the relevant associative areas.[13] For instance, auditory information reaches associative

[11] Schneider [10].

[12] Please note the latter is a narrative link among all the disciplines pertaining to behavioral science.

[13] Damasio [11, 12]; Edelman and Tononi [13].

areas before visual[14] one. We are not aware of this time mismatch precisely because they are automatisms: our senses pick up external and internal stimuli and the body/environment interface and relation so we can inform our brain of the conditions our behavior will have to play out.

Automatic processes require a minimum effort compared to the maximum sustainable effort for the person in question. Furthermore, automatisms are not limited by short-term memory issues: using a fork at dinner is an example of an automatic process. It is an action that requires limited control by the person following an all-round consistent training and learning needed to establish lasting proficiency. A two-handed backhand is taught to advanced tennis learners, but after a lot of exercise, it can become automatic and will no longer require direct control. Training will make the exercise increasingly complex until the player reaches angles and accuracy that will surprise even those who devised this tennis shot. As we will see later on in the book, automatisms have a major impact on our daily routines. By repeating movements or minor choices, they become habits which can be difficult to eliminate, ignore, or modify once acquired.

Serial controlled processes are relatively slow and confined to short-term memory: they require a significant effort by the person, as two simultaneous tasks requiring competing senses and skills cannot be completed. For instance, even after long practice, you can't dance the tango while listening to a waltz, as it is not possible to focus on an interesting speaker on television while speaking on the phone to your CEO about an important decision to be made. Conversely a short interruption in an automatic sequence during routine surgery by an expert surgeon explaining a special technique while performing it on an anesthetized patient typically does not cause any interference with the surgical protocol.[15]

The above shows how controlled processes require a high degree of serial control by the person and the construction of patterns or models (schemata) that make it possible to perform the task in the available time. Our daily lives are a mixture of automatic and serial controls requiring a constant switching between the relevant functional areas of our brains. On the whole, serial processes are used in behaviors required in new unknown or anomalous situations or when they do not offer enough information. As we shall see more extensively below, serial processes may intervene to monitor automatisms and possibly correct the unwanted consequences or mistakes due to automatisms.

According to the classification by Norman and Shallice,[16] there are at least six conditions that require serial or superior—non automatic—mental processes, that is:

---

[14] For instance, a fencer on a *piste* understands the opponent's intensions from a series of sensorial clues and processes the information from the movements on the piste a few milliseconds before the other clues, such as the visual, or position at least till the pass forward which anticipates the thrust la schermaglia and final landing of the point. Parallel processing makes it possible to adapt perceptive motor processes to the many threatening and favorable circumstances that a foil fencer has. See Visciola [14].

[15] From private conversations with expert surgeons using (surgical) robots

[16] Norman and Shallice [15].

(a) Decision-making and planning, such as the purchase of a house or planning spending following a new regular cost such as a mortgage.
(b) Problem-solving and correcting errors.
(c) Learning new sequences for which there are no known solutions exist or are accessible.
(d) Reacting to new dangerous or technically difficult situation.
(e) Changing habits.
(f) Resisting appealing temptations.

I will return to (e) and (f) in Part III because they are especially important for the definitions of sustainable change programs and models. Clearly, the other four conditions also play an important role in sustainable innovation, and we will discuss it later.

The theory of automatic and higher mental processes still prevails in the paradigm of behavioral science as it offers a series of major advantages that account for the many cognitive properties studied in psychology labs at the end of the last century and subsequently proved thanks to research on neuronal processes.

These properties include:

(i) *Selective attention*, that is, the ability to select one auditory stimulus and ignore the others.
(ii) *Divided attention*, that is, the attention deficit, bottlenecks when the sheer number of stimuli exceeds the ability to process them leading to a decline in attention at least until such time as new schemata or models able to integrate sensorial stimulations develop.
(iii) *Focused attention*, that is, the ability to systematically exclude irrelevant information.
(iv) *Distributed attention*, that is, the ability to process simultaneous information from more than one sensorial channel, according to acquired complex patterns, such as interpreting or air traffic controllers.

Furthermore, processing of control by higher mental processes[17] appears to play a key role in bringing about fundamental changes in long-term memory: new patterns or models develop, new problem-solving connections are formed, and new points of view and creative processes are facilitated and may in turn become routines and automatisms.

In conclusion: according to the theory of automated and controlled processes, just like we should not confuse controlled processed with consciousness, we should not confuse automated with the unconscious processes of psychoanalysis. The

[17] Early cognitive theories and models were based on the metaphor of the brain as a central processor of information. According to these models, cognitive processes were either higher process located in the two hemispheres of the brain or cognitive processes that referred to the peripheral nervous system. Higher cognitive processes were thought to process information top-down and therefore regulate inferential, deductive, and inductive processes. Lower cognitive processes were thought to process information bottom-up sending incomplete patterns to the central nervous system

definition of unconscious processes in psychoanalysis[18] refers to pre-attentive processes that give rise to free and causal associations generated by internal and external stimuli. Automated stimuli are pre-attentive processes that give rise to motor regular motor perceptions or to skills. The definition of awareness refers to the processes through which we channel or direct our attention and guide our behavior. In other words, these are processes used to select sensory patterns that can become elements of judgment.[19] Shiffrin and Schneider stated they were unable to demonstrate a correspondence between controlled processes and awareness, in spite of the long series of experiments. No one else has tried to prove if this correspondence effectively exists, and although they have been the object of major passionate studies over the past 20 years, awareness processes are some of the least known processes.

The distinction between awareness and consciousness is less important for the purposes of the present text, and I will refer mainly to the difference between automated and controlled processes, arguing why we have to act on both. The present essay follows the prevailing approach in behavior sciences which rests nearly completely on dual theories.[20]

1.3 Dual Processes and Heuristics in Human Judgment

Amos Tversky and Daniel Kahneman performed impressive research on the heuristics that determine choices and preferences.[21] Their research proved pivotal in understanding behavior and cognition in scientific terms. In the early 1970s, Kahneman started as a researcher of perception, attention, and judgment and pursued this line of research and started with Tversky even after the latter's death. He revised and integrated the theory to the point a synergy between behavior science

---

[18] Psychoanalysis introduced the idea that subconscious processes are part of processing revealing meanings not accessible to consciousness. This idea was taken up by psychologists but is no longer accepted by present-day scientific communities.

[19] According to the most recent neuroscience theories and models, this process occurs in the brainstem, which is also the anatomical and functional location from which all neural connections generated by the autonomic nervous system and the sensory nervous system pass.

[20] As noted above, the theory of "automated and controlled processes" is part of the large family of dual process theory in the behavioral sciences. These include behavioral economics and social psychology, whose contributions to the dual process theory will be presented further, with the aim of expanding and completing our understanding behavior for sustainable innovation. However, Jens Rasmussen's three-level model, known as the ladder model, may also fall under dual process theories. This model is still very influential in the old school of cognitive ergonomics. It distinguishes between *skill-based behavior*, *rule-based behavior*, and *knowledge-based behaviors* [16].

[21] Kahneman [17]; Kahneman and Tversky [18].

and economics was officially recognized and became known as behavioral economics.[22]

The two researchers started by observing the errors of judgment and the difficulties people had in applying notions to simple cases in their daily lives, even people who had knowledge of statistics. In answering a simple quiz like the one that follows, typically over 50% of the people give the wrong answer, regardless of their level of education:

> If a tennis racquet and balls cost 220€, and we know that the racquet costs 200 € more than the balls how much do the balls cost?

It is "natural" to mentally calculate so that 200 € plus 20€ give 220€, while it requires thought to reach the correct result. Our natural predisposition to make mistakes like this and the difficulty in monitoring the mistake when answering the quiz shows that automatisms make it possible to offer a swift answer and that controlled processes might prove ineffective or require more attention or education to solve the problem.

Research on the relationship between judgment and thought or reasoning saw the large number of scientists associated with Kahneman and Tversky shifting from perception and attention—the focus of Shiffrin and Schneider's area of interest—to higher cognitive processes such as judgment, thought, and decision-making. This approach is consistent with the theory of automated and controlled processes which (as we saw) is based on perceptive processes and the studies on the formation of affordance. Kahneman's research shows that intuition—or intuitive judgment—is based on swift implicit associative automatisms not accessible by introspection. Typically, intuition does not reach a level of awareness and often is associated with emotions. Reasoned processes are slow and serial and require effort and concentration, and they are both flexible and not emotionally connotated. It is a dual perspective whereby the two parts of the human cognitive system share the steps or tasks required to govern behavior: System 1 and System 2 are distinct, and most of today's scientific community is founded on this premise. After over 30 years of research, the two components of dual processes have been finally named: Stanovich and West formalized the proposal in the year 2000, but Kahneman was the one who popularized it in his famous *Thinking, Fast and Slow*, quite a feat outlining the ground that behavioral sciences share.

Properties of System 1 can best be illustrated premising three fundamental preconditions to frame its ontological essence:

(i) It is reasonable to suggest that automated mechanisms developed very early on in the course of our evolution, and in fact they exist in all the biological steps of life. Generally, these automatic processes enable us to gather important information from the environment that surrounds us including the inner envi-

[22] I am referring to Kahneman's Nobel Prize for Economics awarded in 2003, in the wake of the other great humanist Herbert Simon, who was awarded the Nobel Prize in Economics in 1963. The same Prize to Richard Thaler followed.

ronment. These mechanisms are necessary for swift answers and have a high chance of survival.

(ii) These mechanisms are strongly connected to what we call "environment." They are a part of our genetic inheritance accrued through the evolution of our species. One can reasonably suggest these inherited automatisms developed under favorable conditions of cognitive development and as a result of a gradual exposure to environmental conditions. For instance, we do not need a good understanding of height and depth to judge whether it is more convenient and less risky to climb a six-foot tree to pick an apple or walk 10 feet to pick an apple from a lower apple tree, where he could pick it by reaching out with our arm.

(iii) We know that they are imprecise and vital mechanisms. In typical situations of uncertainty, in daily life we prefer to have information and form anticipations that can be verified with more detailed information rather than not having a hypothesis to verify. In time we acquire skill and experience and count on the automatisms we have learnt more than on the analytical properties of the available information details. In other terms, in our daily lives, we fail to use all the available information or the information in our memory, but only the one which springs spontaneously to mind.

This said, we can now examine some of the important aspects on System 1 which will prove useful in the discussion on the theory of the evolution of behavior and more generally inform the sustainable innovation strategy building it up which is the central proposition of this book. I am referring to the five pillars of the automatic processes of System 1: a) availability of potential action patterns; b) dependence on context; c) dependence of the model of reference; d) propensity for change; and e) resilience to change.

1.4 Availability of Judgment and Action Patterns

One of the key properties of System 1 is that certain circumstances trigger perception patterns and intuitions whereby the person is able to act or react accordingly. These schemata are triggered spontaneously without any effort resulting from the combination of the characteristics of human cognition and the stimuli generated by the environment. Perceptologist Gibson refers to this as *affordance*, emphasizing the features of the environment and direct access by human perception without mediation and learned mental constructs. Kahneman refers to it as *accessibility* focusing on the ability of human cognition to create judgment and preference mechanisms that will become *accessible* when necessary. Accessibility of perceptive patterns and judgment is determined by ease with which we access mental contents. One might wonder why some contents or mental patterns are easily accessed as precepts or intuitions and why they prevail over others. The answer is relatively simple and can easily be identified in our daily lives. For instance, they refer to how salient an object is: a standard size gold ring is more salient and attracts more than a bronze one, although the latter may be bigger. However, if we ask a person to focus on bronze objects jumbled together in a basket, the attraction for the gold ring will wane. Designers learn very soon to use visual patterns based on saliency or noticeability to trigger the desired perceptive mechanisms and judgments. In fact, salience is one of the easiest properties of *accessibility* to manipulate. Alternatively, consider the emotional valence of the stimulus: words like "cancer" or "rare disease" easily summon up worry. An image that triggers positive or negative evokes mental schemata more easily than an image with no expression. Image designers and photographers know that the stronger the emotional impact of the image, the greater the accessibility to the contents of the image, to the disadvantage of other images and meanings in the person's visual field.

Other *determinants* available to System 1 action patterns or schemata include resemblance and the strength of associations; affective valence; surprise; proximity of cause and effect; and the intuitive judgment if something is "good" or "bad," harmless and attractive, or dangerous and repulsive. As we will see later, they can be manipulated to change the "natural" and spontaneous evaluation by a person at any given moment. To this end, perspicacity and ability are called for as well as being able to argue one's case or present counterfactual elements through System 2 mechanisms. Again, this is discussed in more detail further in the text. One is more likely to be successful using System 1 rather than System 2 corrective mechanisms in addressing the potential these human cognitive features offer, in terms of the impact and of behavior modification. In fact, it is especially difficult to change the inherent meaning of these mental contents especially if they are part to the person's value system and reference culture. Social psychology has studied them at length in terms of stereotypes, normative and informative conformity, racism, and prejudice.

1.5 Context Dependence

The second System 1 known property is the strong *context dependence* for perception and judgment. Research into this and the previous properties have seriously questioned the basis of classical economic theories in the Western world opening the doors of behavioral economics. In fact, to fully understand the implications, let us not forget that classical economic theories presume a perfectly rational decision and thus that people:

(a) Develop a value system that will inform choices.
(b) They will maintain the value system stable once his established. Following Herbert Simon, I will refer to it as an "Olympian rationality" to tell it apart from the "bounded rationality" theory that behavioral scientists uphold. Olympian rationality leads to simplifications according to which one presumes that:
(c) Choices depend on the tendency to maximize one's own best advantage.

(d) Choices are not dependent on the change in context. In other words, we prefer what gives us the best advantage measured according to our value system, and, besides, we are able to have stable preferences we maintain.

Simplifications of decisional processes have deeply influenced economic theory and schools of economics. We are still using analytical tools and data collection from these models with the result that they deform reality and then inform company decisions, market strategies, and positioning of products and services accordingly. For instance, market research based on elicitated preferences presume Olympian rationality in interviewees' answers to questionnaires and surveys—or any other quantitative research. In other words, they presume a voluntary and deliberate (conscious) act underlying each and every decision and also that the person will hold the preference and not waiver in the future. Unsurprisingly, market surveys ask consumers abstract decontextualized questions separate from the real situation where the decision will be taken. Likewise, answers to strategic question are sought in Big Data, although in the best of cases they offer well-known answers, as they disregard specific situations.

Research on choice-led behavior and the influence of context I am referring to offers unquestionable evidence on the fallacy of *Olympian rationality*-based models. It will also highlight the opportunistic side of market strategies counting on people's real inability to opt for rational choices based on chosen architectures that confuse them and make it impossible for them to decide what is good and what is not for them. Part II will discuss this aspect in more detail when examining value and how it conveyed on the market.

As we have seen, the theory of Olympian rationality predicts that the number of alternatives does not influence the criteria used to make the choice. Below we will show the role alternative choices play in determining the judgment and will posit that the number of options the person has shapes the inner context within which the choice will be expressed. *Trade-off contrasts* is the most interesting case as brilliantly proved by Tversky and Simonson in a series of experiments on preference and context influence.[23] Research shows that contrary to the predictions of the Olympian rationality model, preferences do not form with regularity. Furthermore, it proves that heuristics-shaped preferences strongly depend on the presence of alternatives that lead to comparisons and reduce initial uncertainty thus determining one's choice.

For instance, generally we make a choice to make a purchase with limited knowledge of the best price or quality for us. In some cases, we might refer to ideas based on other people's experience, on previous experience of our own, and possibly on our max budget. However, all these ideas will have to be assessed in the actual situation.

Quite early in life, as soon as we acquire some purchasing power, we realize that the commodity market is not stable and can present positive or negative surprises any time. Let us suppose that it is time to change your summer tires and that you

[23] Tversky and Simonson [19].

drive about 10,000 miles a season. The market has many models to offer and although you trust your tire dealer, a quick look around the market indicates that there are two products that differ in price and in terms of the guaranteed mileage as per Table 1.1, offer A. Since your usual tire dealer cannot service your car for a fortnight because of backlog, your partner whom you share the car with, goes to another tire dealer who also offers a binary choice of another two tire brands, according to Table 1.1, offer B. How do you choose and what would your partner choose? According to the Olympian rationality theory (ORT), in this case, the person who assesses the advertised offer will generally go for the slightly higher price tires with a warranty of more than 2 years, and most of the people who receive an offer from the tire dealer approached as an alternative will instead choose much cheaper tires in spite of a slightly shorter warranty. You would probably also fall into the majority and therefore choose the slightly more expensive tires, while your partner, who is unaware of the advertised offer, has already thought of going for the cheaper tires proposed by the new tire dealer.

Now let us presume you receive new information: your usual dealer has called you telling you a slot has unexpectedly become available on the following day and they could do the work. Their offer is described as alternative offering (see Table 1.1). How would you make the decision? According to ORT, your choice will persist and therefore you'd be expected to still prefer the tires that offer a longer warranty even though they are more expensive. Your partner is expected to prefer the cheaper tires at a lower price although they have a shorter warranty. For a moment let's forget the comments or expectations of the difficult situation that might arise between partners, especially if they both cling onto their view as most couples I know. As mentioned above, due to judgment automatisms without thinking about it (reasoning), it will be difficult to see that the two products offered by the usual tire dealer are the same, and the only decision is whether summer tires need to be changed after 4 or 5 years.

Bounded rationality theory (BRT)—the one Tversky and his team refer to—expects the contrast between alternatives, background vs target, favors:

Table 1.1 Choice and contrast between alternatives

Warranty	Price	Choice (n = 111)	Choice (n = 109)
Offer A			
55,000 miles	\$85	12%	
75,000 miles	\$91	88%	
Offer B			
30,000 miles	\$25		84%
35,000 miles	\$49		16%
Alternative offer			
40,000 miles	\$60	57%	33%
50,000 miles	\$75	43%	67%

From Tversky A. and Simonson I.; op. cit. Page 522

(a) The one partner who was offered the best price—the one in comparison with the offer of the usual tire dealer—tendency to go for the better quality and longer warranty for a slightly higher price.
(b) The tendency to choose a longer guarantee and better quality in the case of the partner who was offered a lower price.

In other words, the results of Tversky and Simonson's research show choice being determined by available background information. In the example offered, considering the market search on the Internet and hearing the other tire dealer: the alternatives meant two comparable warranties, and two comparable prices could be considered. This makes it possible to compare and reach a rational decision based on logic inferences among alternatives. In this case the background (information) is in *contrast*, and one can opt between the two available factors in evaluating, that is, price and quality. Results show an aspect not understood by the Olympian rationality theory (ORT): alternatives play an important role in preference forming, and the background plays a role in terms of choice.

A conscientious reader familiar with subtle reasoning such as this could certainly argue that in the end, these are all rational choices: comparisons were possible, and a conclusion was reached albeit with difficulty, that is, that our tire dealer proved worthy of our trust, so whatever the choice, it will be a good choice. However, there is another key element to bear in mind that proves how ORT is oversimplified and unreliable. In a series of later experiments, Tversky proved that background contrasts persist even when it is not possible to offer deductive reasoning and build preferences based on logical inferences. In these experiments, the price and quality variables were handled in the same way, although the object of the choice and the contrast between target alternative and background change and unlike the first case there is neither a trusted usual dealer nor a normative model of choices.

As a first experiment, let's imagine we have been invited to a usability test for a new application soon to be launched. The recruiter offers us the following alternative as an incentive to convince us to spend an hour of our time:

(a) 52 € cash and three book tokens worth roughly 15 € each.
(b) 22 € cash and five book tokens worth roughly15 € each.

Tokens can be redeemed in a bookshop of our choice. What would you choose?

Let us now imagine that the same test is offered in another country where another choice selection is offered:

(a1) 77 € cash and four book tokens each one worth roughly 5 € each.
(b1) 67 € cash and six book tokens worth approx. 5 € each.

Which do you think will be the preferred option? As you can see in Tables 1.2 (test "a") and 1.2 (test "b"), in the first case the choice with more cash strongly prevails, while in the second case the option with more tokens prevails albeit marginally so.

Table 1.2 Choice and contrast between alternatives without a normative model

Cash	Coupon	Choice ($n = 51$)	Choice ($n = 49$)
Test a			
\$52	3	92%	
\$22	5	8%	
Test b			
\$77	4		40%
\$67	6		60%
Alternative bonus			
a2 \$47	5	47%	77%
b2 \$37	6	53%	23%

From Tversky A. and Simonson I.; op. cit. Page 522

Let us now imagine that a month later you are once again invited to take part in a new test for a more advanced version of the same application, having implemented all the recommendations for improvement from the previous test.

This time the recruiter offers the following alternative:

(a2) 47 € cash and five tokens worth roughly 10€.
(b2) 37 € cash and six tokens worth roughly 10€.

What do you think you would choose? How do you think the group of participants from the other country would decide?

I would remind you that ORT does not admit that alternatives or context play an important role in determining choice and also posits that once made, choice will be regular and persistent; the first group will prefer more cash, while the second group will go for more tokens.

Vice versa, BRT suggests that people do not always have well-defined values and build choices according to how the problem is represented—as discussed further—and context. Specifically, context-dependent choices would predict the first group would notice a smaller difference in cash between a2 and b2 and therefore would opt for the choice with more tokens. Consistently with the predictive model, in the second test, the second group will choose the option with more cash.

In conclusion, in both cases as in the case of the tires, the context influences choice even in the absence of a normative model. In spite of the experiment not allowing for rational choices using explicit criteria, people reached a decision according to the information extracted from background contexts (see Test "a") and from targets (see Test "b").

The so-called local context is another important case of context dependence as proved by other experimental activities that highlight how by comparing target and background people are led to choices where there are no consolidated value systems. In this series, a third alternative is added to the two. The third choice offers lower quality and lower costs than the best choice but is close to the second choice. Typically, a context with several quality-price alternatives induces people to avoid extremes (*extremeness aversion*) or *polarization* toward the median values which is an improvement in the quality compared to the lowest quality price and a price improvement compared to the highest price. A larger market share can be acquired by breaking the regularity in comparing two competing products.

Let us say that you wish to buy a new chair for when you are in remote working from home. The salesperson presents an alternative between two chairs by different designers but the same brand. Let us say choice *a1* is 350 € and choice *b1* 200 €. You can select the color, delivery time, and other factors which affect the quality of the product and of the purchasing experience. What and how would you choose? Probably the result would be a virtually identical distribution of preferences.[24] Now let us suppose that the chair manufacturer asked the designer of the *a1* chair to design a stronger model with lighter materials to be manufactured in small numbers as top-of-the-range item and this chair will be put on the market for 500€. What do you think will happen? Results following a series of experiments by several teams of researchers clearly evidence that preferences shift significantly to the two models of the designer chairs increasing the *a1* market share.

The above research offers conclusive evidence that preferences can be manipulated and that when we build our preferences, we compare possible alternatives. We do not compare according to measurement criteria establishing which is the best choice in an absolute and abstract manner beyond any reasonable doubt. We compare according to optimal heuristics and thus develop an opinion there and then: in other words, these choices are situation-based preferences not based on a stable value system. By changing the points of reference between figure and background, target and background, the preference system changes too.

1.6 Dependence of the Reference Model

In addition to context dependence and the resulting oscillation or switching between target and background, System 1 adapts to the ways in which information is presented: by varying the reference model judgments, preferences and choices also vary. As in the case of context dependency, choices are not consistent. Due to bounded rationality, preferences are construed so as to be symmetrical opposed (*preference reversal*) to those expressed in similar situations with different framing. However, in expressing contradictory choices, our experience is not associated with *irrationality* or to the inability to judge, and we are in no way aware we have failed to follow a consistent judgment path. The experiments described below highlight a violation of one of the main principles of Olympian rationality, that is, if some of the framing features change, the preference system should not switch. To quote Daniel Kahneman: “invariance cannot be achieved by a finite mind.” The more accessible features of human judgment are more attractive, although it is not a given

[24] Huber et al. [20].

that the more accessible characteristics are also the most relevant in terms of a correct judgment and a sound decision.

The experiment refers to a virus epidemic. No, not COVID-19. It was conceived in the 1980s, and we have two experimental programs and decide to offer two different representations for each program: a risk aversion and risk seeking frame.

The first offers these two options:

Program A: administering program A, 200 people out of a sample of 600 people in the trial will get over the contagion.

Program B: administering program B, we have a 1 in 3 (i.e., 1/3) probability that the 600 people will overcome the contagion and a 2 in 3 (i.e., 2/3) probability that no one will survive.

Which of these two programs would you give precedence to for a large trial on many people? Are you one of the ones (72%) who opted for program A or one of the ones (28%) that chose program B?

In the second trial conducted by Tversky and Kahneman in another laboratory, the two programs were presented as follows:

Program C: 400 of the 600 people in the trial will be infected.

Program D: we have a probability close to a 1 in 3 (i.e., 1/3) that the 600 vaccinated people will get over the infection and have a 2 in 3 (i.e., 2/3) chance of contagion.

As Table 1.3 shows, in this case preference is the symmetrical reverse with 22% opting for C as opposed to 78% opting for program D.

Programs A and B are comparable to C and D; in fact they are quite similar and overlapping. As we observed, preferences show a propensity to risk when representation—that is the way in which the story is told or the problem presented—emphasizes the possibility of a great loss. There is a propensity to caution when the possibility of saving lives is stressed. We refer to this principle underlying the psychological value of choices (see Fig. 1.1) of *prospect theory*. The theory posits a phase when framing makes it possible to represent a situation and a subsequent evaluation or assessment determined by the representation used when judging. As Fig. 1.1 shows, the model presumes that the representation of a loss or gain each projects a value above or below a hypothetical neutral point. In this function, the neutral value is the reference model chosen as background: without a neutral model,

Table 1.3 Framing and choices

Vaccine programs	Success rate	Choice
Program a	200 in 600	72%
Program b	1/3 of 600 YES 2/3 of 600 NO	28%
Vaccine programs	Infection rate	Choice
Program c	400 in 600	22%
Program d	1/3 in 600 NO 2/3 in 600 YES	78%

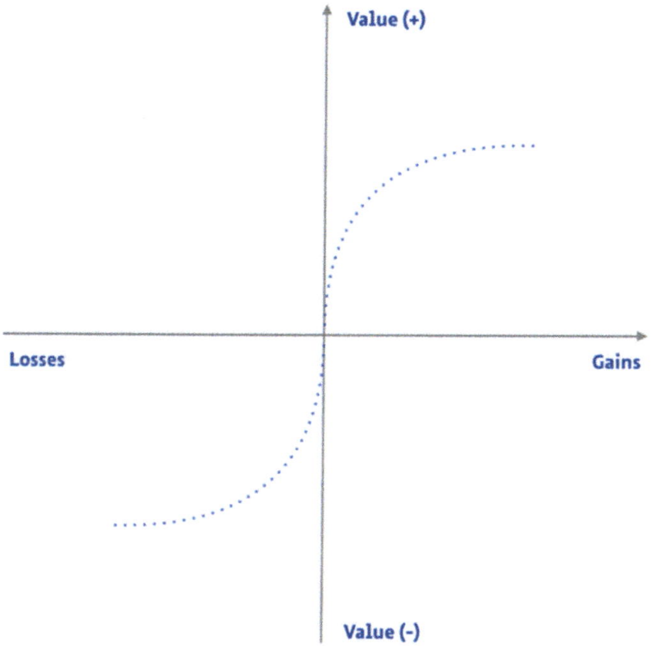

Fig. 1.1 The psychological value of choice. (From Kahneman and Tversky)

it is not possible to evaluate and make a decision or a choice. When below the neutral value, then evaluations shift toward a greater risk-taking, and vice versa when the value is above the neutral value risk exposure, it shifts toward risk reduction or aversion.

Unlike ORT models, the psychological value model predicts where the reference point that guides perception will fall in a hypothetical S-shaped function: for instance, a loss of 1000 € out of 2000€ is a bigger psychological pain than a loss of the same 1000 € out of a 200,000 €. Furthermore, the model predicts that a loss causes a bigger emotional blow and thus the psychological reaction of a loss outweighs that of a win. Psychological reactions are essential in determining the weight of the probability attributed to an event: for instance, in the case of ambivalent or vague situations lacking certain probability values and stable points of reference, events with lower probability tend to bear more weight. And moderately to highly probable events bear lower weight. The *prospect theory* explains this in terms of a greater propensity to risk aversion—not wishing to lose is associated with a higher probability outweighing the opposite perspective—that is a gain. If points of reference are not certain (labile), most people will opt for a more prudential point of view and base their choices on a smaller risk.

The experimental paradigm on the effect the dependence model has on the reference model has been reproduced in many real-life situations, and not just by Tversky and Kahneman. As they say in their preface to *Choices, Values, and Frames*, "We were surprised by how easy it was to construct different versions of a decision problem that were transparently equivalent when considered together but evoked different preferences when considered separately." By manipulating the representations of decision-based problems, the impact of framing has been proved time and time again in medical and surgical decisions, retail sales to consumers, negotiation and legal matters, allocation of resources in the public sector, and voting outcomes.

The impact of framing is all too clear also in the case of innovation: who pays for innovation? Typically, innovation investment costs fall on the consumer whatever the source of the money used for the investment.[25] An investment presumes a return and a higher price compared to a standard product or service: when presenting them as *premium*, one is implying a paradigm of choice. The additional price incurred in means enjoying the advantages offered by the innovation to the consumer who is available to pay for the advantages of the innovation. This in turn implies a slow spread of innovation and the actual creation of an access threshold to access the new product or service, due to the greater cost incurred compared to a standard service or product with a lower innovation value (see more in Parts II and III on this point). Behavioral economics also predict that if the higher price is presented as a discount, more people will be willing to pay for the premium service/product compared to the number of people who would in any case pay the additional price for the premium product/service.[26] In fact, people tend to overestimate the subtractive value in terms of cost rather than the added value in purchasing the innovation. As we will see in Part IV, strategies aimed at manipulating variables contribute to the creation of representations, and narratives accelerate sustainable innovation programs. Good new habits can prevail without waiting for their slow spreading.

1.7 Propensity for Transformation

In the previous pages, I referred to the lability of points of reference (reference outcomes). We noticed how it is difficult to maintain a stable reference to build a decision consistent with our value system in our everyday lives and also that very often we lack a stable value system and count on context information and on the contrast between context and target to reach a judgment. In prospect theory, the reference point can be the current state the person is in and which they have adapted to or it can correspond to the level of aspiration regardless of whether an ideal is attainable or not. However, if we discover that our point of reference is not valid, we adapt to the new point of reference.

As mentioned, when the reference point changes as the result of a discovery, we then change choices and preference. However, we may change our preferences as our reference point changes without realizing it. Theory admits and predicts that

[25] This is also the case for the investments with public funding.

[26] Thaler [21].

reference points change all the time, according to our habits and ability to adapt. System 1 favors this process of easy adaptation with little energy and without counting on System 2. In other words, it favors learning when adaptation is possible, and we can reach an admissible judgment, that is, one consistent with the point of reference (see more in Part II on this point).

As we will see later, neurobiological theories of homeostasis explain the adaptation to new or different points of view: we are prepared to accept another point of view if the new situation enables us to maintain stability, even if only apparent, or to follow an aspiration.[27] In fact, stable change is not possible or not conceivable unless one can adapt to the new reference points. Clearly, we don't have to be aware that our reference point has changed or that we are adapting another point of reference. This proves that propensity to change is an important part of System 1 automatic processes. Health insurance is a case in point: most people decide to purchase health insurance in addition to the national health service (when and where a public system is available, like in most Europe) because they prefer a loss in value over a possible higher loss or uncertainty on speed of access to proper care, despite the onset of disease being uncertain or unknown. The psychological value of the yearly premium is seen as lower than that of the psychological cost associated with dealing with a serious disease with little or delayed coverage.

However, if and when the insured person develops a stable model on the personal or subjective probability of normal and unexpected events such as medical and therapeutic expenses, then they are able to choose which premium to pay and know how to fine-tune the variable cost of the deductible excess. A newly insured person usually opts for a higher monthly premium to have a lower deductible or excess, that is, the amount to pay as a partial coverage of costs above which the insurance steps in. As time goes by, track records of yearly medical costs incurred make it possible to improve and change the reference model, faced with the evidence that a lower excess is not necessarily an advantage of accumulated saving. Policy holders become more knowledgeable and improve the reference point increasing risk threshold more efficiently, accepting a higher deductible saving by opting for lower monthly premiums.

As discussed in Chap. 2, social psychology self-control and self-efficacy describe the ability to undergo comprehensive adaptation and transformation of self-control mechanisms and how this increases awareness on how to manage System 1 automatic mechanisms. The prospective approach of a health policy is acquired when transformed reference models give a better understanding of how to address and manage risk and uncertainty. In fact, reference models would remain stable were it not for experience and the opportunity to correct choices: knowledge makes it possible to prospectively foresee how one will feel in the future. Ulysses asks his companions to tie him to the mast of the ship not yield to the mermaids' call.

---

[27] Visciola [25].

1.8 Resilience

The psychological effect of dependence on the reference model has already been described as the most meaningful violation of the invariance principle underpinning ORT. We also established that System 1 acts actively limiting information access to System 2. We will now move to the last of the key processes properties that act automatically in controlling our adaptive behavior, *resilience to change*, which has major implications on the effective possibility of modifying behavior once individual habits and collective practices have become engrained. The automatic patterns we use and especially our dependence on framing and context determine the decisional behavior of any person, regardless of their level of experience, expertise, and ability to analyze information.

In a series of tests performed in seven different experimental decision-making settings, two US researchers, LeBoeuf and Shafir,[28] considered several hypotheses to verify whether framing effects were experimental artifacts or biases that could be overcome by giving participants the chance to think choices over and possibly change their minds or avoid the effect of reference point dependence. Would we consider reference points and context less important if we had more time to think? Do people who think more (*need for cognition, NC*) escape dependence on reference points (*frame*)? Experimental studies addressed these two questions, manipulating both the situation where variables refer to the level of information and thought and then the situation where one can justify one's choice. In both cases the experiment had to verify whether dependence from the reference model was reduced.

Experiments were set up to verify the following hypotheses:

1. Reference point dependence is confirmed.
2. The effects on reference-dependence are more significant in conditions where there is no possibility to justify one's choice and a greater amount of information is not available.
3. The effects of reference-dependence are less or none for those who were able to justify their choice and those who ask for more time to think of the answer.

To complete the above, I shall illustrate the seven decisional situations examined in the course of the experiments (see Table 1.4): the choice between a certain and an uncertain endowment; the choice between repurchasing a lost ticket or not going to the movies; the choice between two political candidates (Frank/Carl); the choice between surgery and radiotherapy; the choice between cuts and pay increase; and the choice between an increase and a greater tax allowance. Participants were selected using a need for cognition (NC) scale and distributed into two groups, each with a number of people with a high and a low NC. Furthermore, participants in the group where they had to justify their presence were asked to make their preference explicit and explain the rationale underlying their choice.

[28] Leboeuf and Shafir [22].

Table 1.4 Significant experimental effects of "framing"

Framing types							
	Cuts vs pays	Asian problem	Lost ticket	Taxes	Frank/ Carl	400$ endowment	Surgery vs radiotherapy
Main effect	$p > 0.001$	$p > 0.001$	$p > 0.001$	$p > 0.001$	$p > 0.001$	$p > 0.001$	$p > 0.001$
Need for cognition (NC)	Ns	$p > 0.02$	Ns	Ns	Ns	Ns	$p > 0.10$
Justification	Ns	$p > 0.08$	Ns	Ns	$p > 0.005$	Ns	Ns

ns not significant
Adapted from LeBoeuf and Shafir.

The results in Table 1.4 show how the effect of reference model dependence was confirmed by all the experimental tests.[29] The two hypotheses concerning dependence variability proved not significant in all cases except for a low and therefore unreliable significance in the choice of candidate. Reference model dependence remained a cross-effect in all experiments and invariably in all the conditions of decision-making. Stability of established automatic processes was also confirmed. This long series of experiments indicated that people more inclined to analyze their choices in detail and justify their preferences also saw their representation of reference models as resilient in any further choices. Nevertheless, they did not change their minds and confirmed the choice by selecting a *risk averse* profile when offered an alternative between a smaller or greater advantage and *a risk seeking* profile *when* the alternative presented the possibility of a loss. A study of choice rationales shows that participants most willing to address decision-making had a more stable preference and therefore found consistency among the various reference models. As a result, researchers believe it is possible to argue that the more sophisticated participants confirm their choices because they recognize that a different choice—that is, risk aversion or risk seeking independently of the model presenting information—would indicate inconsistent decisions. However, such inconsistency is acceptable because of *how* (the conditions) the choice is made can determine the decision itself.

This overview of experimental tests in psychology laboratories highlights the role of cognitive automatisms in regulating human behavior whose mechanisms are the basis of our daily choices and of the adaptive dynamics to task and context. George Miller's and Herbert Simon's intuitions on our bounded and imperfect rationality have become scientific cornerstones of our understanding of behavior.[30] Possibly the most important contribution to the foundation of sustainable innovation is the evidence that the context and representation of information are decisive in shaping our choices and orientations. One wonders whether situational features,

[29] In statistics, significance measures the presence or absence of an experimental effect and therefore the validity of the tested hypothesis. The probability that the hypothesis is correct is considered very high when the significance is greater than 0.001.

[30] Miller [23]; Simon [24].

that is, the variables that characterize the environment we live and act in and dispositional variables that describe the distinctive traits of our behavior, interact with how we interface (our interaction) with the environment, how we represent reality, and our ability to adapt.

Highlights

- The idea of human-computer symbiosis and the consequent invention of the Internet and all technological apparatus are the result of a magnificent multidisciplinary cooperative program.
- The intention behind the human-computer symbiosis paradigm is to transform work-related behaviors, by increasing decision-making, creativity, communication, and cooperative skills.
- Emotions underlie cognitive automatic processes and can misguide behaviors.
- Good design is human-centered in facilitating the learning of perceptive-motor routines that can easily become habits requiring a low cognitive involvement.
- Dual processes are referred to the distribution of human cognition between parallel sensory motor processes (i.e., System 1) and controlled serial processes (i.e., System 2).
- Errors of judgment are typical in everyone daily life.
- Cognitive automatic processes are not accessible by introspection.
- Mental automatisms are triggered by easily accessible perceptual and judgment patterns.
- Mental automatisms are manipulable.
- Preferences do not form with regularity.
- Alternatives between choices play an important role in preference forming.
- The choice in the background plays a role and persists even when it is not possible to offer deductive reasoning.
- People do not always have well-defined values and build choices according to how the problem is represented.
- Context dependence sets preferences: the median value is preferred because of extremeness aversion.
- Preference reversal is the explanation for contradictory choices: when preference reversal happens, our experience is not associated with irrationality nor with the inability to judge.
- We are not aware when we fail in following consistent judgment paths.
- When presenting an innovative product as "premium," we are implying a paradigm of hierarchical choices with exclusive selection criteria, which in turn means a slow spread of innovation.
- People can change preferences without being aware of it.
- Change is not possible without a "reference point."
- Propensity to change is an important feature of automatic processes.
- Automatic mental processes are resilient.

References

1. Watson, J. B. (1913). Psychology as the behaviorist views it. *Psychological Review, 20*, 1–16.
2. Watson, J. B., & Rayner, R. (1924). *Psychological care of the infant and child.* Chicago University Press.
3. Skinner, B. F. (1974). *About behaviorism.* Kopf.
4. Licklider, J. C. R. (1960). *Man-computer symbiosis, IRE transactions on human factors in electronics* (Vol. HFE-1, pp. 4–11).
5. Licklider, J. R. C., & Taylor, R. W. (1968). The computer as a communication device. *Science and Technology*. Vol. 76, pp. 21-38.
6. Norman, D. (2013). *The design of everyday things. Revised and expanded.* Basic Books.
7. Gibson, J. J. (1979). *The ecological approach to visual perception.* Houghton Mifflin Harcourt (HMH).
8. Norman, D. A. (1993). *Things that make us smart: Defending human attributes in the age of the machine*. William Patrick Book. Basic Books.
9. Norman, D. A. (2005). *Emotional design: why we love (or hate) everyday things*. Basic Books.
10. Schneider, W., Dumais Sue, T., Shiffrin, A., & Richard, N. (1977). Automatic/control processing and attention. Detection, search, and attention. *Psychological Review, 84*, 1–66.
11. Damasio, A. (2011). *Self comes to mind: Constructing the conscious brain. The Evolution of Consciousness*. William Heinemann.
12. Damasio, A. (2018). *The strange order of things. Life, feelings and the making of cultures.* Pantheon Books.
13. Edelman, G. M., & Tononi, G. (2001). *Consciousness. How matter becomes imagination.* Penguin Press.
14. Visciola, M. (1985). *Attention patterns in fencing*. Scuola dello Sport. Rivista di cultura sportiva. November, n.2
15. Norman, D., & Shallice, T. (1986). Attention to action: willed and automatic control of behavior. In R. Davidson, R. Schwartz, & A. D. Shapiro (Eds.), *Consciousness and self-regulation: Advances in research and theory IV*. Plenum Press.
16. Rasmussen, J. (1986). *Information processing and human-machine interaction: An approach to cognitive engineering*. North-Holland.
17. Kahneman, D., Slovic, P., & Tversky, A. (1982). *Judgement under uncertainty.* Cambridge University Press.
18. Kahneman, D., & Tversky, A. (2000). *Choices, values and frames*. Cambridge University Press.
19. Tversky, A., & Simonson, I. (2000). Context-dependent preferences. In *Choices, values and frames*. Russell Sage Foundation.
20. Huber, J., Payne, J. W., & Andand Puto, C. (1982). Adding asymmetrically dominated alternatives: Violations of regularity and similarity hypothesis. *Journal of Consumer Research, 10*(31–44), 29.
21. Thaler, R. (1980). Towards a positive theory of consumer choice. *Journal of Economic Behavioral and Organization, 39*, 36–90 7,8,9,33,38.
22. Leboeuf, R., & Shafir, E. (2003). Deep thoughts and shallow frames. *Journal of Behavioral Decision Making, 16*, 77–92.
23. Miller, G. A. (1956). The magical number seven, plus or minus two: Some limits on our capacity for processing information. *Psychological Review, 63*(2), 81–97.
24. Simon, H. (1979). *Models of thoughts*. Yale University Press.
25. Visciola, M. (2020). Thinking as behavioral scientists and acting as designers. In A.Samson (Ed.), *The Behavioral Economics Guide 2020* (with an Introduction by Colin Camerer) (pp. 69-79).

Chapter 2
The Determinants of Behaviors

I shall be drawing from social psychology in discussing the relationship between situational and dispositional determinants, that is, on the close relationship or interdependence between the characteristics of our cognitive automatisms and the structural and environmental characteristics of the cultures in which we live. Furthermore, I'll also refer to the latest research in evolutionary biology and cultural anthropology that links the theory of evolution to behavioral sciences, as these are the domains that best highlight the variety of adaptive behaviors (heterogeneity) and their evolution in the cultural traits that go beyond individual differences.

Situationism—as described by Kurt Lewin's school—offered a major perspective for research. So did the later developments of other great psychologists such as Leon Festinger, Solomon Asch, Lee Ross, and Richard Nisbett. Fundamental research on these subjects assumes that behavior results from personal and environmental factors. However, the strength of this research is to demonstrate how environmental variations can impact on behavior to the point it can give unexpected and surprising results. Situations are so powerful that they can undermine all certainties and beliefs on free will and the actual possibilities of an individual to avoid the control and strength of environmental and social determinants. The most widely accepted interpretations of experimental outcomes of these demonstrations (a person's stable traits or dispositions) prove to be less significant than what observers might presume. People tend to absorb the influence of their reference groups(s) and to assimilate their values without asking themselves basic questions: social communities or more widely a person's ethnic group are the normative reference for an individual, who tacitly compares with them to determine whether their behavior is adequate.

There are many good examples of "nonobvious" experiments:[1] I would like to recall the experiments on conformity, where a person is induced by a group of

[1] These are experimental situations whose results contradict common sense; Ross and Nisbett [1].

M. Visciola, *Sustainable Innovation*,
https://doi.org/10.1007/978-3-031-18751-3_2

accomplices to freely deny visual evidence and to state the opposite of what they have just seen.[2] The experiments on obeying to authority figures where the participants do not rebel against the instructions to administer electroshock to a "victim" in the room next room.[3] The studies on non-moral behavior such as the research led Zimbardo at Stanford *prisoners* and *guards*: guards were selected among normal people with low levels of aggressiveness, and their aggressive and punitive behavior developed directly as a consequence of the prisoners' rebellious behavior.[4] Many experiments were organized to show how surprisingly behavior adapts to expectations determined by circumstances, the leading one being many interpretations of the so-called prisoner's dilemma.[5] In a version of this simulation,[6] the game's name is changed although the rules remain the same: it is either presented as a stock exchange, the *Wall Street Game* in the first case, or as a community, the *Community Game* in the second one, a typical experiment designed according to the framing paradigm. The researcher reminds participants that they can either cooperate or resort to conflict. Simulation rules reward the outcome of the decision at the end of each round, rather than truth or readiness to cooperate. Table 2.1 shows the matrix used to assign points or prizes to each participant according to the choice made when it is their turn: each player knows the prize-giving matrix and is aware it can be consulted at any time; clearly, they will only discover if the other has chosen to cooperate or conflict at the end of the round. As Table 2.1 shows, if they both cooperate, they both gain, and if neither do, they both lose out. However, if one cooperates in the round where the other has opted not to, they will lose an important share of their prize to the advantage of the other. Results clearly show that whatever the personal nature of the participants, two thirds of those told it was the Wall Street simulation chose conflict, while two thirds chose to cooperate when told it was the Community Game. In other words, the framing effect was very strong and was also confirmed in more complex decision-making settings.

Table 2.1 The matrix with the reward or penalty system for each of the four possibilities provided

		Player 2	
Player 1		Collaboration	Conflict
	Collaboration	Player 1 + 40 cents Player 2 + 40 cents	Player 1–20 cents Player 2 + 80 cents
	Conflict	Player 1 + 80 cents Player 2–20 cents	Player 1 zero cents Player 2 zero cents

[2] Asch Asch [2].

[3] Milgram [3]

[4] Musen and Zimbardo [4].

[5] Axelrod and Hamilton [5]; Axelrod [6].

[6] Liberman et al. [7].

Table 2.2 In the simulation game you collaborate more in cooperative community contexts than in competitive contexts

Percentage		Wall Street simulation	Cooperation simulation
	Collaboration	30%	66%
	Conflict	70%	34%

This confirms that in our daily routines, we are typically unaware of the relative lability of the most frequently used reference outcomes, as we are unaware of the potential effects and consequences of the reference outcomes we are using. We fail to realize the possible contradiction between and among the schemata being used. Social psychologists and cultural anthropologists developed their sphere of investigation and gamut of knowledge on the basis of varied perceptions and representations and how they generate expectations, to then say that our expectations and goals shape our anticipations of perceptions and representations (Table 2.2).[7]

By examining the functional "distortions" ensuing from these cognitive shifts—from perception to representation and action—we are touching the core aspects of the debate on dispositional determinants. It is especially important to deal with individual determinants in cognitive processes because when analyzing real life, we tend not to clearly distinguish between the incidence and weight of situational and dispositional aspects. One can easily sway and under- or overestimate the relative incidence of each set of variables. Frequently, behavioral investigation questionnaires or protocols in any field—say health, consumers, finance, or insurance—clearly identify and tell all the variables apart. Although dispositional variables clearly contribute in a significant and paradigmatic manner both to willingness and to preference and habit shaping, they are often within the boundaries of a limited management of motivational aspects related to behavior and personality theories. In fact, they are variables that go beyond motivational and personality classifications. One of the distortions highlighted by Lee Ross's research team is the so-called naive realism,[8] that is, the unspoken assumption that there is a sort of isomorphism between subjective and objective experiences. Groups that wish to build their identity's image on characteristics, beliefs, and values corresponding to positive images tend to read their subjective experience as if they were objective. Even as individuals, we tend to select the information that reinforces some of our identitarian features from our environment. Naïve realism gives rise to biases, tendencies, and distorts or simplifies reality. *Confirmation bias* is a perception bias based on the assimilation of biased information and partial perceptions to validate beliefs and inaccurate theories even when faced with evidence to the contrary. Such biases lead to further perception paths such as *self-fulfilling prophecies*[9] and *selective comparisons* toward people who are perceived as having a lower status when in a difficult situation or with a better status when in a stable situation.

[7] Bruner [8].

[8] Robinson et al. [9].

[9] Robert et al. [10].

Selective comparisons play an important role in maintaining a degree of perceptive stability of the self. Bias uses representations and narrations that attribute a positive result to one's actions and skills and a negative result to external factors (*self-serving bias*).[10] This behavior reduces the possibility of exploiting opportunities for change. A self-serving bias can twist the actual situation in one's favor but also to one's disadvantage[11] and can be considered on a par with cognitive automatisms.

Just like automatisms affect our ability to express judgments and make choices, likewise, self-perception automatisms evolve and can be manipulated. Schachter and Singer's[12] studies on the relationship between physiological and cognitive states of experience provide some of the most interesting evidence. The two researchers from the Festinger School proved that when we experience neurovegetative arousal, we look for an explanation and attribute the emotion to the cognitive categories available to us at the time. The two-factor theory of emotions is linked to the large family of dual processes: we are aroused every time the situation we are in presents with a new factor, and this generates an emotion and thus behavioral reactions. Our reactions are the result of an emotion and therefore of behavioral reactions. Such reactions correspond to an implicit or explicit (overt) definition of the cognitive explanation of the emotion.

Let us dwell on these two definitions: implicit and explicit. According to the dual theory, our emotions are what we experience in arousal. We seek an explanation of arousal only if the event triggering our emotions is unfamiliar, and, in these cases, we rely on the cognitive evidence in the situation we are in, assessing it to name and define the emotion experienced. This is the explicit phase where System 2 intervenes.[13] The neurovegetative state can give rise known, acquired emotions that do not require further explanations because they are implicit. In this case, we are dealing with automatisms that trigger automatic behavior without going through conscious evaluation. In Schachter and Singer's experimental conditions, arousal and synthetic adrenaline (epinephrine) were manipulated artificially as is cognitive attribution by *priming* that is directing experiment participants to happiness or anger. Results showed that the same neurophysiological state can give rise to opposed emotional evaluations—rage or happiness—and that manipulation when evaluating the causes of the arousal can give rise to misattributions.

The effects of misattribution give rise to research on the manipulation of emotions although there is no unequivocal interpretation of Schachter and Singer's experimental results. The two-factor theory has not been universally accepted.[14] The

[10] Miller and Ross [11].

[11] Higgins et al. [12].

[12] Schachter and Singer [13].

[13] Clearly the two researchers did not use these words, but they refer explicitly to a phase of conscious evaluation which can be described and rationalized.

[14] Cotton [14].

effects of misattributions are documented in research on aggressiveness, attraction, sexual reactions, discomfort, and mood.

I shall be illustrating some conclusions that might prove useful: automatisms giving rise to attribution biases cannot be easily manipulated, as once established they are not accessible to self-examination and have the properties of resilience as above described.[15] People often settle for incomplete or naïve models to explain their emotional state, that is, they are unable to understand if they are misattributing the emotional experienced. Lastly, they tend to avoid conditions where it is difficult to identify the reason underlying the emotionally triggered physiological arousal.[16]

In our daily lives, we use attribution biases. There has been no experimental research on how the biases interact with situational factors, but it is reasonable to suggest that the interface between attribution biases and situations gives rise to a series of adaptation or behavioral patterns that can lead to individual differences. Studies on individual differences relevant to the present text include self-regulation of behavior, ability to control, and cultural dimension of the self (interdependence).

A first fundamental observation of the so-called *priming* effect[17] or preparation of the task takes us back to the previous comments on cognitive automatisms and the impossibility of consciously accessing to their inner mechanisms as we are acting. The term *priming* refers to the pre-attentive nature of the signs and its implicit nature in influencing our behavior. An interesting set of experiments shows that if the clues or pointers of a task are presented as positive expectations, we are more successful as opposed to when they have a negative connotation: we adapt to the context in an acritical manner, especially in the presence of stereotypes. In other words, we are able to pick those pointers that orient us, although we are unaware of the effect they will have on us. Emotional, facial, and postural expressions of the people are some of the pointers we immediately latch on to.[18] Emotions and body postures communicate the signs which we perceive whatever culture we belong to. Conversely, in spite of their universal cultural value and context dependence, there is no definitive evidence on the impact that the recognition/acknowledgment of emotional signals has on people. For instance, some signals are known to hit the target. In other words, they generate reciprocal reactions—for instance, calling for help—or of attraction, such as standard or culturally beauty, or repulsion, disgust, and fear when they occur in a context where attention is free. However, when attention is not available, positive messages signaling a possible gain are more successful if they support evidence, that is, if they are consistent with the goals the person is intending to achieve: dieting is a good case in point. If it is a matter of preventing undesirable consequences and maintaining a stable condition, messages described as a loss work better. It is known as *attention myopia*, which as we shall see in Part

---

[15] See Izard [15]. See also Chap. 1.

[16] Bargh [16].

[17] Nisbett and Wilson [17].

[18] Ekman [18].

IV is especially relevant in accounting for and improving behavioral self-regulation of behavior to remain healthy.

Every human being finds it difficult to maintain behavioral control, to reduce switching between virtuous and loose and avoid behavior leading to undesirable consequences. However, experience and common sense tell us that we don't all act or react in the same way to similar circumstances. Scientific evidence indicates that individual differences start shaping early in life:[19] for instance, some well-known longitudinal studies [20]proved that the youths who had the ability to postpone gratification in the course of the experiment were also the ones who attained more ambitious aims in life—in terms of universities and careers—compared to those who had sought immediate gratification.

Albert Bandura's studies and research on the self-regulation of behavior, human agency, and the effectiveness of the self[21] are known for the influence they had on social psychologists and sociologists. According to Bandura, as time goes by, some of the positive individual traits can lead to choices that in turn determine opportunities and create conditions which can objectively bring out the person's positive characteristics. This pioneering research from the last century has become part and parcel of today's economic theories on social impact[22] suggesting that skills acquired in one's early years play a key role in developing good habits, both in terms of looking after one's health and also to maintain conditions of well-being. Such differences are not just due to different personalities or to the presence (or absence) of psychological illnesses. The ability to develop one's individuality and interdependence within one's reference community is a skill developed over time through obstinacy. As Bandura puts it, *self-efficacy* is a person's belief or set of beliefs in their ability to succeed that determine how well one can execute an action in prospective situations.[23]

The belief that one *can* succeed triggers patterns of thought and action that speak of determination, perseverance, and resistance to frustrations. The ability to self-regulate and "find one's path"[24] is clearly the result of having proved it was possible to have success. Despite being based on emotional and cognitive constituents established in the early years of one's life, it is a skill, and as such it needs to be exercised; it requires constancy and results. When people with these distinctive traits are asked in the context of their actions, they show or describe the mental routines which they use to channel choices and behavior consistent with the profile of their life's goals.

[19] Ever since John Bowlby's early studies gathered in his brilliant collection on the theory of primary attachment, see Bowlby [19]

[20] Ross and Nisbett [20].

[21] Bandura [21–23].

[22] The initiative of the so-called brain economy and the Brain Capital Index (BCI) is also interesting, in that it aims to measure the impact that economy generates on cognitive well-being and how capital and investments can be measured and evaluated according to the generated well-being indices. See Cunha and Heckman [24].

[23] Bandura, 1977 op.cit.

[24] Bandura [23]; Mann and Ward [25].

In addition, they actively choose positive reference points, people, or life events that share the idea they have of themselves or to an idea close to it. This mental activity contributes to the creation of adaptable and flexible psychological states, which in turn act as a basis to receive positive feedback, such as encouragement and explicit recognition. The ability to feel at ease with others is one of the key ingredients of self-efficacy: it makes one feel comfortable with one's self and generates the need to be perceived as a rational and consistent person, worthy of trust because morally deserving it. One of the results of learning social life skills is the ability to measure one's self against reference points or models[25] that offer a context and an inspiration to refer to in assessing one's behavior and to define one's line of conduct.

Bandura's theory of self-efficacy and social learning virtually bridges the gap between behaviorists such as Watson and Skinner (the possibility of modifying behavior by reinforcing positive experiences) and the early twenty-first-century Seligman and Csikszentmihalyi, two American psychologists who suggested the definition of "positive psychology" to research the psychological states that lead to well-being.[26] Positive psychology studies focus on psychological states such as happiness, hope, gratitude, forgiveness, love, optimism, and creativity. Although these studies are not directly linked[27] to epigenetic research, increasing evidence indicates the close relationship and the interdependence between psychological states and hormonal components and how these affect expectations about life, cell physiological and biological states. Serotonin, oxytocin, and dopamine are considered feel-good hormones that stimulate positive thoughts, reassuring mental routines, and these in turn facilitate the reproduction of these neurotransmitters and hormones according to virtuous cycles. Relevant psychobiological research is in its early stages but already offers interesting glimpses into the relationship between our biome, the microorganisms of our digestive system, and how the biological states and cycles of our brains are regulated. As explained below, the cognitive abilities that play out in positive psychology are the same one underlying cooperation and the ethical development of our behavior.

2.1 Cumulative and Additive Effects of Experiences

The individual propensity of developing a positive self-image leads to agentive behavior and the resistance to negative feedback. Action plan drafting leads to cumulative effects where situational and dispositional features are intertwined in ever-changing ways. However, the cumulative exposure to stressors and negative feedback tests an individual's ability to build positive images and to reduce negative systematic tendencies, cognitive automatisms, and mental routines. In the absence

[25] See Bandura's notion of modeling, which is not the same as the one used in the present text.

[26] Seligman [26]

[27] Snyder and Lopez [27]

of positive reference points, we tend to assimilate negative reference points and to reproduce them until such time as those are penalized in practice.[28] Inequalities, design flaws in access systems to resources, and narrations that disproportionately justify and reward the individual's ability to gain high profits impact negatively and have consequences on one's self, on equality (fairness), and in society. Accumulated subjective negative experiences, starting from an objectively disadvantaged situation, have a deep impact on one's self-perception and on the resulting representations of what is possible and legitimate.

The different theories of behavioral change (see Part III) all recognize the great impact that negative experiences and stress have on humans and how they act in a cumulative manner: as a result, people find it very difficult to change the basis of their behaviors. Negative mental routines lead to lower levels of attention, a worse self-image, limit introspection, and develop negative expectations even when they are not necessarily backed by evidence. Lastly, the cumulative effects of social, situational, and dispositional determinants have now been studied in many fields and not just social psychology and anthropology. Evolutionary biologists and physiologists, epidemiologists, and doctors have added their work to that of psychologists and anthropologists.[29]

All these studies point to a person's agentivity having social and relational features. They show how the latter play an essential role in understanding the cumulative and additive effects of experience and of the risks to well-being and health. More in general, they indicate how to withstand and foresee social pressure caused by change. We should not let our assumptions on Olympian rationality spill over into how we understand ability of factors able to modify perceptive, mental, and cognitive routines that can lead to accumulating negative experiences. Narratives about free will and the freedom of choice are delusive and cloak the many nuances that reality reveals if the appropriate lens is used.

The question then is how can positive psychology, the ability to adapt and promote collaborative social behavior in themselves, establish the premises for sustainable innovation? What is required for individual well-being and cooperation to progress? How can innovative services facilitate agentivity, the ability to navigate complexity, positive self-regulatory skills, and the ability to promote change? Furthermore, who has the moral responsibility to improve life conditions and favor rightful participation to change for the social good? Such are the questions that I will try and address in the next pages. These themes will then be reiterated in Part III, where how to shape change for sustainable innovation is discussed.

Cumulative effects of experience contribute to the shaping of life stories. In a series of activities linked to ethnographic research and systematic observation (2010 to 2020), we collected the personal stories of tens of participants in our research activities that highlighted the cumulative strength of lived experience. The

[28] See further a study of the consequences of deviatiation of social behavior in cooperation.

[29] Snyder-Mackler et al. [28].

experiential sphere accrued over time guides individual perception on the possibility to act and impart a direction to one's life.

Research was aimed at:

(a) Understanding situational and dispositional factors to map clusters of participants selected with guiding criteria.
(b) Identifying opportunities to innovate services and products to promote greater agentivity and regulatory capacity for behavior.

In the course of this research, we related participants' ability to describe and show their reactivity or proactivity in managing their lives with reference to a number of key research topics, the ability to move in social context able to support their individual, family objectives, or more generally those of their personal ecosystem.

2.2 Elderly Lifestyles and Sustainable Services in Singapore

One such research project was commissioned by the Design Council of Singapore.[30] The aim of the project was to understand the lifestyles of the elderly population (60- to 90-year-olds) by studying how they took care of their health at close quarters and access to services for the elderly in the city-state. The project required a lengthy and careful preparation, and field research lasted 4 months. Twenty-four people were selected according to the percentage of their ethnic group in Singapore. Other socio-demographics such as income level, gender, and cohabiting household were also considered, so as to include all the variables of the social ecosystem. Field activities included contextual interviews in the participant's house. Furthermore, the team carried out targeted observation sessions aimed at understanding meaningful daily life routines of the research samples, with a focus on health, transport, nutrition, assistance, free time, and social life. Results showed a great variety and wealth of subjective personal experience, a hallmark of Singapore's ethnic and cultural diversity, comparable to the biodiversity of the Galápagos Islands in terms of range and harmonious coexistence.

The research protocol was agreed with the team and validated by experts with a knowledge of the local social welfare and healthcare systems. The protocol stated the areas to be investigated in depth to trace the typical days and journeys in terms of access to care, welfare, and health services for the elderly. A number of assumptions to be validated were also included: how the architecture of the services for senior citizens—available as a public resource—welfare and benefit policies, matched the sample's ability to navigate the complex sphere of rules and access procedures (see Fig. 2.1 Map of the Health Ecosystem in Singapore). Specifically, we wanted to verify the understanding and ability to access resources made available to the public to continue to benefit from assistance in the absence of a pension

[30] Visciola et al. [29].

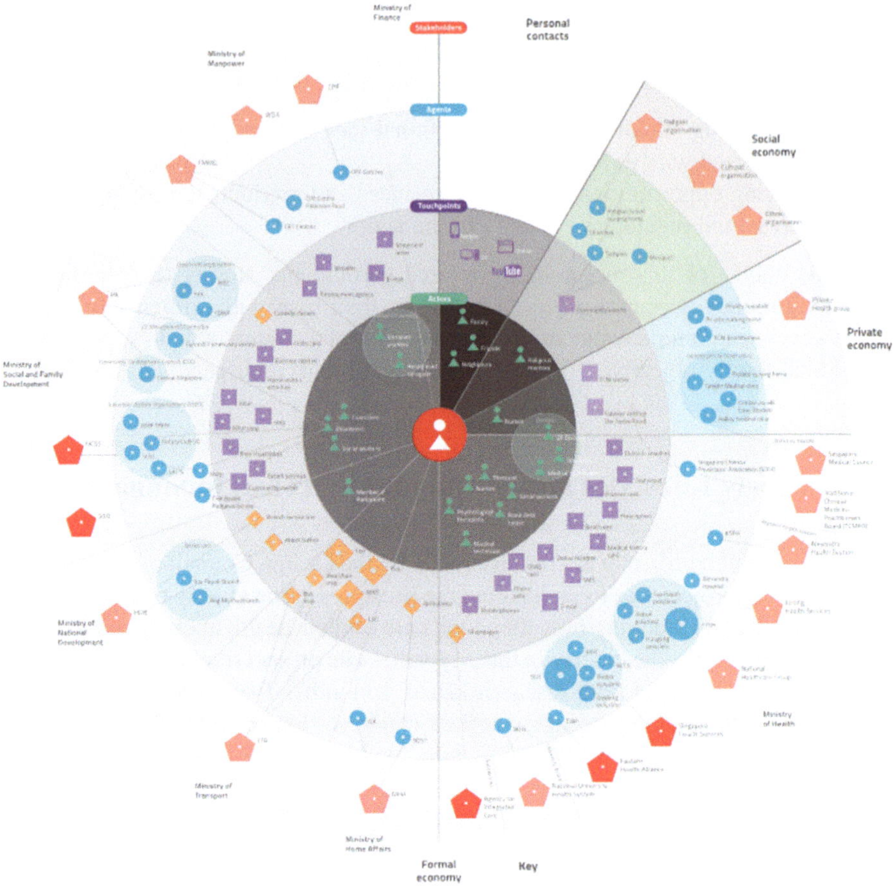

Fig. 2.1 Map of the Health Ecosystem in Singapore (year 2015). (Thanks to Erin O'Loughlin, Ciara Green, Gina Taha, Xiangyi Tang, and Jan-Christoph Zoels who were contributing to the definition of the map)

system coverage.[31] The study also intended to evidence the opportunity to rethink the welfare system; improve orientation, onboarding; and innovate the offer of available services.

Qualitative data gathered in the field were analyzed according to the practices of ethnographic research and subsequently represented as insight, drawn from experiential and narrative data. Lastly, insights were grouped into distinctive cluster. Results defined a sort of algorithm organizing the 24 participants in 6 groups and 2 subgroups. Each group was then mapped along two virtual axes contrasting agentivity (on the x-axis), that is, reactivity and proactivity, and social competence (on the

[31] Singapore's pension system is relatively young as the state is very recent and, as a result, there is a very high number of Singapore's elderly without insurance coverage or with partial coverage.

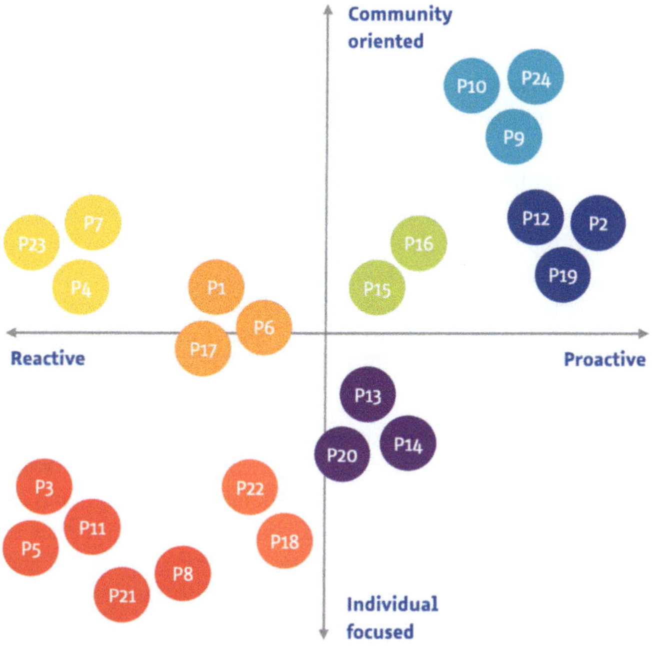

Fig. 2.2 The clusters of elderly population in Singapore. (Thanks to Erin O'Loughlin, Ciara Green, Gina Taha, Xiangyi Tang who participated in the definition of the axes)

y-axis), that is, social isolation vs belonging to one or more community. The distribution of the sample of participants grouped by their cluster is shown in Fig. 2.2. Given the same socioeconomic conditions, the clusters differed in their ability to identify welfare and care aid and to navigate the service system to access resources made available to the public sector as participation in community activities, free transport passes, booking prevention services, housing services, and so on. The different personal histories, the impact of their cultural heritage still present in daily lives, highlighted the diversity of behavior and a limited and mottled understanding of policies to access public services. Clearly the heterogeneity of the potential demand for services was high. To address such large individual and cultural differences, service programs cannot be easily standardized and homogeneously weighted across the board.

2.3 Security Perception and Urban Regeneration in Northern Italy

In the course of another research project carried out in Turin, we investigated and analyzed perceptions of safety in a neighborhood with a majority of non-EU first- and second-generation migrants. The research followed a European Commission co-funded plan to regenerate an urban fabric plagued by the slow industrial decline of the city. The neighborhood close to the old city center had slowly lost the previously working-class residents and had been repopulated by non-EU migrants attracted by the availability of low-cost housing. Although violence and crime rates in Turin are not higher than the country average, the press and political campaigns described the neighborhood as no-man's land, especially at night, pointing to drug dealing and use along the river and in some areas with empty buildings. The City of Turin was aware of the state of decline in the neighborhood and also took on board what the Municipal Police (*Polizia Municipale*) reported on a negative perception of safety, especially where women and mothers were concerned. Furthermore, the concerns on the risks of gentrification of the area raised the need to act promptly. The aim was to gather the personal stories/histories of the new residents to understand how they differed in terms of their perception of safety in the neighborhood streets and renaissance of the neighborhood's social life and on how space was used at night. A certain number of assumptions were verified, on whether we could expect community participation to regenerate the urban fabric, to design and co-plan night-time services. The underlying idea was that people perceive a higher level of security if there are more community participations, through projects and policies to improve social competence and cultural agentivity.[32] The project was designed according to the procedures of ethnographic research. A research protocol was agreed upon during preparation and was then validated by local experts. A methodological mix of contextual interviews, video ethnographic activity, targeted contextual observation, questionnaires, participatory design workshops, and a series of workshops to ideate new services followed.

Research, modeling, conception, planning, and design were finalized in a call for proposals and funding of innovative night services and filling the spaces identified by the research.[33] Research participants were accurately selected so as to include several ethnic groups and business figures, crafts, shopkeepers, and full-time homemakers. Migrant associations, schools, and vocational training centers traditionally operating in Northern Italy were also included.

Research results highlighted critical points and polarizations that gave rise to conflict and threatened social cohesion. Ethnographic research insights led to identify specific behavior that mirrored the very different experiences perceived by members of the community. Results included the relative distance between each cluster and the virtual reference model of an active deeply rooted member of the community. As Fig. 2.3 shows, clusters were mapped along two axes with the level of community or territorial rooting and neighborhood agentivity. Identified behavior models pinpointed a strong drive to partake in the renewal of the neighborhood's social and economic fabric and the need to generate new models of participation to improve social competence, with a special focus on groups that were furthest from or disenchanted with the model of the active community member or citizen.

[32] Tomasiello et al. [30].

[33] https://tonite.eu/ricerca-etnografica/

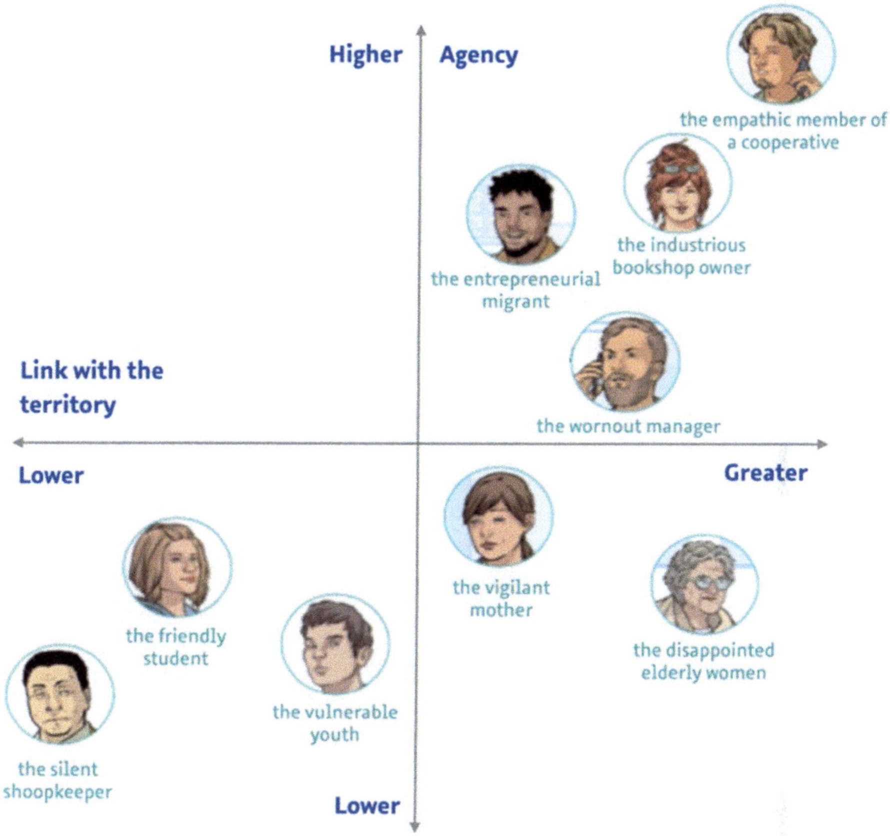

Fig. 2.3 The map of behaviors: territorial rooting and neighborhood agency. (Thanks to Elena Guidorzi and Giulia Teso who participated in the definition of the axes)

In conclusion, ethnic and generational differences—even within each ethnic group—present cultural challenges referred to:

(a) Closing the gap between neighborhood renewal decision-making and community action potential to implement projects and service innovation.
(b) Reducing isolation of first-generation immigrants who have few opportunities/possibilities of being active members of the community.
(c) Harmonizing the different feeling and sensitivity of day vs night use of public spaces.
(d) Improving the perception of security by managing public spaces and increasing the sense of belonging to neighborhood life.

In conclusion, both the research project on the elderly in Singapore and on the perception of safety in a Turin (Italy) neighborhood at high risk of losing social cohesion pointed to a vast range of perceived experiences and to a very mixed range of behaviors. Variety and heterogeneity are objective challenges both in identifying the levers to favor agentivity and social competence and to plan flexible service models able to cope with and mirror positional and situational complexity. Both projects showed that individuals and social groups had different initial conditions: this implies that strategies to reduce inequality and favor the change in individual and collective behavior must consider the impact of cumulative and additive effects of negative experiences and how the negative impact can be replaced by actions with a positive effect.

2.4 Access to Cure and the Proximity Ecosystems in China

In another project recently carried out in the PRC in cooperation with one of the big Asian pharmaceutical companies, we completed an ethnographic research of the Beijing's and Shanghai's urban agglomerations and in some rural area of Sichuan and Guangdong. The aim was to understand the typical journey from the onset of lung cancer symptoms to the search for treatments and lastly access to treatment. The project was planned according to ethnographical research practices and followed the process for ethical approval of a research protocol. This included contextual interviews[34] and some participatory workshops to validate insights and behavioral models from the study. The research team consisted of Asian and European anthropologists which made it possible to gain a better understanding of the complex organization of the Chinese health service, regional specificity, and difference in coverage between urban and rural areas.

Research results offered a clear understanding of how different and varied behavior is when comparing urban areas with medical and hospital services and rural areas that have very scanty resources and a limited presence of specialized doctors.

At least six macro-variables directly and indirectly influencing the possibility of a timely diagnosis and access to treatment centers were identified:

1. Proximity to a specialized hospital.
2. The frequency of consultations with the family doctor (*kanbing*).
3. Personal and family relational network (*guanxi*).
4. The relative burden of the illness on the family (*jiating zeren*).
5. Income.
6. The type of medical insurance and the reimbursement the patient is entitled to.

A person with strong social and family ties had a greater chance of finding their own path in the treatment journey, both because of the support from his/her family members and for the indirect support from the relational system to navigate and accredit themselves in the medical treatment system. These are the people who can

[34] Our research started at the end of the second COVID-19 wave of the pandemic in China, and therefore it was not possible to conduct the targeted observation activities. Contextual interviews were carried out using netnography and digital ethnography techniques.

count on an adaptive or flexible *proximity ecosystem* that can self-adapt and accommodate resources. During the steps of the Journey leading to the therapy/treatment, patients with a proximity ecosystem have a greater chance to overcome frustration and possible structural deficiencies of the medical and care systems, such as the lack of transparency on treatment options, the little time doctors devote to the patient, untrained nursing staff, little information and training on the consequences of the treatment and how best to address them, little informational on the appropriate nutritional regimen, and so on for many other issues which impact on habits and daily routines. Conversely, patients who cannot count on an adaptive/flexible proximity ecosystem or who in the worse cases are socially isolated, or have failed to establish meaningful relationships of interdependence, are met with a series of painful negative experiences marred by precariousness, uncertainties, and bad service that impact directly on the possibility of finding a new balance in behavior and daily routines. As a result, it is not uncommon for these patients to develop specific resistance to target therapies and present with more severe symptoms. Fig. 1.5 shows the four clusters identified in the course of the project and mapped along two axes, the one referring to *agentivity* and the other *readiness to accept* the illness by the

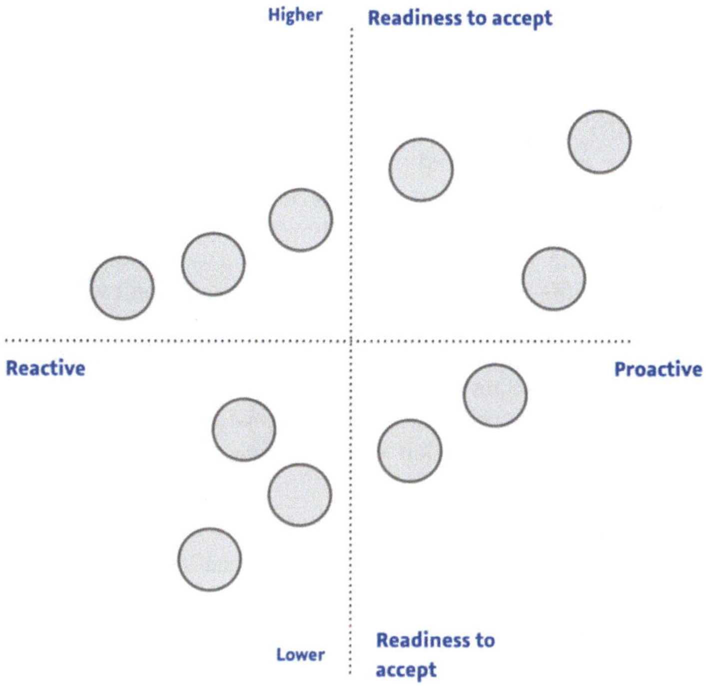

Fig. 2.4 The behavioral map of "agency" and "readiness to accept" the diagnosis of an oncological disease (cancer) in China (PRC). (Thanks to Feifei Li, Yubei Gong, Yuxin Zhao, Elena Messina, Chiara Agamennone, and Sara Innocenti who participated in the definition of the axes)

proximity ecosystem and therefore its ability to adapt to the new living conditions of the person throughout treatment (Fig. 2.4).

Lastly, opportunity analysis underscored at least four service areas to improve the understanding of the treatment and recovery journey, as well as the establishment and creation of an adaptive proximity ecosystem. The four areas are:

(a) Patient education and understanding and their care circle on the illness and treatment journey.
(b) Educating doctors, nurses, and carers to evaluate the actual state of the patient and any extra-treatment needs.
(c) Tools to facilitate coordination and cooperation between patients and the care/treatment circle.
(d) Tools to monitor results and failures throughout treatment/care journey.

The stories we gathered conformed some observations and shared achievements that we summarily presented herein in Singapore, Turin, and China. Observations can be generalized and establish the tenets for a shared ground for sustainable innovation strategies:

1. Situations and dispositions are intertwined in all personal histories, giving rise to stable adaptative models. Such models can lean toward a positive model or toward a precarious and prejudicial balance.
2. The variety of behaviors can be mapped in homogenous clusters on two axes which refer to the ability to control one's routine (reactivity vs proactivity) and the ability to navigate the rules and policies (high or low social competence). See more in Part III.
3. Significance or pregnance[35] and proximity of reference models, i.e., proximity ecosystems in each story play a key role in the possibility of each person to evolve naturally turning old equilibria into new ones.
4. Individual and cultural differences play a role in understanding behavior which is why a one-size-fits-all (false homogenous) approach won't work for everyone. Vice versa, strategies, solutions, and services thought for and designed (tailored) to support individual agentivity and social competence of the proximity ecosystem the person refers to are necessary.
5. People who can refer to positive social models where interpersonal cooperation prevails over conflict can develop a more flexible agentivity and a more adaptable social competence.

Highlights

- Behaviors are the resultant of personal (dispositional) and environmental (situational) factors.
- Situational variations can impact on behaviors to the point they can give surprising results.

---

[35] The term pregnance is analogous to the use of the term in Gestalt psychology. Specifically, it refers to the semantic strength that a perceptual field offers relative to other possible perceptual fields.

- Manipulating the situational variables in experiments shows the fallacy of common sense.
- Typically, analyzing real-life events, we do not easily distinguish between the incidence of situational and dispositional aspects.
- Naïve realism is the unspoken assumption of an isomorphism between subjective and objective experiences.
- Confirmation bias is a perception bias to validate inaccurate theories even when faced with evidence to the contrary.
- Self-fulfilling prophecies are confirmation of structured expectations.
- Depending on the self-assessment of one's own status or situation, people show selective comparisons toward low status or higher status situations.
- Self-serving biases and misattributions like positive results are because of one's actions, whereas negative outcomes are attributed to external factors.
- Individual differences start shaping early in life.
- Self-efficacy is a person's belief or set of beliefs in own ability to succeed that determine how well one can execute an action in prospective situations.
- A person's agentivity has social and relational factors.
- Innovative services should facilitate agency.
- The heterogeneity of the potential demand for services is typically high.
- Social competence and cultural agentivity can improve people perception of social security.
- The heterogeneity of behaviors is objective challenges for the design of innovative services that can promote change.
- Strategies to reduce inequality and favor agentivity must consider the impact of cumulative and additive effects of negative experiences.
- Strategies to favor agentivity should clarify how the negative impact of experiences can be replaced by the actions which will have a positive effect.
- People who can refer to positive social models, where interpersonal cooperation prevails over conflict, can develop a more flexible agentivity and a more adaptable social competence.

References

1. Ross, L., & Nisbett, R. (1991). *The person and the situation*. McGraw-Hill.
2. Asch Asch, S. E. (1956). Studies of independence and conformity. A minority of one against a unanimous majority. *Psychological Monographs., 70*(9), 1–70.
3. Milgram, S. (1974). *Obedience to authority: An experimental view*. Tavistock Publications.
4. Musen, K., & Zimbardo, P. G. (1991). *Quiet rage: The Stanford Prison Study. Video recording*. Psychology Dept., Stanford University.
5. Axelrod, R., & Hamilton, W. D. (1981). The evolution of cooperation. *Science, 211*(4489), 1390–1396.
6. Axelrod, R. (2006). *The Evolution of Cooperation*. Perseus Books Group.
7. Liberman, V., Samuels, S. M., & Ross, L. (2004). The name of the game: Predictive power of reputations versus situational labels in determining prisoner's dilemma game moves. *Personality and Social Psychology Bulletin, 30*(9), 1175–1185.

8. Bruner, J. (1986). *Actual Minds; Possible Worlds*. Harvard Univ. Press.
9. Robinson, R. J., Keltner, D., Ward, A., & Ross, L. (1995). Actual versus assumed differences in construal: 'Naive realism' in intergroup perception and conflict. *Journal of Personality and Social Psychology, 68*(3), 404–417.
10. Robert, K., Merton, M., & King, R. (1996). *On social structure and science*. University of Chicago Press.
11. Miller, D. T., & Ross, M. (1975). Self-serving biases in the attribution of causality: Fact or fiction? *Psychological Bulletin, 82*(2), 213–225.
12. Higgins, R., Snyder, C. R., & Berglas, S. (1990). *Self-handicapping: The paradox that isn't*. Plenum Press.
13. Schachter, S., & Singer, J. (1962). Cognitive, social, and physiological determinants of emotional state. *Psychological Review, 69*(5), 379–399.
14. Cotton, J. L. (1981). A review of research on Schachter's theory of emotion and the misattribution of Arousal. *European Journal of Social Psychology, 11*(4), 365–397.
15. Izard, C. E. (1971). *The face of emotion*. Appleton-Century-Crofts.
16. Bargh, J. A. (1984). Automatic and conscious processing of social information. In R. S. Wyer & T. K. Srull (Eds.), *Handbook of social cognition* (Vol. 3, pp. 1–43). Lawrence Erlbaum Associates Publishers.
17. Nisbett, R. E., & Wilson, T. D. (1977). Telling more than we can know: Verbal reports on mental processes. *Psychological Review*, *84*, 231–259.
18. Ekman. (2003). *Emotions revealed: Recognizing faces and feelings to improve communication and emotional life*. Times Books.
19. Bowlby, J. (1982). *Attachment and loss* (Vol. 1, 2nd ed.). Basic Books.
20. Ross, L., & Nisbett, R. E. (1991). *The person and the situation: Perspectives of social psychology*. McGraw-Hill.
21. Bandura, A. (1977). Self-efficacy: Toward a unifying theory of behavioral changE. *Psychological Review, 84*(2), 191–215.
22. Bandura, A. (1977). *Social learning theory* (Vol. 1). Prentice-Hall.
23. Bandura, A. (1997b). *Self-efficacy: The exercise of control*. Freeman.
24. Cunha, F., & Heckman, J. (2009). The economics and psychology of inequality and human development. *Journal of the European Economic Association, 7*(2), 320–364.
25. Mann, T., & Ward, A. (2007). Attention, Self-Control, and Health Behaviors. *Current Directions in Psychological Science, 16*(5), 280–283. https://doi.org/10.1111/j.1467-8721.2007.00520.x
26. Seligman, M. E. P., & Csikszentmihalyi, M. (2000). Positive psychology: An introduction. *American Psychologist, 55*, 5–14.
27. Snyder, C. R., & Lopez, S. J. *Handbook of positive psychology* (pp. 214–230). Oxford University Press.
28. Snyder-Mackler N, Burger JR, Gaydosh L, Belsky DW, Noppert GA, Campos FA, Bartolomucci A, Yang YC, Aiello AE, O'Rand A, Harris KM, Shively CA, Alberts SC, Tung J. (2020). *Social determinants of health and survival in humans and other animals* (Vol. 20). Science. May 22;368(6493):eaax9553. doi: 10.1126/science.aax9553.
29. Visciola, M., et al. (2015). Design for aging gracefully. Rethinking health and wellness for the elderly: Public services. Asian insights and design innovation. Singapore Design Council. Retrieved from https://issuu.com/aididsg/docs/exp_dsg_ageing_booklet_e-book_issuu
30. Tomasiello, C., et al. (2005). Understanding and sharing intentions: the origins of cultural cognition. *Behavioral and Brain Sciences, 28*(5), 675–691.

Chapter 3
The Fragility of Cooperation

By observing and studying the behavior of people in real-life situations, listening to their stories, and understanding their stories' cultural and social contexts, you see how the strength of automatisms interacts with power of the situations where the stories develop. In other words, there is a tension between each individual's need to develop agentive control of behavior and the opportunity to foster cultural agentivity. Those are the specific competences we require as humans to promote interdependence relations in our proximity ecosystems. Such skills are neither evenly nor univocally shared out, and above all they are sophisticated complex cognitive structures, a sort of moral code that needs time and the right conditions to grow.

Social psychologists, cultural anthropologists, and evolutionary biologists have carried out large-scale research on how interpersonal cooperation develops and which conditions enable collaboration and reciprocity to prevail over individualism. They investigated the reasons why unknown people—foreigners or strangers—cooperate and the evolutionary roots of such a behavior. One of their shared practice targets is the rebuttal of the *homo economicus* theory as the early interpretations of Darwin's theory of evolution and Wilson's socio-biology and the other theories which in time associated simplified visions of human nature. If we turn to the dominant pre-twentieth-century theories and models of prevailing economic doctrines,[1] *adaptive human behaviors* were synonymous for opportunism, selfishness, and rationality. The rougher interpretations of Darwin's theory of evolution emphasize individualism, the narrative of the need to fight and compete to live and on the survival of the fittest. Maybe it is plethoric to observe that the economic liberalism doctrine is well matched with pseudo-Darwinist narratives.

I mentioned how limited our rationality is and that perception, choices and decisions are in fact guided by the heuristics and reference models available in the context. In the pages that follow, I will refer to "why is cooperation, not competition,

[1] Such doctrines have a cultural matrix rooted in philosophical doctrines and in particular in the liberal doctrines dating back to John Stewart Mill.

M. Visciola, *Sustainable Innovation*,
https://doi.org/10.1007/978-3-031-18751-3_3

always been the key to the evolutionary complexity" to quote computational evolutionary biologist Martin Nowak.[2] Yet, cooperation is always at risk. And for the great challenges that lie ahead for the next 5 to 10 years, collaboration for the good will have to be cultivated, safeguarded, and maintained so that it prevails. We scientists and designers of change understand its complexities and difficulties. For instance, we assume that by feeding our interdependence, establishing relations, and building mutual trust systems, we reduce the risk of falling prey to selfish and opportunistic behaviors. Cooperation and conflict are in fact both present in everybody's life and experience. How do we form trust relations? What ingredients favor them, and which undermine them?

Another fundamental assumption is that by establishing mutual trust, relations require us to remember what happened in previous exchanges with others: if exchanges had led to mutual satisfaction, it generated a new synapse conveying an actual passage of positive energy. When this spark of energy is rekindled at every interaction, then the exchange becomes collaboration. As a result, previous experience starts to shape a theory of the advantage and pleasure of cooperation in the person's mind. This implicit theory is also based on an estimate of the different and additional circumstances where one might interact with the other individual and also depends on their propensity to cooperate: what would happen if one came out of the exchange with the feeling or the evidence of not having received one's due? Clearly the reaction can vary according to the individual and circumstances. The premise of research on collaboration is that it is in practice a loss if one fails to receive a tangible sign of collaboration a situation well depicted by the simulation game known as *the prisoner's dilemma*.[3] As in the previously described experiments where participants were given a role (see page 27), in the original format of the game, there is a clear matrix like the one in Table 2.1, where both players gain in the event of cooperation but only the player who responds by defecting (self-protection) to the detriment of the other gains. Lastly, it can be relatively negative for both that is neither gains nor loses in the event of both opting to defect.

What is the dilemma? As you can see in Table 2.1, a rational analysis would suggest that self-protection pays more than cooperation: there is always an advantage regardless of what the other player's choice is. However, when both opt for noncooperation, then the overall result is less than in the case of both cooperating. The dilemma stems from the fact that cooperation pays off as the combined balance of the two exceeds all other outcomes. In the early version of the prisoner's dilemma, published by the psychologist Axelrod and the biologist Hamilton in *Science* in 1981,[4] participants in the simulation game could play several rounds with several others, i.e., simultaneously, and/or repeat the game with the same participants, i.e., iterated. Thus, the experiment layout mirrored real-life conditions, that is, the possibility of establishing cooperation models. That is to say, a participation strategy

---

[2] Nowak [1].

[3] Axelrod [2].

[4] Robert and William [3].

can improve following iterations and therefore present a range potentially very varied and rich in possibilities and opportunities. Clearly in the extended version be it simultaneous or repeated, the exchange matrix in Table 2.1 is the same and scalable ad infinitum.

According to Axelrod and Hamilton, by playing the *prisoner's dilemma*, one can understand the development of *mutualistic symbiosis* in biological ecosystems and therefore illustrate the formation and survival of collaborative systems. They believed a cooperative strategy must be based on three tenets: stability, soundness, and the possibility of training in a typically competitive environment. The implementation of the game's interpretation strategies explains the need for microorganisms to establish stable relations. Thanks to the sound cooperation, they are equipped to cope with the event of rare external mutants prevailing with other strategies.[5] This means that strategies have to develop and survive in a competitive environment. To verify which and how many strategies bore the three characteristics, Axelrod had the brilliant idea to get a series of academics and professionals enamored with simulation games to play: economists, sociologists, biologists, and psychologists were among the players. At the end of the experiment, each participant had tried out their strategy which could then be compared with all the others. A mathematician psychologist by the name of Anatol Rapoport developed the strategy that contained the three key features and decidedly prevailed over the others: it is known as the *tit for tat*, and it is very simple. You start by cooperating and do exactly what the other participant did in the previous round. One could call it *reciprocity-based cooperation*, and it scored highest in all the versions of the simulation outperforming mathematical and Bayesian approaches, created to establish and foresee how fruitful other strategies are in the long term.

Inevitably when both participants defected after a few rounds, the strategy ended by eliminating options for cooperation. However, if one is prepared to assume that the choice was due either to mistakes or errors of judgment or to passing carelessness due to circumstances, a small variation of the model, such as an occasional cooperative response after a series of defections (aka *generous tit for tat*), proves it more advantageous than other strategies. This variant introduced by Martin Nowak[6] shows that the model resists and outperforms especially in the extended iterated version of the game. Computational simulations by the same author show that the strategy is less effective in more complex simulations, with more participants and in both iterated and simultaneous conditions where the latter automatisms tend not to work well, and a strategy of unconditional cooperation known as *win stay-lose shift*[7] outperforms. Under different conditions, the unconditioned cooperation strategy leaves the player vulnerable and can be exploited by strategies based on systematic defection.

---

[5] A mutation can be benign and not have any negative effect or malignant with dire consequences.

[6] Martin Nowak; ibid. note 1

[7] Nowak and Sigmund [4]

Nowak's interpretation both confirms Axelrod's evolutionary theory of cooperation and suggests that it is possible to identify and prove its ecological validity throughout evolution. Despite nature having no stability and the prevailing ongoing selective pressure, in the long-term biological cooperation outperforms the other strategies: aggressive and conflictual members of a community can exploit altruistic and cooperative people, but groups or communities of selfless and cooperative individuals prevail over groups and communities of conflicting individuals.

Let me focus on one of Nowak's interesting assumptions: in nature cooperation is never stable as there are destabilizing factors that interrupt it and hinder or interrupt the possibility of cooperating. Furthermore, the continued existence of conditions favoring cooperation depends first and foremost on the selfless (altruistic) behavior prevailing and secondly on the possibility that they will evolve into a moral system (or super organism[8]). The precondition for cooperation to continue the expectation of gaining has to be more widespread and greater than the expectations of the associated costs. The question therefore is: How does one assess gain/loss expectations? What is required for cooperation to evolve into a moral system? The evolution of our species can be best described as the sum of our individual and community behaviors. This begs for the question whether *benevolent nature* will always be able to offer us further expectations of gain. What are the known costs, and which are the hidden costs of our behavior?

In the next pages, I will show how creativity facilitating altruistic (selfless) behavior and the establishment of a moral system are essential to prevail over selfish behavior that weakens the sustainability of our ambitions to innovate. Garrett Hardin certainly offered the most brilliant demonstration of how fragile cooperation is in his article *The Tragedy of the Commons'*[9] that the American ecologist published in 1968. The article cogently argues that if you leave a resource, say pastureland in open access without imposing shared rules,[10] an exploitative behavior of the limited good will inevitably prevail. The paradox, and hence the tragedy, is that the race to exploit resources is triggered by the concern that the good may not be available in the future, as others could overuse it and deplete it. According to Hardin, *in an overcrowded world, unmanaged commons don't work*, and there are no easy solutions to the tragedy of common goods, unless we extend ethics that preserve resources from selfish behavior and to use his words "Freedom in a commons bring ruin to all."

According to research on limited judgment and the possibility of inferring correctly using incomplete information, referred to in this chapter, it is deceptive to believe that self-regulatory behavior will work: our minds are not equipped to

---

[8] The term used by Wilson and Sober in 1989 was *organism* to reduce the impact of such a high-sounding term. The term organism offers a a special angle to the idea that the laws of evolution apply to the biological individual as well as to groups of individuals. Today we generally have replaced the term biological *organism* with the more inclusive term *biological ecosystem*

[9] Hardin [5].

[10] Regulation need not be established outside the community that enjoys the commons; the absence of written rules but shared by all members of the community in fact performs the same function as a written regulation. See the work of Nobel laureate Elinor Ostrom [10].

forecast using Bayesian probability.[11] Furthermore, the narrative on individual rights to freedom refers to models that lead to conflict with self-regulation. A moral code that justifies selfish behavior authorizes individuals to organize and attain their goals exploiting resources and situations to their advantage. We are therefore left with the need to answer the question on how we can develop an ethical code which on the contrary will make altruistic (selfless) behavior prevail: Garrett Hardin advocated an unparalleled extension of human morality. Is it possible? And if so, how? We can seek an answer in some of the studies that examined how collaborative behavior gives rise to an altruistic behavior and to the possibility that collective efforts and social pressure should give rise to reputation-based systems.

Research started from assumptions laid down by previously described results of group psychology investigations. Group or community social life is subjected to selective pressure promoting conformity, imitation, and the development of systematic trends excluding behavioral and value-based dissonance. Pressure presents itself in the guise of automatisms which strengthens and maintains group bonds as well as preserving differences among groups. In turn automatisms for group formation and preservation give rise to forms of reciprocity. However, to fully appreciate what reciprocity is, one has to first define how communities with shared expectations and joint intentionality come to be: goals and rules to attain them, as well as an implicit monitoring of other people's behavior are needed. Every member's behavior contributes to the establishment of reputation-based system which then becomes the yardstick to monitor and judge singles behaviors.

In 1987, Richard Alexander[12] wrote a seminal text distinguishing between direct and indirect reciprocity: the former is the result of a relationship between two people that exchange value for mutual convenience; the latter is the force that generated reputation. Expectations of a reward for having followed a generous and altruistic conduct are directed to the community or to society as a whole. Indirect reciprocity is the key for status and reputation[13] although there is an implicit assessment by others.[14] It is precisely this ongoing assessment that lays the social foundations of common morality and moral judgments. Direct reciprocity contributes to trust building between two people, while indirect reciprocity establishes the trust conditions regardless and beyond a specific person's experience; thus accounting for altruistic behavior has a greater impact when publicly acknowledged. With no recognition by society, one's community, or reference group, there is no meaning to reciprocal actions and contributes to the legitimating of selfish and opportunistic behavior. Furthermore, monitoring and implicit valuation of others' behavior tell us whether there are conditions for cooperation: we expect society to punish

[11] According to the *Cumulative Prospect Theory* Kahneman and Tversky [6]—judgments under conditions of uncertainty are not based on an estimate of the observed frequency of an event, but on an estimate of the probability inferred from the available reference points

[12] Alexander [7].

[13] Generosity and altruism are an investment in reputational social capital. See Wedekind [8].

[14] We should not imagine an explicit value system but rather automatic schemata enabling us to make a comparison with the adopted reference models.

opportunistic behavior or contain their impact. Results of tension arising within the community and in society between virtuous and opportunistic behaviors can either lead to cohesion in society or to group competition.

An extremely interesting study by a group of German biologists[15] assessed the propensity of individual people to make personal sacrifices and reduce the collective risk of climate change. The dilemma is very present in our day and age: to what extent are we prepared to accept sacrifices for the common good? What different behaviors are we prepared to implement when faced with a collective risk? What buttons can we push to align behavior well aware of the fact that not everyone will subscribe to personal investments and sacrifices for the common good?

According to the German researchers' definition, social dilemmas of collective risks differ from other social dilemmas in so much as:

(i) People have to make decisions repeatedly before the outcome is evident.
(ii) There is a cost; investments [to maintain the conduct] are lost and cannot be refunded.
(iii) The effective value of the public good is unknown.
(iv) Reliable estimate on the likelihood that the risk threatened collective goods may be lost due to the absence of collective and consistent behavior.

In the simulation game, there were 30 groups of 6 students each, each having an endowment of 40€ to spend, and the goal was to attain the collective sum of 120€ needed to reduce collective climate change risk. In each of the ten rounds, every participant could contribute with 0, 2, or 4 €. The sum each person had given and the total sum were known at the end of each round so that in the following round, each participant could determine the sum to pay in. In this dilemma, the higher the individual contribution to the community goals, the more likely it is collective risk will be minimized. However, individual monetary resources also decreased as a result. Monitoring the contributions by other participants has an important role in determining one's own contribution in the following round and what can be done to save money without jeopardizing the social goal. The game has three conditions: if the group failed to collect at least 120 €, all group members would lose, respectively, 10%, 50%, or 90% of their savings. In the 10% condition even if they had not contributed to the pot, they would have been left 36 €. In the condition of 50%, in any case they would receive 20 € and a 50% likelihood of having 40 savings at the end of the game. Lastly, in the 90% condition, if they failed to attain the goal, participants would have had an average of 4 € each. According to the game if a participant is a *free rider*, then the maximum personal gain will happen in the case of the 10% option. If a participant is a *fair sharer*, then their maximum advantage in the simulation is with a 50% risk. Lastly, if a participant is an *altruist*, the simulation with a 90% change of losing everything offers the greatest advantage. In this case, the individual advantage fully corresponds to the collective advantage, as well as to the

[15] Milinski et al. [9].

misfortune of losing everything equally for all participants as the goal is not achieved.

Results are of great interest for possible future even on large-scale experiments. It will not surprise readers that in the 90% simulation, the risk of losing everything meant that five out of ten groups attained the 120€ goal, while just one out of ten in the 50% condition and no group in the 10% condition attained their target sums. Results indicate that when the risk of losing everything is very high, individual behavior aligns toward an altruistic profile. In spite of the fact that this propensity prevailed in five groups out of ten, in the other groups, the *free riders* and *fair sharers* aligned with the goals of contributing a sufficient sum only late in the game by which time it was difficult to achieve the aim. In any case the five groups just missed their targets and that in the second half of the game, there was a prevalence of altruistic behavior. In the 10% risk condition, the *free riders* managed save a good percentage of their endowment eight times out of ten. However, there were many examples of irrational behavior with changes of strategies during the game in the condition of 10% of risk as well as in the risk condition of 50%. In the latter (the 50% condition), participants with an altruist behavior tried in vain to improve the situation and to compensate the opportunistic *free riders*.

Since games are clearly conducted anonymously, it is not possible to act by putting pressure on opportunistic nor on merely irrational players. The research clearly shows that anonymity does not favor collaborative behavior and therefore implicit persuasion is effective only in the case the risk of losing everything is very high. Results suggest a number of ideas of collective social risks consistent with what observed in other studies described in this chapter:

(a) In the presence of mixed behavior (*heterogeneity*), one cannot follow a single (*univocal*) line of communication nor risk reducing strategies (*mitigation*) based on implicit (*indirect and generic*) pressure.
(b) Behavior has to be monitored to apply stronger and more overt strategies for *free riders* and opportunists, while more involving educational models are required in the case of irrational unresolved or ineffective behaviors.
(c) Awareness is not always sufficient to produce adequate individual objective.
(d) Individual and collective advantages have to be balanced to have effective cooperation.

We will address the consequences of these insights in Part III. Sustainable innovation requires deep and diverse change strategies to promote individual and cultural agentivity on one side and to reduce the space for opportunistic strategies and false narratives, on the other side.

Highlights

- "Mutualistic symbiosis" develops in biological ecosystems to foster collaboration.
- Reciprocity-based cooperation outperforms mathematical and Bayesian approaches for cooperation in conflictual conditions (e.g., competitive environments), like the simulation of the prisoner's dilemma game.

- Aggressive and conflictual members of a community can easily exploit altruistic and cooperative people.
- Groups or communities of selfless and cooperative individuals prevail over groups and communities of conflicting individuals.
- "Freedom in a commons brings ruin to all."
- The narrative of unbounded individual rights to freedom refers to models that lead to conflict with self-regulation.
- Direct reciprocity is the result of a relationship between two people that exchange value for mutual convenience.
- Indirect reciprocity is the form that generates reputation.
- When the risk of losing everything is very high, individual behaviors align toward an altruistic profile.
- Anonymity does not favor collaborative behaviors.

References

1. Nowak, M. (2011). Super cooperators.
2. Axelrod. (1984). *The evolution of cooperation*. Basic Books.
3. Axelrod, R., & William, H. D. (1981). The evolution of cooperation. *Science, 211*, 1390–1396.
4. Nowak, M., & Sigmund, K. (1993). A strategy of win-stay, lose-shift that outperforms tit-for-tat in the Prisoner's Dilemma game. *Nature, 364*(6432), 56–58.
5. Hardin, G. (1968). The tragedy of the commons. *Science, 162*(3859), 1243–1248.
6. Kahneman, D., & Tversky, A. (1992). Advances in prospect theory: Cumulative representation of uncertainty. *Journal of Risk and Uncertainty, 5*, 297–324.
7. Alexander, R. (1987). *The biology of moral systems*. New York.
8. Wedekind, C., & Braithwaite, V. A. (2002). The long-term benefits of human generosity in indirect reciprocity. *Current Biology, 12*, 1012–1015.
9. Milinski, M., Sommerfeld, R. D., Krambeck, H. J., Reed, F., & Marotzke, J. (2008). The collective-risk social dilemma and the prevention of simulated dangerous climate change. *Proc Natl Acad Sci U S A*. 2008 Feb 19;105(7):2291-4. doi: 10.1073/pnas.0709546105. Epub 2008 Feb 19. PMID: 18287081; PMCID: PMC2268129.
10. Ostrom, E. (1990). *Governing the Commons: The Evolution of Institutions for Collective Action* (Political Economy of Institutions and Decisions). Cambridge: Cambridge University Press. doi:10.1017/CBO9780511807763

Part II
Disclosing Value Through Behavioral Design

Abstract All human endeavors aim to have an impact on society, but this book maintains that an interdisciplinary convergence between cultures based on *know-how* and those based on *humanistic knowledge* is needed to address the challenges of the next 10 years. Design practices fall short of analytical understanding of important intangible and immaterial constraints, in shaping new possibilities and behavioral development. The design challenges we are concerned with require us to act on intentionality and to persevere in our innovation goals. Design could play a key role in releasing the real value society expects from sustainable innovation from the language of those protecting business. The classical academic separation ascribes a descriptive role to human sciences and a prescriptive role to design. I believe we have accrued great experience, and we can say that by merging design and behavioral science we will be able to act more effectively than in the past.

> The proper study of mankind has been said to be man. But I have argued that man—or at least the intellective component of man—may be relatively simple, that most of the complexity of his behavior may be drawn from man's environment, ... If I have made my case, then we can conclude that, in large part, the proper study of mankind is the science of design, not only as the professional component of a technical education, but as a core discipline for every liberally educated person [1].

In the closing pages of *The Science of Artificial*, Herbert Simon argued that the complexity of human behavior can be traced back to the complexity of the environment human beings have designed and built throughout their evolution. Following this key intuition, design can be identified as the best discipline to develop aids or prostheses in our environment, thus expanding our intellectual skills. As we imagine and design these extensions, we are in fact shaping our environment, better tailoring it for our purposes. Design, as we now know it, has inherited *Homo sapiens*'s vernacular culture, where it is the equivalent of *knowing how to*, that is, skills that make it possible to transform ideas into things, the immaterial nature of imagination into tangible artifacts.

Statements such as the above are very suggestive as well as raising key questions: What transformative skills are embodied in design? How do ideas shape in the course of design thinking? How does ideation develop? Part 2 explores the features of thinking and acting as a designer. In addressing these questions, I shall further develop issues outlined in the first chapter, making use of ideas developed by designers and design scholars. The cross referencing or intersecting among a range of disciplines can add value following methods that favor a sustainably oriented evolution of behaviors and cultures. Nowadays, all human endeavors aim to have an impact on society, but this book maintains that an interdisciplinary convergence between cultures based on *know-how* and those based on *humanistic knowledge* is needed to address the challenges of the next 10 years.

I will argue that design as a discipline is based on practice and methods that can be fruitfully combined with research on human behavior, both in laboratory conditions and in real life. The very particular nature of some of design features determines (designers') remits. Practice is aimed at shaping representation of the real world. It introduces innovations that inevitably have an impact on experience and behavior. I will show that design practices are relatively *weak*, that is, they fall short of analytical understanding of important intangible and immaterial constraints in shaping new possibilities and behavioral development. However, design practices also have a high impact potential, in that they determine the intentionality and direction of design action for change. In conclusion, I shall prove how it is possible to compensate the shortcomings that impact on the value of a product or service by focusing on intentionality.

The value of a product or service is protected and upheld by legal instruments used to market them in the Western world and in the wealthiest countries as a whole. Marketing artifacts are also—in fact especially—used to document the value of products and services. However, as we will see in the course of Part II, the legal instruments used to disclose and safeguard the value of goods—be they products or services—mean one cannot impact on intentionality and on the intended effects of innovation.

The design challenges we are concerned with require us to act on intentionality and to persevere in our innovation goals, thanks to *business with purpose* strategies. Design could play a key role in releasing the real value society expects from sustainable innovation. These arguments differ substantially from the narrative usually employed when explaining what designers do and what their special ways of thinking and acting are. Traditional narrative needs to be revised and updated to identify the important relationships that develop when integrating design, social science, and behavioral practices. Usually, design practice is described as if separate from humanities, anthropology, and biology that study the evolution of behaviors and cultures.

This asyndeton used to be justified by the different nature of the problems design has to deal with, as opposed to the scientific nature of scientific problems. Design is seen as solving problems that cannot be solved using linear and easy solutions, holistically called *wicked problems* [2]. Conversely, humanities are seen to deal with issues that require a deeper understanding and a definition of the underlying issues. The accepted *classical* separation used by academia ascribes a *descriptive* role to human sciences and a *prescriptive* role to design. Although such a separation can help streamline, it hides the fact that the so-called *wicked problems* are present in nearly all complex challenges including those of the Sustainable Development Goals (SDG) agenda. These are challenges that require not so much a solution to problems as a strong collaboration between the sciense and practices of change. Furthermore, I feel that all the attempts to integrate design practice with the body of knowledge generated by social change science disciplines are lacking. In this respect I agree with what Bryan Lawson, architect and designer, wrote in 2005: *"By and large this liaison between design and social science has not been as practically useful as was first hoped. Social science remains largely descriptive while design is necessarily prescriptive, so the psychologists and sociologists have gone on researching and the designers designing, and they are yet to re-educate each other into more genuinely collaborative roles* [3]*"*.

Fifteen years after designer's stated his mistrust, I believe we have accrued great experience and it is therefore possible to say that by merging design and behavioral science we will be able to act more effectively than in the past, meeting the innovation challenges I referred to in Part I. In the next two chapters I will discuss the shift in focus and the necessary interface required to promote a more transdisciplinary approach for behavioral and cultural change and the impact required to develop the complex work of sustainable innovation.

References

1. Simon, H. (1981). *The science of artificial.* MIT Press: Cambridge, MA.
2. Rittel, H. W., & Webber, M. M. (1973). Dilemmas in a general theory of planning. *Policy Sciences, 4*(2), 155–169.
3. Lawson, B. (2005) *How designers think,* 4th Ed. London: Blackwell's.

Chapter 4
Design Paths

The classical idea used to describe design processes distinguishes between *design by drawing*, that is, visualizing an idea which is taking shape during a conversation on design using sketches, graphic images, and other visuals, and *design by science*, following procedures, rules, and a methodology to disclose the constraints present in the case.[1] The two paths are neither mutually exclusive, nor do they complement each other. During a typical design process, graphic and visual representations of ideas are specific to a designer's mode action and profoundly characterize the specific competence one expects of a person trained in the field of design. Were we to describe a designer's rules and procedures, we would notice that methodological specificities branch out in many directions, partly as the result of the role evolving.

A fascinating idea of Richard Buchanan's[2] played a seminal role in the designer community. It suggests a sort of progression in the specific areas that pertain to design. His four orders of design are a practical way of describing the problems design addresses.

- The first order concerns communication and includes printed graphics: signals, signs, symbols, visualizations, and icons encompass and present meanings of communication.
- The second order refers more specifically to artifact or industrial product design such as engineering, architectural systems, and objects used for mass production.
- The third order refers to interactive systems mediated by computer and digital technology, including human-computer interaction skills, interaction, and service design. This order includes designing interactive objects, wearables, and anything else which allows interaction with things and relating with people—such as detection, IoT systems, and the like.

[1] Lawson [1].

[2] Buchanan [2].

M. Visciola, *Sustainable Innovation*,
https://doi.org/10.1007/978-3-031-18751-3_4

- The fourth order refers to the design of built environments and of complex cooperation systems such as public and private organizations, government institutions and NGOs, and education agencies.

Each order includes the previous one, and thus the fourth includes all the others. According to Buchanan, the fourth is also the most complex and the one which offers an important practical (pragmatic) perspective for the development of design as a discipline.[3] Unquestionably, this model is based on a strong concept which means it can be adapted and tailored. Behavioral, systemic, digital economy, circular economy design and design for green economy are definitively part of the fourth order.

A closer look at these "orders" will help us understand how synergies between design practice and humanities can be established, so as to think of new sustainably led programs on behavioral evolution. Design processes depicting the first and second design orders have a natural matrix and vernacular design that highlight creativity as well as the synthesis that ensues from designing itself. Clearly designers also develop an analytical side to it, but it is purely aimed at turning their intuition into something tangible and practical. Intuition is information fed into an idea and concerns the problem to be solved or the point of view that develops during the creative act.

The information the designer normally uses is neither necessarily accurate nor tailored, and therefore the analysis is aimed at materializing some of the intuitions. That is exactly what we expect of design and designers: for them to materialize an intuition, interpret a problem and imagine a solution. Think of the design of an extremely popular product or objects, chairs, tables, furniture, but also computers, keyboards, and peripheral devices, cellphones, cars, and so on. Information and analysis have an important role which is typically laid out in the client's brief or in the definition of the problem to be solved. Information has an anecdotic role, and no one expects it to lead to an in-depth and punctual analysis. In the words of Rowe, the architect and planner "*...design is a process in which problem and solution emerge together*".[4] Value is determined by how original the interpretation of the brief is, making the designer a creator and a leader who follows an act of creation. Design and sometimes the designer themselves are the special feature.

In the first and second order, designers also do not necessarily follow a precise sequence of tasks, but rather an intuition that leads to solutions. As a result, industrial designers will inevitably switch seamlessly from a project on a new series of machine tools to food packaging, or even organizing space in bank branch. The processes for these designs share very little: schedules and methods can vary according to the complexity of the issues and the time needed to reach presentable and communicable solutions. It is only when one is ready to communicate the solution(s) that the hierarchy of information used, its/their quality, or usefulness become clear.

[3] Golsby-Smith [3]

[4] Rowe [4]

Unlike the first and second order, I believe that in the other two orders, designers' work and the design itself are of service. Imagination and creativity still have to do with it even if they follow more structured paths. Let us see why: in projects referring to the third and fourth order, intuition is the result of an extremely complex analytical process. It must consider many points of view and a large amount to information. The center of the design process is no longer in the problem-solving idea. In fact, one can describe it as a multicentered, multifocal, multidimensional picture as design paths intersect with specialist ones that use explicit information and an implied knowledge of the dominion. The ideation process is repeated cycle after cycle, as many times as required to reach a sufficient understanding of the available opportunities, of priorities in pursuing opportunities, design goals, and the directions to be followed.

Following to Buchanan's classification, I feel that in the third and fourth order, ideation is *subjected* to a larger number of external constraints unrelated to design cycles. I believe the opposite should be sought and that merging or integrating is essential to offer a strategic focus and vitality to design consistently with sustainable innovation goals.

4.1 Design Constraints

A comprehensive description of design processes calls for us to first focus on constraints and their types and specificity, an extremely important issue. Usually design processes focus on the so-called formal constraints including laws and security, for instance, *laws and regulations* such as privacy and security, *technologies* such as open or proprietary platforms, *functionality* such as types of functions and their integration, *economics* such as budgeting and schedule, and *aesthetics*, that is, aesthetical models of reference.

Following the development of digital economy, that is, the buildup of experience and the many new avenues opened by AI software technology applications, other kinds of constraints have emerged and play a dominant role. I am referring to *immaterial* constraints that may include design culture—such as the particular school of design; the designer's academic preferences; use and user requirements such as context of use and user profile which were described in Chap. 2 as dispositional and situational variables; behavioral models, such as ability, capacity, and competence; and agentive levels, such as evolutionary adjacency (see also Part III).

The immaterial constraints discussed in the previous chapters included action constraints such as affordance, mapping, and cognitive automatisms which were discussed at length. I also debated situational and dispositional constraints at length. Acknowledging constraints and discussing them in depth are a milestone of design planning paths. In this perspective, analytical paths cannot be limited to nor are they merely data collection. The analytical phase includes the definition of the constraints and great care in how to translate constraints into actionable requirements. In other words, requirements must be turned into design solutions so that users can implement their intentions achieving goals in a few simple steps, without having to understand how everything works.

Designers with a traditional education find it difficult to grasp the notion of constraints. The number and complexity of constraints reduces designers' creative potential narrative in conventional design schools. Designers free to imagine and pursue imagination-based construction have a greater creative ability. However, one can easily prove that anecdotic data gathering weakens analysis or makes it instrumental greatly reducing the credibility of ideation. Under these circumstances, it takes on the guise of a deliberate act, the result of an opinion, or a bias. The more complex the dominion to discuss—even if based on expert opinions—the less anecdotic information or opinion count, compared to evidence and how alternative possibilities are presented.

A sound analysis of constraints must supply the evidence of what informs design decision-making processes and what weight it should bear. Constraints due to the technology application context, *usage constraints*, are a case in point that highlights the tension between a creative side ensuing from the freedom of interpretation by the team of designers and the considered use of constraints to find effective, efficient, and satisfying solutions for the end user.

The digital economy world as we know it, that is, the Internet after 15 years of browsers and search engines, has players who have consistently worked on *constraints* or *usage requirement definition* or management. This relentless activity carried out by a global army of usability and interaction designers has made it possible to use digital technologies for economic, social, and cultural transactions. This activity has yielded the greatest possible advantage from domesticating motor perceptual and decision (judgment) automatisms discussed at length in Part I. After years of usability tests aimed at proving immediate access to information and contents, web signs and signals have been standardized in ways that leave little room to syntactical ambiguities. HTML codes standardize hypertext navigation enabling content designers to emphasize information prioritizing according to the user's task. A digital environment with the appropriate visual hierarchies and the right contrast between figure and background no longer resembles a jungle but well-planned garden. Patterns like *one-click buttons*, the use of navigation buttons, simple and practical navigation trees, cooperation filters, icons appreciating semantic analogies, and minimalist designs, all make interaction designers' task very practical. A designer's main task is to increase the metrics used to measure the success rates of technological solution, such as *stickiness*, i.e., the time spent on the application and frequency of use, the number of clicks required to access the useful information, and the conversion rate, i.e., the percentage of single visits that lead to transactions.

A good design aims to understand how to improve people's decision-making skills and how to make time worthwhile. It must see that navigation times in a digital environment reduced to a fraction ending up with a satisfactory transaction. *Don't Make Me Think*[5] is the title of a book on the usability of web environments

[5] Krug [5]

that has proved highly successful among interaction designers. It epitomizes in a quasi-operatic manner what is expected of designers' creative efforts, in other words, how one can facilitate the acquisition of perceptual motor automatisms and habits that swiftly lead to the digital goals. Once implemented in interactive environments, design patterns enable a person to fulfill their aims *without thinking* as the online service designer has already thought and developed a process that will swiftly lead to the transaction. When a few smooth keyboard or display touches are all that is needed to make a purchase, a motivational trigger is no longer required.[6] The digital process that the designer has created by building on digital platform usage constraints facilitates satisfying a real or a passing need, a wish, or a fancy. At the end of the transaction, the user will have had a seamless experience bolstered by positive emotions.

Another set of immaterial constraints that design considers in (designing) complex systems concerns the *user requirements* and thus learning what the service user profiles are. As a result, planning it will be the hallmark of the relationship between the service and the various types of expectations and goals to achieve. In Chap. 2, I illustrated how cultural and individual differences make it necessary to see how to favor *individual agency* defined as the ability to control one's mental and behavioral routines and *cultural agentivity* defined as the social competence required in navigating the system of formal rules and policies, as well as formal and informal relational systems. Chapter 2 also documented how the abundant research on bounded rationality mechanisms shows that perceptual motor and decision-making automatisms create biases. The latter are not easily corrected while performing a task or completing an action. Biases refer to all action, judgment, and decision-making processes, that is, to *constructive* process based on reference models, context, and available information, and they are framed, as illustrated in Part I.

In marketing psychology, individual differences are usually attributed to specific personality differences and motivations. Personality theories such as the *five-factor model*[7] aka as Big Five or OCEAN (*openness, consciousness, extraversion, agreeableness, neuroticism*) are based on theories or theatrical constructs that at a closer look appear not to be based on experimental research, with the systematic research approach used for cognitive processes in neuroscience. Furthermore, these theories fail to consider situational factors that are key to understand and describe the nature of bounded rationality in behavior and decision-making (see Chap. 1). Features generally considered in literature and marketing practice to describe personality differences suggest they do not remain the same (stable) when situations change. As a result, they do not offer a sound enough theatrical basis for activities aimed at sustainable innovation.

Personality theories are open to criticism and not very usable due to prodigality, that is, for having included a large number of traits that cannot be traced back to

---

[6] In Part III, I shall discuss how most programs to facilitate the change/evolution of behavior can use incentives and constraints that do not require motivational tools.

[7] Goldberg [6]; McCrae and John [7]; Costa and McCrae [8].

essential ones and integrate all the possible nuances of the dispositional features.[8] However, personality theories are not easily usable also for the opposite reason. They arbitrarily exclude many other traits such as propensity for religion, masculinity, femininity, individualism, and the like.[9] This is why personality theories cannot be considered as reliable points of reference for the goals discussed herein.

Similar considerations apply to the theories of persuasion such as that of "seven principles" of social influence by Cialdini.[10] Persuasion theories are open to the same criticisms on non-essentiality and multidimensionality. Both the Big Five and Cialdini's seven principles or Fogg's persuasion strategy through technology[11] were conceived for marketing rather than as behavioral theories. So far, we have been unable to translate them into design principles, not can we envisage turning them into models to facilitate change and promote sustainable innovation.[12]

However, one cannot rule out that marketing practices could find those principles useful for tactical-commercial reasons and in particular to start a dialogue based on conversation styles corresponding to the lexical profile of the potential buyers. This is true for both marketing technology design and for communication strategy design. Rather than being descriptive behavioral models, they are mini taxonomies or classifications of everyday language where some words prevail over others and can therefore characterize some types of the purchasing behavior. Characterization makes it possible to hypothesize some of the user's aims and thus their profile as the purchaser of goods or services. Linguistic taxonomies have the potential to create pre-attentive conditions that might prove useful in attracting users. Once a user's attention has been captured, one can draft the right path leading to marketing campaigns influencing choices and preferences by personalizing contents.

However, taxonomies fail to offer insight and principles for behavioral evolution design. If we consider marketing technologies, they do not allow to develop proven/provable hypotheses on the rationality of user goals and on how to consequently favor aware decisions matching the purchaser's profile. Taxonomies create the preconditions to compare and measure the possible architectures of choice (see further in the text). Marketing practices based on personality profiles do not have a predictive value and are partly or totally blind as to the characteristics which differentiate behavior and choice. In a certain sense, we could say that personality profiles cannot be used as triggers to inform design strategies referred to the requisites of service requirements, and, as interaction designers well know, they are not even necessary.

Once the attention of a potential client has been captured and the mechanisms for service on boarding have been developed, motor-perceptual and decisional automatisms have to be facilitated to lead the transaction along the desired path. The

[8] Eysenck [9]

[9] For instance, see the many critical reviews [10–14].

[10] The six principles included in the first version Cialdini published in 1984 reciprocity, commitment/consistency, social proof, authority, liking, and scarcity. Subsequently Cialdini added a seventh, the unity principle. See Cialdini [15].

[11] Fogg [16]

[12] Harri [17].

possibility of establishing a digital relationship justifies the observations on the ease thanks to which it is possible to "manipulate" people's behavior during digital transactions. As we saw in Part I, manipulation is possible because people typically make decisions without having a stable preference structure. Choices are decided there and then, on the basis of available information and of how it is presented. By working on the metrics that establish the quality of the experience and the fluid interactions, marketing managers and the contents and interaction designers can prepare an experiential pathway aimed at leading to selecting one choice among the available ones. By adding an item to the existing ones, replacing, or eliminating other items, one acts on *prominence* or on the hierarchy of choices, thus impacting on decisions. After repeated tests, it is relatively easy to create different paths according to the analytical data gathered using experimental techniques and heuristics.

Design cannot take on a merely neutral or technical role if it wishes to influence user requirements in view of sustainable innovation. It is not enough to satisfy the "*usage* and *user requirements*" pair by facilitating motor perceptual and decisional automatisms and using empirical tests to complete any of the possible transactions. The alliance between behavioral scientists and designers takes place in the framework of behavioral design for sustainable innovation. It is aimed at creating the conditions to evidence the intended aims we need to work toward becoming aware of the architecture of choices and the hierarchy of aims. As you will see below, we need to work on pursued intentionality, thus creating the conditions for the orientation of the consumers to be built on an ethical basis and on a clear assumption of responsibility by the designer, as well as by the service provider.

I will now focus on two topics to explain in more depth and more detail what I mean by *intentionality* and *responsibility* in design planning: the so-called web dark patterns and nudging.[13] It is not inappropriate to illustrate the two side by side: both show how it is possible to have a decisive influence on choices and preference for quite the opposite reasons, just by acting on mental automatisms.

4.2 Dark Patterns

Harry Brignull[14] a designer User eXperience specialist invented the definition dark pattern in 2010 to describe which manipulations of interactive design can act and get a person to do things they had no intention of doing. His *darkpatterns.org* site lists and described the 12 types of manipulation (see the Table 4.1) that can be used to create misleading, frustrating experiences or other negative psychological states. When the web was initially used for commercial reasons, interaction designers made several mistakes. Some were due to the application production regimes, the

[13] In Part III, I will be discussing in more depth the construction of service models to improve literacy and agentivity.

[14] Harry Brignull also holds a PhD in cognitive science.

Table 4.1 The 12 dark patterns of the web and applications. From Brignull, https://www.deceptive.design/

Trick questions
Sneak into basket
Roach motel
Privacy Zuckering
Price comparison prevention
Misdirection
Hidden costs
Bait and switch
Confirmshaming
Disguised ads
Forced continuity
Friend spam

web sites that required swift execution, and others were due to the lack of reference points to build valid experience-based models. After 15 years of digital mass-produced solutions, interaction designers can count on an endless number of good practices that make manipulative and misleading experiences inexcusable. However, some manipulations are still widespread in digital economy. One of the reasons is that they are subtly misleading mechanisms, so one does not realize what is happening making it difficult to become aware of them in time. Consumer legislation has so far failed to list these subtle and skillful manipulations as offences that can thus be pursued. It is therefore up to the users to find the mechanisms they need to defend themselves. Still, the defense of one's right is deliberately hindered, or it is practically impossible to achieve.

Let us see some of the most frequent manipulations:

Privacy Zuckering, that is, Zuckerberg-styled privacy manipulation, is very subtle and gets its name from the Facebook founder Mark Zuckerberg. It recalls a very common digital practice: users are asked to publish information on their private lives with an endless number of photos, data, videos, and traces of their daily lives to share with acquaintances, relatives, friends, and colleagues. Naïve users typically find good reasons to continue publishing personal information, but the trick is in the fact that they are not aware the information they have made available are accessible to others too. Above all they ignore the fact that Facebook can use this information at any time for commercial purposes, and no one can stop them from doing this.

Confirmshaming (shamed into confirming) is one of the oldest tricks in the book: a person not wishing to continue with a purchase (intention to buy) or a subscription when navigating on the web or with a mobile device app feels unworthy or unsuited if they cancel. Typically, this happens before leaving the page where the user had lingered on, following a procedure to order something. A pop-up window appears with the last button to press and confirm a visible purchase choice, while underneath, a less visible option (*No, thank you*) to not follow up the intention as if stressing the mistake one could incur in was one to opt for the refusal to continue. For instance, let us imagine a user who does not want to proceed with a "miracle diet" subscription. They will have to first press a link where they state they are not interested in it anymore, giving the reason which attracted them first. At the same time, the message also leads one to think something that connotes the person who decided not to purchase, for example, by displaying a message that reads: *No, thank you, healthy food is not for me.*

Likewise, sites appreciated for their ability to generate *stickiness* and high *conversion rates*, like *booking.com*, adopt a number of such subtle mechanisms to mortify a person and hasten the users' decisions, reducing booking time. They offer unrequested information in the guise of transparency, but in fact just make it easier to opt for a particular choice. For instance, let us say you are looking up a hotel and you get a notice saying *the last room was booked 10 minutes ago* or *only 3 rooms left at this hotel* or again *another two people are interested in this site on the dates you selected* and so on. This kind of information pushes you to choose, while you are in no hurry. And as happens when you have little time to make your choice, you cut down on decision-making time.

One of the most common dark patterns is the *forced continuity*. For instance, let us say a user completes a transaction by subscribing to a service and did so with a degree of ease. However, the day after they decide, they wish to cancel the service, and they cannot easily find the way to cancel the subscription. The mechanism is all the more hateful because the site requests automatic renewal, and many users agree to it without giving thought to the fact that one it might come in useful to be able to cancel the service. In the many cases, it is not possible to cancel unless you contact a call center or send a registered email—cases known as the *Roach Motel*. In most cases, service cancellation is not very accessible thanks to a series of tricks that confuse even the most expert of users, such as unclear labeling, a link positioned in a remote area of the service, and the function hidden among access data in a scarcely visible and accessible point.

Lastly, the *bait and switch* dark pattern is the one which was typically adopted by Microsoft to force the user to download the new version of the operative system at a cost, something which is now used by Dropbox or LinkedIn to convince the user to purchase the so-called premium or added value services. The latter are more versatile functions that offer greater versatility and ease of use for an additional fee, and in the worst cases, they are necessary to be active and in control. One might object that there is a very fine line between lawful and misleading patterns. At least in some cases, it is an honest way to offer a more expensive service that requires a justification for the extra service. However, one should note that when functions are essential to access resources that enable users to carry out more complex professional, sophisticated, and advanced tasks, it is a de facto violation of one of the basic principles of what free market opportunities purport, that is, situations where monopoly regimes can develop and where competition becomes virtually impossible or difficult to access. In the digital economy when a company builds a competitive advantage, it is exceedingly difficult for other companies to catch up. In addition, there is hardly any chance of emerging, establishing a company, and finding an *independent* environmental niche that is not compatible or absorbable by one of the big players. At this point in time, Apple, Alphabet, Amazon, Facebook, and Microsoft, the five largest digital economy companies in affluent part of the globe, have attained a dominant position. They have emerged unscathed from any attempt to reduce their advantage, for instance, with fines and investigations by Parliamentary Committees to undermine their reputation with the wider consumer public. Interaction design built its own toolbox to favor motor perceptual and decisional automatisms that played a key role in establishing monopolies in the digital economy. The toolbox is used by well-funded start-ups whose main aim is to be bought by one of the large corporations.

4.3 Softly Nudging and Selective Drifts

Nudging is the development of strategies to facilitate choices that promote people's well-being. They are procedures and ploys that highlight a particular frame over other possible ones. This makes the choice for the person confronted with it more convincing although they might in fact have alternatives. Nudging uses design judgment automatisms to influence preferences and behaviors, in a systematic manner and according to the context. Influence is openly exercised while maintaining the possibility of alternatives and opting for something other than the predefined, suggested, or priority choice. According to Thaler and Sunstein's explanation[15] in all cases where consumers are asked whether they are interested in opting-in for a feature of the service that would give the company an advantage (*opt-in*), the recommended choice is presented as a priority, and possibly consumers are asked whether they wish to exclude it (*opt-out*). In fact, the *opt-out* should be the predefined option: for instance, if you wish to increase the number of organ donors, donation should be presented as the predefined option. Likewise, if you wish to increase charitable donations in the yearly tax return, donation should be the predefined choice. If you wish to promote savings, then you ought to suggest a part of wages should be earmarked for a savings fund. In all these examples, consumers are faced with a decision, and opting out is seen as the exception, only to refuse the predefined choice.

Designers have other options to use nudging in creating consumer choices. Another way to nudge is to use social or group pressure. Take insurance: if you add a well-visible note specifying the most frequently subscribed excess—with the highest percentage compared to others—that is an especially useful and informative nudging for people who have no comparable reference for the sort of health expenditure on a yearly basis. This immediately gives the future policy holder a good point of reference to navigate choices (see Fig. 4.1). Another case of nudging referred to energy consumption is the bill showing the user's regular consumption levels comparing it to the neighborhood average. In the event of that specific user

[15] Thaler [18].

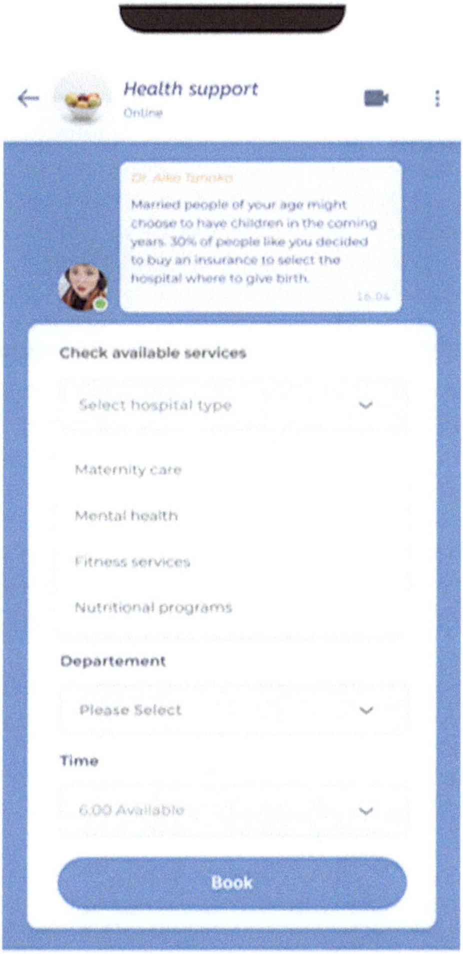

Fig. 4.1 Example of nudging: health policy excesses

exceeding the expected standard, they offer practical advice on how to improve consumption patterns. For instance, it might read: *80% of people do not use their high consumption domestic appliances at peak time* (i.e., 6 to 9 pm). In our example the user will either continue to behave as previously or will have the necessary information on what to do to not hit peak levels.

Example
Married people of your age might choose to have children in the coming years. 30% of people like you decided to buy an insurance to select the hospital where to give birth.

Awareness raising information is not a case of nudging: for example, listing all the wrong types of behavior as an electricity consumer does not bear the hallmarks of a suggestion in the context of decision-making. Likewise, it is not nudging to advise on insurance excesses and supply information on the percentage of policy holders per tier. Nor is it nudging in the case of a change of incentives, such as favoring some choices over others, for instance, higher taxation on cigarettes or on using fossil fuels to produce energy. In all these cases, it is left to the person's own understanding as to which is the base choice under the circumstances: in other words, on the opportunity of a rational choice. Lastly, policies forbidding certain choices or limiting possibilities are not included in nudging. As Selinger and Whyte point out, nudging strategies operate using judgment biases and not other mechanisms to influence and modify people's behavior.[16]

When Sunstein and Thaler's book first came out, it was followed by criticism and observations on the potential curtailing of the freedom of choice due to intrusions in a person's decisional sphere by manipulating information.[17] All these concerns can be grouped under the heading that nudging is nothing but another form of coercion and reduces freedom by manipulating choices.[18] We should not confuse manipulation of behavior or decision-making using tricks or deceit to obtain advantages as is the case of the dark patterns, with manipulations on how information is presented leading to advantage both to the company and to the person making the choice as is the case of nudging. One of the key outcomes of the dual theory cognitive process illustrated in Chap. 1 is that perception and judgment automatisms can lead people to act against their own best interest. You do not have to solve decisional dilemmas every day: that notwithstanding our daily lives are peppered with routines that require us to make decisions and we would all prefer to make good decisions rather than bad ones. As the theory of dual mental processes suggests, we do not generally fully appreciate the consequences of our choices. We are unable to make comprehensive and in-depth assessments of what the best choice is. We are prisoners of mental and behavioral routines that prevent us from seeing more favorable alternatives in the medium and long term. As discussed at length in Part I, our system of preferences changes according to how options are presented, despite us believing our behavior is consistent. Lastly, individual and cultural differences due to the level of maturity of individual literacy and cultural agentivity are pointers of how diverse behavioral patterns and the possibilities that are produced by the many (behavioral) patterns and nuances in the range from autonomous to heteronymous agentivity.

4.4 The Inescapability of Design's Responsibility

Evidence that bounded rationality characterizes behavior and decisions and that motor perceptual automatisms and judgments prevail over rational mental processes is per se a decisive answer to the criticism to *libertarian paternalism* used by

[16] Selinger and Whyte [19]

[17] Selinger [20] and Bovens [21].

[18] See the critical review by two researchers who defend libertarian theory on freedom Wright [22].

Sunstein and Thaler who defended the democratic and liberal nature of nudging.[19] This evidence has major consequences for design and designers' work for nudging. Let us look at them separately.

The first important consequence is that one must deal with the intangible design constraints due to bounded rationality. A good design highlights the constraints and makes them clear and transparent at the right moment. Design is a powerful tool and plays a key role in achieving market leadership by the digital economy big players. Interaction and choice design make it possible to act on context and on people's preferences, thus influencing their behavior in a decisive way. The alternative to not using this power is *non-design*. In the case of digital economy, but not just that, information presented in a chaotic or random manner does *not* enable users to develop preferences and make it exceedingly difficult to compare and accurately frame possibilities. Furthermore, when faced with a wealth of information, users tend to avoid choosing or instinctively follow an intuition that could lead to unpleasant consequences. The psychologist Schwartz described this concept very clearly[20] showing how the over-emphasizing self-determination favors the conditions for unrealistic expectations. For the average consumer, too many options generate an information overload that can lead to the *tyranny of freedom*. If designers fail to consider bounded rationality constraints or simply ignore them, they are denying their responsibilities.

The second major consequence is that design cannot wallow in the illusion of neutrality. Design of information architecture such as structure and hierarchy and its contents affect people's behavior and choices. The only practical alternative to *non-design* is to describe the goals one wishes to achieve with design and then assess the effects obtained pursuing a given direction: design's responsibility is inescapable in this respect. Critical literature on design also refers to the option of *non-committal design*, that is to say avoid taking position, allowing for a natural evolution of choices. However, this option is not neutral but rather the refusal to take on direct responsibility which can be possibly procrastinated to the point when the impact of design on behavior becomes clearer. It is not always possible to understand all the implications and offer a final assessment of all the effects following design decisions. If one openly states one's intentions, then it is possible to better understand and define expected behavior and possibly correct design execution accordingly. This also makes it possible to assess distance for the statement of intent over time. When the necessary modifications have not been completed, it helps those supervising and upholding consumer rights so that they may signal it and take any required steps, if need be. A nudge is a very important tool to point designers to solutions, to behaviors, and to clearly indicate goals and the effects they might have.

The third important consequence concerns content design: a range of different effects can be obtained with semantic variations, on two levels, individual and cultural. In the former, there is a wide range of behavioral patterns which means biases

---

[19] Thaler and Sunstein [23, 24].

[20] Schwartz [25].

and decisional automatisms are not all the same. As we saw in Chap. 1 and will see in more detail further in the present chapter and in Chap. 8, there are differences in the level of maturity and in controlling self-efficacy, thus determining strategies to adapt to different tasks. For instance, given the same level of education and income level, the propensity to save is not the same across the various saver profiles. Likewise, given the same health, lifestyles are not the same. Individual differences concern good and bad habits, just as so-called health literacy[21].

On an individual level, nudging can be used to pursue two complementary goals: *prompting* and *framing*. While the former, *prompting*, facilitates motor perceptual automatism, the latter, *framing*, is an invitation to stop and think for a moment, although it too acts on automatisms of judgment. In prompting, designers can act on behavior creating the conditions whereby the solution encourages the user to choose the desired option without the need to make a decision (other than accepting yes or rejecting no). In the latter case, designers manipulate information architecture highlighting the choice which favors accepting the desired aim, offering at least two alternatives.

Example
This month you saved 500€, which amount do you want to put into your plans? Currently you have 3 plans—add 1 more plan, put 200 in plan holidays, put 100 in plan new shoes; make 200 fungible.

In fact, in real life things are slightly more complex than what appears at first sight. In a certain sense, prompting and framing are major factors in a designer's consistency of purpose: in both cases, designers make choosing easier or reduce the tyranny of freedom effect due to the user's potential difficulties in choosing. However, as repeatedly stated, one of the most complex tasks of a contents and information designer is setting up choice and information architectures mirroring the user profile mix. In other words, designers will have to help service users by highlighting the choice considered most suited for their profile.

Let us now suppose that the designer is aware of the fact that the target user has chosen to put a certain sum aside every month whatever the reason. For example, let us presume Claire wishes to go on holiday in a wonderful Mediterranean resort. The application could automatically set aside part of her monthly earnings and automatically making the sum non-spendable. It is a simple case of prompting (see Fig. 4.2). Let us now presume that a designer imagines that a user has several options or plans in mind and that they are not clear about their priorities. For instance, Claire would like to go on holiday this summer, but she would also like to buy top of the range shoes for a party she is going to with friends. She also wants to put aside money for a post graduate course starting the following autumn. Let us now presume that Claire is not sure she can manage to do all of this since she has a fixed monthly income. What could the content designer do to help Claire? For instance, the

[21] Ang Li [26]; *also see "Health Literacy"*. https://www.nih.gov/institutes-nih/nih-office-director/office-communications-public-liaison/clear-communication/health-literacy *National Institutes of Health (NIH). 2015-05-08*

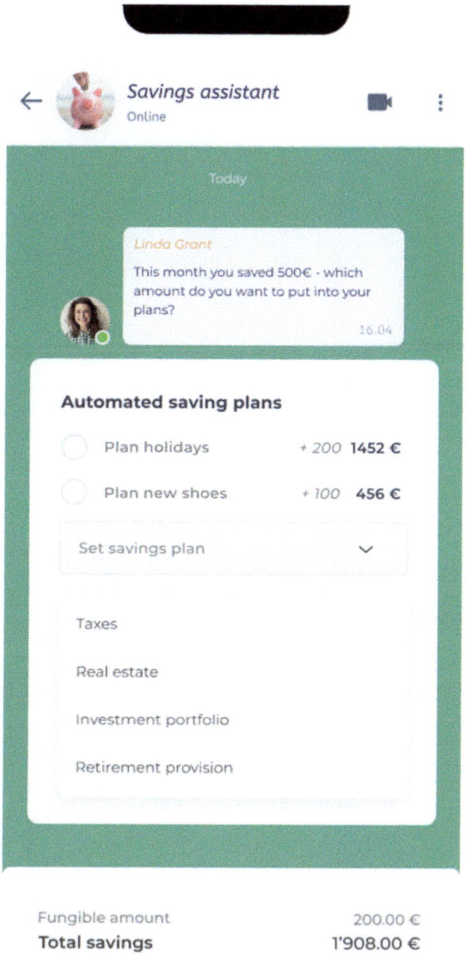

Fig. 4.2 An example of prompting to save

application could help put a larger sum aside by proportionally reducing current spending increasing the sum set aside proportionally to the objectives (see Fig. 4.3). This still falls under the definition of *prompting*. If we now turn to *framing*, the application could still help modulate choices listing a priority of the three objectives and highlighting the most *edifying* choices to then facilitate hedonic choices, according to a progressive and cumulative modularity.[22] According to the

[22] The semantic difference between *edifying* and *hedonic* choices clearly refers to the profile of the person and bears a relative weight. As the example suggests, if Claire were a promising and ambitious working student, then clearly she is the edifying master driver. However, the aim of a holiday in a pleasant resort can also be as edifying if it helps deal with autumn commitments in a more fruitful way after a restoring and restful period. Clearly the juxtaposition between edifying and hedonic features might be less conflictual for other profiles (see Fig 4.3).

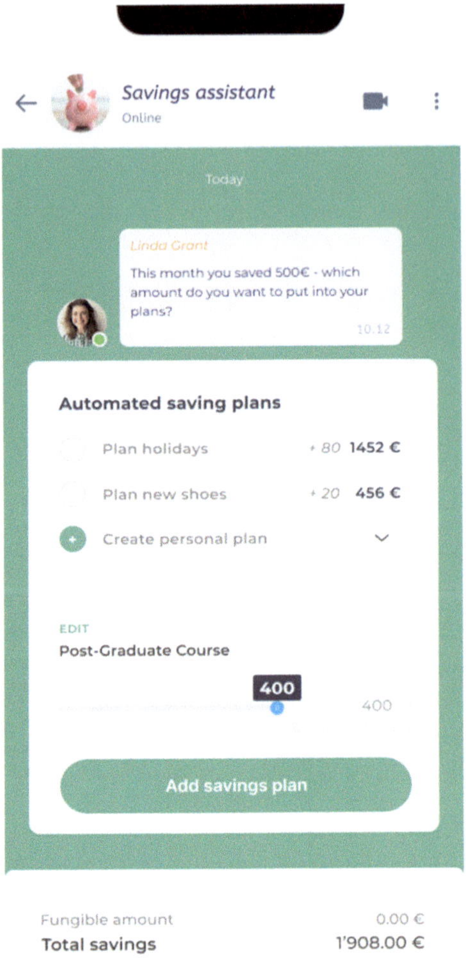

Fig. 4.3 An example of framing planned saving

recommendations of the applications and agreeing each time to set aside as suggested by the application, Claire would increase her chances of attaining the largest number of *desiderata* without having to really labor each time to decide how much to set aside and what for.

This architecture of choices based on framing is more complicated than prompting but lacks the level of complexity required to facilitate an improved behavior. We can imagine situations where self-reliance (autonomy) and control are limited and place users in a heteronymous position.

Example
This month you saved 500€, which amount do you want to put in your plans? Currently you have 3 plans—add 1 more plan, put 400 in plan "Post-Graduate

Course," put 80€ in plan "Holidays," put 20€ in plan "New shoes"—make 000€ fungible

A further level of complexity is introduced by acting on a cultural level, and it would be reductive to think it could be managed with nudging strategy. Strategies of contents design taking cultural differences onboard require information architectural designs to be consistent with the cultural expectations of their target users. Tailoring the choices to the person's use is especially complex for designers who want to avoid generating semantic confusion. In this case, designers will have to avoid supplying details that do not help distinguish and fine-tune choices. The main task of a designer is to create a hierarchy of information to exclude nonrelevant information and favor the choice best suited to the profile. However, in so doing, they will have to go beyond nudging strategies. As Thaler and Sunstein's articles and interviews outlined, to define the limits of nudging, this way of presenting information does not include a limitation of choice.[23]

By excluding a certain number of possibilities, a selective drift develops and acts covertly on the desirability and acceptability of behavior. A selective drift is one of the possible strategies to implement a responsible and intentional design that excludes the choices considered unacceptable for a given user's culture and/or profile. It happens to be one of the more effective ways, although a design team deciding to exclude some options and possibilities and abide by the principles of responsible and intentional design can always set hierarchies and priorities so as to exclude or include according to the modeling they adopt. We could presume that in a group with individuals sharing the same profile, semantic invariance will prevail. It is also reasonable to suggest that differences among groups of individuals are characterized by semantic variance. The most important advice, which designers are well aware of in diverse cultural contexts, is without the guide of ethnography, sociology, and cognitive psychology, in the best of cases, designing information architecture is an empirical and anecdotic activity with little evidence and data to support. In this respect, it is useful to reiterate the importance of integrating design practice with social science and behavioral practice. A study of individual and cultural differences can yield the requirements and useful insights to define more inclusive strategies. Furthermore, it will be possible to define behavioral models that offer a direction on how to facilitate the evolution of behavior and cultures in a sustainable way, acting on information and contents. Chapter 8 discusses this point more in detail.

The last consequence for designers and design—implied in the above-description—is that the impact of actions implemented through nudging does not include cultural variables and individual differences. The repertoire needed for sustainable innovation is much broader than what nudging strategies can imply and adopt. Nudging in itself is not enough to support inclusive and personalized responsible and intentional strategies. We have seen that nudging is based on building information architectures that preserve the freedom of choice without using

[23] Thaler and Sunstein [23, 24].

mechanisms of manipulation based on incentives and selective drifts. As discussed further in the text, sustainable innovation design has other possibilities too, so that the expertise needed to be a designer can be expanded to facilitate a progressive evolution of individual literacy and cultural agentivity.

4.5 Descriptive and Prescriptive Paths

According to the prevailing narrative among practitioners, design is a prescriptive activity. Unlike the scientific method which is usually described as the approach to describe a problem, a trend, or a phenomenon, design can imagine and invent what solution there *could be* or which *should* be the solution indicated. According to this dichotomy, scientists help us understand the present and foresee the future, while the designers prevalently develop ideas, prescribe, and create the future. As a result, to tell scientific from design thinking, one normally makes a difference between analytical paths, focused on rules and methods, and syntheses, focused on results and solutions. While scientific thought follows clear, logical, and open paths, design is chaotic, sniffs out the track of information, and compares advantages and disadvantages comparing alternative hypotheses. Designers are not interested in fully understanding how the world we live in presents to us. To a degree, designers are researchers of the future that rise to the challenge of putting into practice what they imagined.

This narrative find is explained by the nature of design itself, as it is taught in schools and in how it is practiced. However, if we wish to pursue sustainable and responsible innovation, it becomes essential to limit the biases that a designer inevitably produces and generate the evidence required to support and validate design decisions. Design is one of the disciplines that enable us to pursue strategies of change and shares a propensity for progress and seeking to improve people's lives, a trait it shares with behavioral science.

Nowadays all the disciplines of change must come to terms with the challenges of sustainable innovation. Do we really think that all the relevant systemic challenges can be addressed without producing evidence? We are all immersed in a new phase of globalization: both if we focus on the center and on the periphery of the global economy, design solutions must be based on evidence produced by methods and practice. Evidence must be developed using the most appropriate scientific practices, with analytical tools and targeted/longitudinal observation. We must move on from the traditional design practice of the digital economy that has developed in these past 15 years. We should reward managerial practices and design methods enabling us to appreciate differences of points of view; complexity of processes to generate cohesive evidence; cultural constraints; and heterogeneity of behavioral patterns and thus rebalance the enormous level of disparity between those who manage information and give the service and those who access information and services. For more details, see Part III.

4.6 Behavioral Modeling

Design is action of change, and designers are facilitators of change. Designers are generally taught to form opinions and believe in their creative abilities. Can we say the same of behavior and change scientists? Scientists also have a more technical education, but evidence building follows paths and procedures that question the truth of the evidence that emerges. Behavioral scientists learn to develop critical thought to define the limits of the evidence produced and to define the conditions whereby that evidence is valid and reproducible. In a certain sense, designers too must learn to develop a critical view and question the directions and insights underlying their work.

A critical point of view is the result of a development aimed at gathering diverging ideas and points of view to converge on one or more working hypothesis. Designers cultivate their own critical propensity, collecting a host of ideas and points of view during ideation. In this respect, we have to make a distinction between points of view and ideas: the former inevitably reflect the opinions and the interests and have a degree of legitimacy which the designer has to take into account. On the other hand, ideas are educated and reflexive results to stimuli, information, and points of view presenting a problem to be solved or an opportunity to grasp. An exercise like this can develop in sessions whose duration may vary. They have rules that define the criteria to declare the *stop rule* and arguments that are central or related (*peripheral*), *majority*, or *minority*. A designer's task is to see that minority-related (peripheral) ideas should have the opportunity to express themselves and develop all their potential throughout the diverging paths and also that majority central ideas should emerge in converging design paths.

Interestingly, the procedure mirrors the practices used for inclusion and to modify attitudes toward social inclusion that divide interest groups.[24] In fact, the aim of designers and design processes is to create participation systems where each relevant issue affected by the problem or solution of the design can be adequately and legitimately expressed. This makes it possible for them to partake in the decisional process that leads to choosing the direction for the subsequent design interactions. Another important aim is linked to the importance of creating moments of participation with the techniques that guarantee the right to create innovative solutions: telling a good idea from a bad one and selecting the ones that will receive consensus and will be more meaningful than less valid routes. According to the psychologist Csikszentmihalyi, following divergent and convergent paths is one of key practices of creative thinking in that it makes it possible to reach an agreed-upon solution: "Divergent thinking leads to no agreed-upon solution. It involves fluency, or the ability to generate a great quantity of ideas; flexibility, or the ability to switch from one perspective to another; and originality in picking unusual associations of ideas. These are the dimensions of thinking that most creativity tests measure and that most workshops try to enhance. Yet there remains the nagging suspicion that at the

[24] De Dreu [27].

highest levels of creative achievement the generation of novelty is not the main issue. People often claimed to have had only two or three good ideas in their entire career, but each idea was so generative that it kept them busy for a lifetime of testing, filling out, elaborating, and applying. Divergent thinking is not much use without the ability to tell a good idea from a bad one, and this selectivity involves convergent thinking.[25]"

What we have seen so far clearly shows that switching from divergent to convergent processes is not so obvious as it requires selective abilities and judgment but above all it needs to be able to identify all the variables that bear weight in determining what is best suited and how to develop new solutions that offer value to the recipients or users, be they people, organizations, communities, or society as a whole.

Behavioral modeling is one of the new ways to help switching from a divergent to a convergent process, a plastic and dynamic representation of the characteristics the innovation is required to have. Behavioral modeling enables us to prefigure what the services are intended to do for each special cluster of users or consumers. Ideally the process is positioned between the divergent and the convergent processes. Modeling of behavior has an in-between role, as seen in Fig. 4.4.

I suggested the idea of modeling after about 7 years of activity as a professional (2005–2012), when my colleagues and I were trying to integrate research and design into a number of projects. In these projects our attitude was that we needed data, stimuli, points of view, and stories to inspire design cycles, before proposing potential directions for the development of digital solutions. However, at a certain point, I realized that to appear convincing with designers, it was also necessary to put forward live and dynamic representations of what we had gathered in research and field observation, as well as offering a vernacular representation of what we learned, useful in *doing*. Our research activities were mainly ethnographic and either *netnographic* or digital ethnographic or training and context-related activities. They were based on qualitative research protocols mainly centered on targeted observation of people, selected with criteria by thematic interest domain, so as pick up on all the nuances and understand routines, habits, relations, and meaning in everyday ordinary settings.

After year of research carried out according to the cutting-edge standards in mainstream practice of the design industry, I realized something was missing especially when it came to describing the nuances in the intense and concentrated activities of qualitative research. I wondered what we could do to create and offer a useful structure to explain what we had learnt to the stakeholders and the team who had been unable to follow research sessions in the field. My ambition was also to use scientific theories to generate these models, adapting data and the intuitions ensuing from the analysis of the empirical data gathered in identifying the distinctive traits, the various levels of agentive maturity, and the behavioral clusters. In my eyes the

---

[25] See Csikszentmihalyi, Mihaly. *"The Creative Personality"*. In Psychology Today https://www.psychologytoday.com/intl/articles/199607/the-creative-personality. 1996

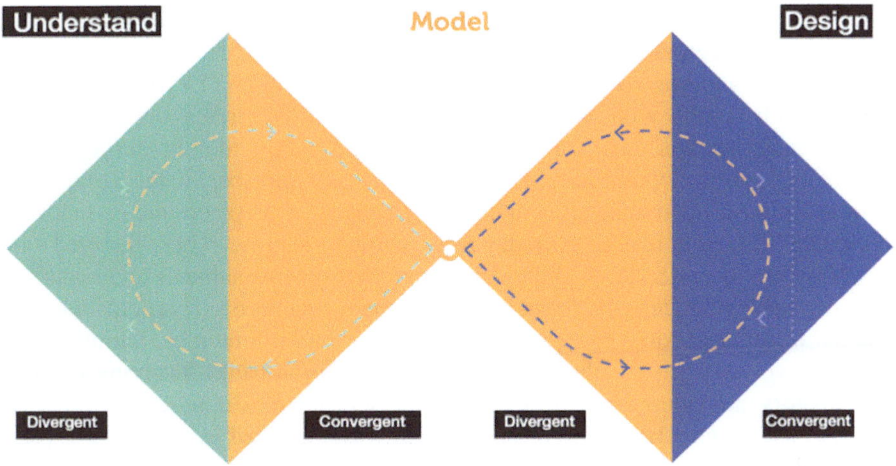

Fig. 4.4 The double diamond shows the divergent and convergent thinking steps in design processes. The diamond to the left shows processes referring to understanding the object of study through research. The other diamond refers to the actual design processes or implementation. The lens at the center that links the two diamonds includes modeling processes. This figure draws inspiration from the London Design Council. Modeling is not included in the Design Council's (See https://www.designcouncil.org.uk/news-opinion/what-framework-innovation-design-councils-evolved-double-diamond (accessed May 2021)) version

modeling of observed behaviors could definitely be considered as a design artifact, a versatile tool, and a guide for designers, educators, and developers. My intuition told me that modeling could prove especially useful as a narrative tool to inform design cycles and illustrate what needed to be done, which requirements needed to be satisfied differentiating by categories or clusters of people, and what staging to enable software engineers to develop the necessary integrations suited to the development of applications. Behavioral modeling is a very versatile tool that can also be used in many more functions, other than the above-listed ones. Part III will discuss functions useful in outlining strategies based on empirical evidence, to shape change, and Part IV will discuss how behavioral models can inform randomized experimental programs for change. I discovered that behavioral modeling can be used also for functions I had never imagined at the beginning, such as teaching people serving the public how to understand the expectations of the people who arrive to have an investment or insurance advice. Another function I saw apply was the use of models to define a strategy for chatbots and advanced interaction programs using AI. I now also see a potential use of modeling techniques to improve protocol adherence in clinical trials and to improve predictive models in chronic diseases.

One of the first behavioral models I was able to work on with several colleagues referred to behavioral models in saving. We wanted to develop an app to help families save and enable them to plan short-, medium-, and long-term expenses. In this case behavior modeling guides the digital service concept design. As you can see in Fig. 4.5, it was seen as a concept or artifact of design, as I explain below.

Research was carried out in 2012 and 2013 in 3 Italian cities (1 each in the North, Center, and South) with 40 people and their family circles or households. Ethnographic surveys were carried out in the field over 4 months during which researchers had the opportunity to interact with each member of the group over several cycles of interaction, concluding with a day spent in places the participants chose and referred to in their everyday lives. Throughout, researchers gathered videos, photographs, interviews, and culturally probed specific subjects and materials made available to understand the daily routine and the habits each participant had in relation to savings. Analysis and result assessment lasted 5 months, during which the team worked with the client (an important European bank) involving them in participatory activities where results were presented and discussed in feedback workshop sessions. The wealth of information was organized in raw data for each participant to identify distinctive and characterizing features. Data were then processed at different levels to identify shared and structural elements. Shared elements and the identified distinctive traits made it possible to identify behavioral clusters and then to classify each participant accordingly. Such clusters helped us identify characterizing routine consumption and saving behavior for each group of people (see Chap. 8).

I applied the dual theory of behavior to describe routines, making a distinction between automatisms aimed at maintaining stability, balancing consumption behaviors within one's spending range, and processes controlled to cultivate short-, medium-, and long-term goals, or aspirations. All those who took part in the research illustrated some daily or periodic routines applied to control spending management mechanisms, to balance income and expenditure. There was a range of different

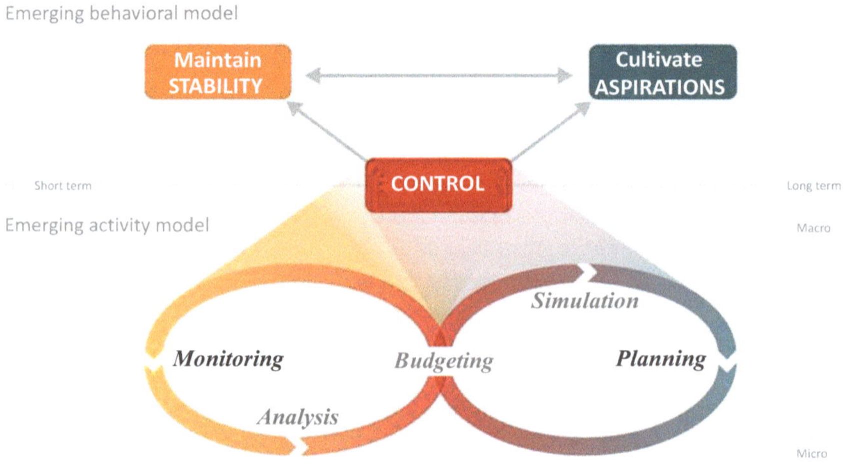

Fig. 4.5 The behavioral model used to inform the design of a personal finance management tool. (Thanks to Takumi Hoshida for his help in finalizing the visual representation of the model)

behavioral patterns even at this level of behavioral model shown in Fig. 4.5: given the spending power, behavioral regulatory patterns were not all the same. People able to budget (forecast expenditure) and offer relative characterization also proved able to offer a precise allocation of each category of repeated expenditure. These same people also displayed a sophisticated *budgeting routine* (see the center of the activity model in Fig. 4.5, where we have routine budget building), which showed behavioral regulation. They also routinely *monitored* and *analyzed* their spending patterns and those of their families. They also were the ones who more readily recognized the value of a digital app to support control and management routines, as if for a business.

The main aim of resource allocation was clearly not to overspend to be able to cope with unexpected expenses or to be able to set savings aside. However, only 30% of all participants appeared to follow that routine and to be aware of existing routines. This first important result shows that so-called mental accounting, that is, the ability to routinely allocate resources for expenses in an automatic or controlled manner,[26] is an unevenly spread distinctive feature. In some cases, there were attempts to allocate resources and to make a distinction between spendable and non-fungible resources, although these attempts do not necessarily generate the ability to allocate resources according to a budget. In some cases, there were attempts to allocate resources and to divide spendable and non-fungible resources, but such attempts do not necessarily mean resource allocation is according to a budget. People who allocate resources for budgeted expenses displayed a greater capacity to monitor spending and set aside repeated and controlled savings. Self-regulation in monitoring spending appeared to be shared by nearly all participants. This is the first step of the model of activity in Fig. 4.5. *Monitoring* routines give rise to an implicit behavioral regulation. They are automatic judgment mechanisms like those described in Chap. 1: for instance, at the beginning of the month, the person may spend more freely than the end of the month. This simple routine operates also when indulging and spending: say you have bought a new clothes item, that day or that week you might limit spending behavior in, say, food or leisure. It is probably a primordial form of the mental accounting Richard Thaler refers to that typically surfaces to balance two systematic trends: *hyperbolic discounting* and *confirmation bias*. Both the former and the latter are dominant behaviors in people who fail to save at the end of the month and are inclined to seek immediate gratification which they later regret.

Implicit or explicit *analytical* attitudes are the next and additional step in control. If they are all implicit, that is to say performed with sub-vocalic mental routines, a degree of management ineffectiveness becomes apparent to the person themselves. However, these people are characterized by a limited propensity to understand how they can improve their spending patterns. In the other case, that is, explicit analysis, for instance, limited to the end of the week or the end of the month, participants displayed a propensity to keep track of spending, for instance, keeping receipts and

---

[26] See Thaler [28, 29].

fixing spending limits (parameters) to have a better grasp of the situation. In Southern Italy where there is a more limited spending capacity, participants displayed a greater propensity to more detailed analytical accounting. That said, not all the people with an explicit analytical propensity necessarily moved on to the next step, as illustrated in the model shown in Fig. 4.5, the ability to allocate resources by spending item. These people use a different form of bias whereby there is no fixed point of reference in time for variations and relative analyses: they are the ones who do not know how to balance oscillations between pessimistic and optimistic views.

The model described in Fig. 4.5 shows how the ability to maintain a comprehensive consumption and spending behavior stability occurs when there are routines that include spending monitoring, spending behavior analysis, and allocation among spending items. The most elementary form of budgeting requires separating fungible (spending) resources from savings. Although all participants understood what saving meant and aspired to have *non-recurring* spending, less than a third of the participant sample displayed a propensity for resource allocation following a path like the above-described one. This subset of participants was definitely able to make substantial spending plans (i.e., *planning*) such as for the house mortgage, their children's university, holidays, and the like. *Simulating* spending capacity is an important feature of mental accounting (see Fig. 4.5), aimed at dynamically verifying the consequences of resource allocation in the medium and long term and identifying the part of fungible saving. They were the people who simulated specially to prevent the possibility of mistakes in deciding, to manage income uncertainty and improve spending behavior regulation. In many cases, simulation was finalized and intended to verify the possibility of moving resources to face unexpected occurrences. In some cases, the simulation was used to confirm disinvestment hypothesis on new or existing objectives.

Analytical management of budgeting, simulation, and planning are deliberate activities which thus require a deliberate decision-making that is prone to mistakes and requires people to apply themselves and be attentive and accounting skills, albeit basic ones. Our research has shown that self-regulatory activities can be satisfying enough but greatly improvable with the special support of instruments and artifacts to reduce fallibility of self-regulatory systems. Self-regulation did not prove very reliable in situations of income variability or uncertainty. But even when income was certain, homeostatic behavior to balance income and output generally proved to have a limited effect for the overwhelming majority of participants. One possible explanation for this ineffectiveness can be found in the notion of homeostasis as used by the neurologists Antonio and Hanna Damasio.[27] Human self-regulatory behavior, and for that matter behavior in most vertebrates, is a two-tier system: a physiological component that regulates instincts such as hunger and thirst where no

[27] Damasio and Damasio [30].

voluntary behavior or awareness is required[28] and then a voluntary part known as *homeostatic feelings*. The latter is a mental function, and it generates representations that give rise to an emotional experience in the affective sphere, whose nature changes the person into an agent regulating their behavior. According to the Damasios, agentivity is the positive feature of the essence of awareness of these regulatory mechanisms. The fact that the behavior is voluntary means that control is less accurate and more prone to mistakes. The two researchers believe that *homeostatic feelings* are the most advanced solution biological organisms have found to answer regulatory problems that they could not address with automatic and physiological mechanisms in life. Nevertheless, these mechanisms have a fundamental flaw: instability. A wonderful sentence enshrines this notion "Reflexivity promotes unstable oscillatory behaviors."

Digital aids for personal finance management can be seen to support agentivity and improve it. Digital solutions were developed by the design team in four phases (see Fig. 4.6) and were conceived as a reference model of decision-making leading to better control financial stability and the planning of spending objectives. The behavioral model which informs the solution can be best described as a normed model of financial education aimed at savings. This confirms and highlights the activities characterized by mental accounting.

As the figures show, the interface of the digital solution facilitates decision control to maintain regular stability between income and output (see Fig. 4.7), making a progressive automation of spending analytical processes possible, and to both simulate and plan spending aims (see Fig. 4.8), automating impact analysis on the aspirations of spending objectives.

We can imagine the evolution of the application aiming to improve literacy in a contextual and dynamic manner, in everyday life: given the technological limitations and inter-banking policies in place when the behavioral model was established, steps forward have been made to further improve the application. For instance, it is now easier to have several bank accounts and accounts from different banking groups in one app so that users may enjoy a comprehensive view of financial resources. It is also relatively easy to class expenses when receipts for spending flows are automatically traced, which can improve also budgeting techniques. The aim of the first completed version of the app was to improve saving ability and favor a better overall balance in managing personal/household finance, as well as one off (not regular) expenses. It was a matter of rationalizing decision-making in allocating financial resources and modeling proved useful in understanding the mental routines of each reference model. In addition, it offered guidance on how to improve agency to bolster saving-oriented behavior and spending plans. Future versions of the app for mobile devices could focus on a more ambitious aim: facilitating *homeostatic feelings* and as they surface using *cooling off techniques* and simultaneous

[28] The two Damasios illustrate the automatic part of the physiological self-regulatory mechanisms whereby the release of sugars is managed by hormones that automatically stop storing it in cells to make it available, while body fluids are managed by the kidneys that automatically slow diuresis to restore hydration levels.

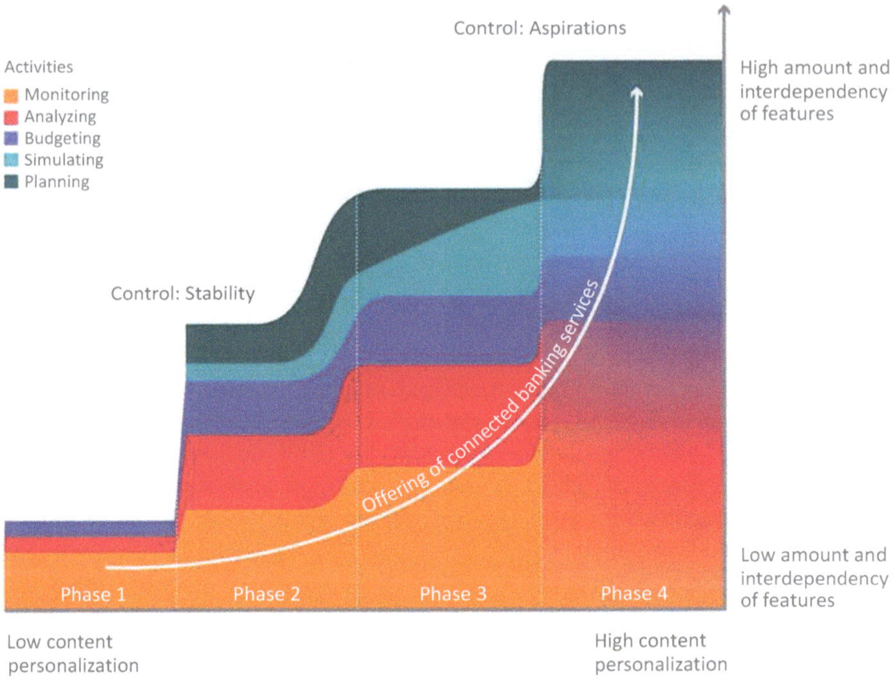

Fig. 4.6 Software roadmap to design support applications for personal and household finance following the behavioral model of this Figure. (Software design roadmap, informed by the behavioral model and activity model shown in Fig. 4.5)

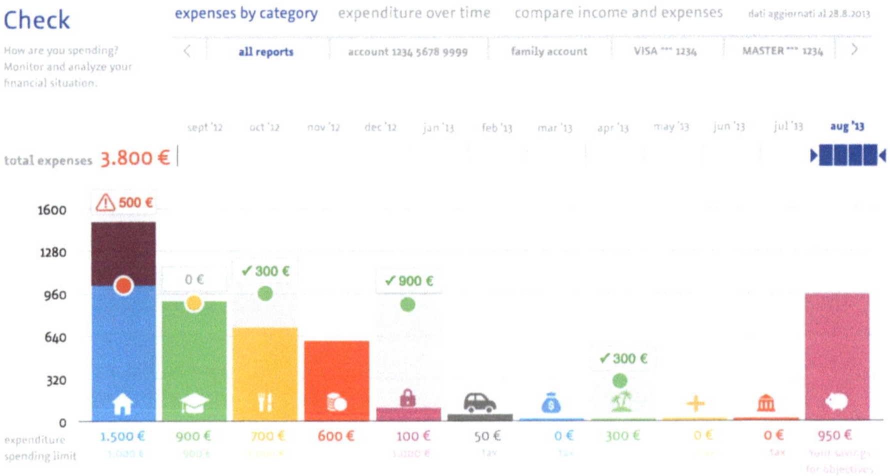

Fig. 4.7 Dashboard used to monitor expenses and allocate resources. Expenses can be traced by category, in a time window, and compared versus income

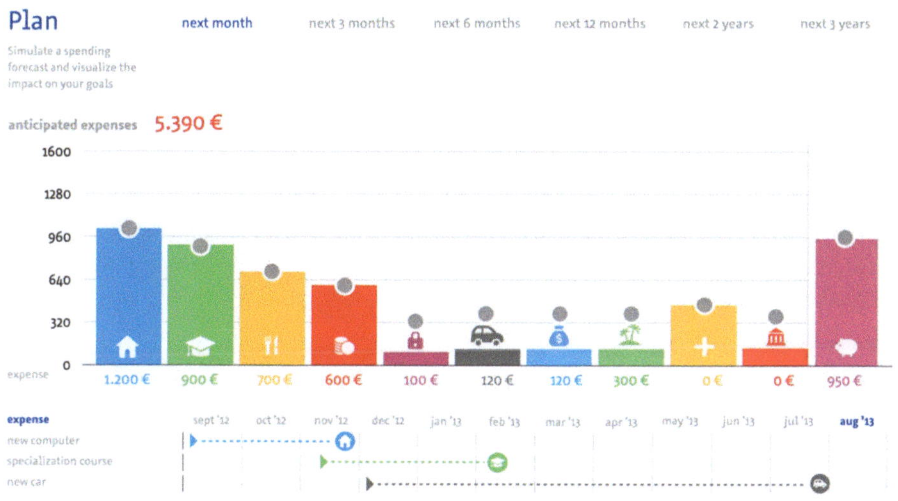

Fig. 4.8 Dashboard to simulate goals and allocate fungible resources to plans. Planning according to different time windows, i.e., any 3 months, 6 months, and so on up to 5 years

simulation, i.e., correcting bias and the inevitable impact due to oscillating decision-making behavior when needed.

Highlights

- The classical separation between the descriptive role of human sciences and the prescriptive role of design is not helpful to address the variety of wicked problems found in all current societal and global challenges.
- Design by drawing is the basic expression of design; it builds on the designers' preferences, styles, and biases.
- Design by science is the most advanced expression of design; it builds on the factual evidence produced by structured observation and experiments.
- The four orders of design help us to understand how synergies between design practices and humanities can be established.
- In the highest orders of design imagination and creativity is the result of complex analytical processes.
- In complex challenges the center of design processes is no longer in the problem-solving ideas.
- Behavioral design is a multicentered, multifocal, multidimensional effort.
- Intentionality and responsibility are two key factors of behavioral design planning.
- Web's dark patterns and behavioral nudges act on mental automatisms and can be used to have a decisive influence on choices for the opposite reasons.
- The "inescapability" of design's responsibility is to describe the design goals and to assess them iteratively.
- Non-committal design does not mean neutrality.

- Prompting and framing are two complementary information design techniques to implement nudging and to facilitate choosing.
- Selective drift is a design technique to implement a responsible design.
- Following divergent and convergent paths is one of the key practices of creative thinking.
- Behavioral modeling is a design artifact, a narrative tool to guide designers, content manager, educators, and developers.
- Behavioral clusters are qualitative data set to identify distinctive behavioral traits.
- Mental accounting is an unevenly spread distinctive feature among savers and bank account holders.

References

1. Lawson, B. (2005). *How designers think* (4th ed.). Blackwell's.
2. Buchanan, R. (1992). Wicked problems in design thinking. *Design Issues: JSTOR, 8*(2), 5–21. https://doi.org/10.2307/1511637. Accessed July 26, 2022.
3. Golsby-Smith, T. (1996). Fourth order design: A practical perspective author(s). *Design Issues, 12*(1), 5–25.
4. Rowe, P. G. (1987). *Design thinking*. Mass. MIT Press.
5. Krug, S. (2006). *Don't make me think*. Published in Italian by Tecniche Nuove.
6. Goldberg, L. R. (1993). The structure of phenotypic personality traits. *American Psychologist, 48*(1), 26–34.
7. McCrae, R. R., & John, O. P. (1992). An introduction to the Five-Factor Model and its applications. *Journal of Personality, 60*(2), 175–215.
8. Costa, P. T., & McCrae, R. R. (1992). *Revised NEO Personality Inventory (NEO-PI-R) and NEO Five-Factor Inventory (NEO-FFI) manual*. Psychological Assessment Resources.
9. Eysenck, H. J. (1992). Four ways five factors are not basic. *Personality and Individual Differences, 13*(8), 667–673.
10. Livneh, H., & Livneh, C. (1989). The five-factor model of personality: Is evidence of its cross-measure validity premature? *Personality and Individual Differences, 10*, 75–80.
11. Block, J. (1995). A contrarian view of the five-factor approach to personality description. *Psychological Bulletin, 117*, 187–229.
12. Boyle, G. J. (2008). *Critique of the five-factor model of personality. Humanities and Social Sciences papers. Paper 297*. http://epublications.bond.edu.au/hss_pubs/297.
13. Saucier, G. (1994). Mini-markers: A brief version of Goldberg's unipolar Big-Five markers. *Journal of Personality Assessment, 63*, 506–516.
14. Saucier, G. (2002). Orthogonal markers for orthogonal factors: The case of the Big Five. *Journal of Research in Personality, 36*, 1–31.
15. Cialdini, R. (2001). *Influence: Science and practice*. Pearson education.
16. Fogg, B. J. (2003). *Persuasive technology: Using computers to change what we think and do*. Morgan Kaufmann Publishers.
17. Harri, O.-K., & Harjumaa, M. (2009). Persuasive systems design: Key issues, process model, and system features. *Communications of the Association for Information Systems, 24*, 28.
18. Thaler, R. H., & Sunstein, C. R. (2009). *Nudge: Improving decisions about health, wealth and happiness* (2nd ed.). Penguin Books.
19. Selinger, E., & Whyte, K. (2011). Is there a right way to nudge? The practice and ethics of choice architecture. *Sociology Compass, 5*(10), 923–935.
20. Selinger, E. (2011). *Concerns over nudging* (p. 2). Initiative for Science, Society, and Policy Essay Series.

21. Bovens, L. (2008). The ethics of nudge. In T. Grüne-Yanoff & S. O. Hansson (Eds.), *Preference change: Approaches from philosophy, economics and psychology*. Springer, Theory and Decision Library A.
22. Wright, J. D., & Ginsburg, D. W. (2012). Behavioral law and economics: Its origins, fatal flaws and implications for liberty. *North-western University Law Review, 106*(3), 1033–1090.
23. Thaler, R., & Sunstein, C. (2003). Libertarian paternalism. *The American Economic Review, 93*, 175–179.
24. Thaler, R., & Sunstein, C. (2003). *Libertarian paternalism is not an oxymoron* (Vol. 70, pp. 1159–1202). The University of Chicago Law Review.
25. Schwartz, B. (2012). Self-determination: The tyranny of freedom. *American Psychologist, 55*(1), 79–88.
26. Li, A. (2021). Individual and organizational health literacies: Moderating psychological distress for individuals with chronic conditions. *Journal of Public Health*, fdab133. https://doi.org/10.1093/pubmed/fdab133
27. De Dreu, C., De Vries, N., Gordijn, E., & Schuurman, M. (1999). Convergent and divergent processing of majority and minority arguments: effects on focal and related attitudes. *European Journal of Social Psychology, 29*(2–3), 329–348.
28. Thaler, R. H. (1990). Saving, fungibility and mental accounts. *Journal of Economic Perspectives, 4*, 193–205.
29. Thaler, R. H. (1999). Mental accounting matters. *Journal of Behavioral Decision Making, 12*(3), 183–206.
30. Damasio, A., & Damasio, H. (2016). Exploring the concept of homeostasis and considering its implications for economics. *Journal of Economic Behavior & Organization, 126*, 125–129.

Chapter 5
Intentional Behavioral Design

As previously observed, *responsible design* is based on the idea that it is impossible to be neutral. *Intentionality* means you must reveal and declare what goals the product and service intend to attain. As a result, if possible, you must validate and measure if and when there is a possible shift that could develop from the stated aims. There are two major implications of intentionality-based design:

(a) It makes it possible to plan for aims according to level of service and/or user maturity, which may or may not correspond to a higher or lower level of integration.
(b) It makes it possible to state that deliberately dismissing intentional design is like saying one is waiving the power of design.

The power of design lies in understanding the constraints to be considered and their implementation in the aims we intend to facilitate. Hence, the main task of responsible design is defining the intentions of the proposed solutions using many strategies aimed at facilitating behavioral changes and to generate an impact for the sustainable evolution of cultures. The aims place design as a natural ally of human, social, and life sciences: design and behavioral science share many features as both share a propensity to generate sense-making possibilities, that is, meanings that enhance the positive sense of people's lives and strengthen them. Furthermore, both operate on desirability and satisfaction of personalized objectives. In this sense, behavioral design acts on individual and collective values, helping people develop an awareness of how they evolve and how they could evolve. This is made possible by behavioral modeling. Lastly, in the synergic action developed through modeling, design appears as a discipline able to further the state of the knowledge developed in scientific labs.

In real life, behavioral design makes it possible to generate new awareness, *evidence-based* and *action-based* awareness. It is a necessary form of knowledge for the agenda of sustainable innovation to progress, as it supports the improvement related to how people form mental images, understand, think, and make choices.

M. Visciola, *Sustainable Innovation*,
https://doi.org/10.1007/978-3-031-18751-3_5

Intentional behavioral design is a form of knowledge which has an educational and emancipatory role because hopefully it conveys a more adequate knowledge, operating on content architectures that improve people's expertise and agentivity. Furthermore, behavioral design balances autonomy and heteronomy, dynamically transferring the locus and the focus of consumer-service control. In traditional user-centered design, responsible design plans services and systems that can tolerate human error. They are permeable to human error and variability of judgment. It also sees to it that users can develop knowledge about the interface of the service, which will improve an individual's bounded rationality regulatory capacity. Behavioral design is an approach that contributes to the considerations where services and solutions generate value for users and consumers, clearly compensating for the entrepreneurship expressed. This yields value for society as whole and therefore for the common good. The moral value of taking a stand can be also found in this identitarian dimension of design and designers: when behavioral design is based on modeling, it becomes intentional. Cultivating design intentionality is a form of taking on responsibility to promote a common good. I believe this side of the matter calls for further thinking and remarks.

5.1 Four Values of Behavioral Design

When intention behavioral design intends to develop sustainable innovation, unique value elements surface. Let us take a closer look (see Table 5.1): the central value of behavioral design is to favor individual literacy and cultural agentivity. As attentive readers will have probably already understood, agentivity presents major challenges for behavioral designers. Some of these challenges have been raised in a critical debate on "the freedom to choose and to make mistakes" which has witnessed behavioral philosophers, economists, and experts of behavioral law debate.[1]

The discussion sees a juxtaposition between a libertarian point of view which identifies consumer policies aimed at behavioral protections as coercive and restrictive and libertarian paternalism which upholds the need to protect consumers from potential decisional or behavioral errors. By favoring agentivity, behavioral designers establish the conditions whereby service users can count on information architectures that improve the ability to judge. In that sense, behavioral design defines

Table 5.1 Four foundational values of behavioral design

1. Favor individual literacy and cultural agentivity	2. Reduce misjudgments due to information asymmetries
3. Promote lifestyle balance and aspirations for improvements	4. Facilitate participation in ideation and creative processes

[1] See the digests of the main Law Schools, i.e., Zamir and Teichman [1]; Jolls, C. *Behavioral Economics and Law.* Also see the European Commission [2, 3].

normed/standardized or reference behavioral models, used for personalized or scalable solutions that foresee conditions of heteronomy. In conditions where the consumer-user acts according to habit (*habitual routines*), there are conditions of autonomy. The definition and design of behavioral models clearly is choice of the side one is on, when designing cognitive aids that favor the management of motor perceptual and judgment automatisms, improving literacy in the dominion of choice, help positive experience and psychology prevail.

Another fundamental value of behavioral design concerns the reduction of the unbalanced information and the resulting errors of judgment. Highlighting the unbalance between service providers and users with reference to the quality of data and information, as well as knowledge sophistication from information and data, is one of the most important contributions of behavioral law.[2] The unbalance of information and knowledge is generally the result of a bias aimed at building the price system on the basis of the product or service functions. The unbalance is made worse by the emphasis on the desirability and utility of functions, which systematically generate false perceptions. Typically, the service provider has to maximize the *perceived net benefit* of the service by the customer not to lose a client or to gain new ones. The value differs systematically from *the actual net benefit.*[3] Information on utility tends to increase the immediate advantage for the consumer and not to give enough information on future associated costs. By working on intentionality and expected behavior, benefit perception paradigms shift from the immediate satisfaction of a need—and therefore from perception of a short-term ensuing from the purchase of the product or service—to attaining the aims the service or product facilitates.

Information emphasis shifts to the actual use of the service and on the medium- and long-term associated benefits. The effect of shifting the balance in transactions is to improve people's agentivity and their understanding of how one can pursue sustainable choices, thus attributing legitimacy to the *quality* of the service performed.

Behavior acceptability and desirability are other important values of such design, listed third but not least. In this sense, service interface design seeks a balance between the sense of surprise and discovery that using a new service elicits, as well as familiarity with the objectives it enables one to attain. The definition of agentivity aims is an important challenge for design as it makes it possible to consider individual and cultural differences for each choice dominion. User profile definition by modeling makes it possible to establish dispositional and situational constraints to be considered, their articulation in distinctive traits for each profile, and the percentage of people for each profiled cluster (see Chap. 1). Once behavioral desirability and acceptability have been defined for each profile of consumer users, then you have behavioral homeostasis, and one can seek a balance between behaviors of stability and change. By building this strategy, that is, behavioral homeostasis, design

[2] See Bar-Gill [4].

[3] See Bar-Gill O. ibid.

contributes to make choices for each profile meaningful that can then build its identity, its own belief, and value system. The effect of this action is to legitimate business with a purpose, putting sustainability and behavioral evolution in the desired direction at the center of one's action, for the individual, their community, and society in a wider sense.

Lastly, participation and involvement of consumers and service users in ideational and creative processes are the facets of the fourth value of behavioral design. Design thinking practices include stakeholders, expert users, and mere users during service-led co-creation and ideation. Behavioral design adds major elements in evidence on user profiles, on the constraints to satisfy, and on the journeys to implement. Furthermore, behavioral models—and hence later phases of exploration and research activities—add design sprint sessions involving all users in detailed design activities of solutions created for each profile or user cluster. Unlike typical participation processes where users are generically interested in the development of the new service, behavioral design is especially attentive where user selection is concerned to offer a greater match and continuity with the research steps. The underlying idea is that the users who can see themselves in the cases where they will be involved will have a greater empathic drive to transfer to the team, consistently with the tradition of Northern European participatory design.[4]

The main aim of participation in behavioral design practice is not just to favor generic user *representatives* in the creative phases of solution development but also to accelerate design progression and define the desired impact in terms of sustainability and usability. I would like to conclude this section with a brief note on behavioral designer identity and on the moral drive that leads their actions: the role of designers is shaping into an important figure mediating between community and users, producers and service managers, regulators (watchdogs), and spheres that define privacy. I believe the phase where designers could develop beautiful, useful, usable, and desirable things is over: we are entering a more committed phase, and nowadays design in terms of behavioral design can play a key role in indicating and outlining the development of sustainable innovation strategies. Intentional behavioral design will enable us to do something new, which is what is discussed below.

5.2 Value Disclosure with Design

I maintained that architecture designing of information and choice structure has moral implications not just because it can be manipulated using bounded rationality generating opportunistic advantages. In fact, thanks to information architecture, behavioral design can play a major moral role with beneficial effects on society. Aware and intentional design of information and structures of choice architecture

[4] See Bjerknes and Kyng [5].

has an impact on people and on their possibility to improve agentivity and cooperative ability.

In seeking to attain these aims, one contributes to the development of cultural values whereby the common good prevails. Sustainable innovation enshrines both values pertaining to the individual sphere and community and social values. In this respect, behavioral design highlights both the value of individual agentivity and cultural interdependence and methodically pursuing their implementation.

I would now like to show how in revealing the value of a service, behavioral design exceeds the limits within which it has operated so far, and at the same time it is able to point how to move beyond the limits of accepted practices, thanks to which economic players of market economies define and reveal value. There is a link between design and usability, interaction design, and behavioral law that I believe can be usefully highlighted. One of the shared aims is to simplify the use of technologies and make contents and information accessible. In the digital economy, the stress on the word simplification is all the stronger among usability designers. This area of design places users at the center, and during design development, it becomes a point of reference for the team, to reduce access barriers and make it possible to easily achieve a wide range of aims.

Interestingly usability designers typically are seen as service user advocates. Likewise, interaction and usability design see its main value in the paradigm of universal access to information, like consumer protection laws. The analogy is especially appealing in this case: just as interaction and usability design endeavors to facilitate the average user so that they may attain their goals favoring perceptual motor and judgment automatisms, behavioral law and policy-making strategies aim to reduce the *cognitive load* the consumer is required to have to read and understand the contracts and rules of transactions.

Consumer rights and behavioral law experts wonder if laws in defense of consumers and those regulating business transactions are open to accept knowledge from behavioral science. In the past decade, there has been a great interest in updating laws and regulations in the light of the fact that imperfect information and bounded reality lead to a misperception of a service's or product's value. Although some different nuances and criticisms have emerged between Europe and the United States,[5] the debate appears to focus around a key point: although laws and regulations try to create conditions to influence consumer behavior and improve perception of the actual value of transactions, their impact is minimal.

I believe it is useful to discuss some of the remarks and conclusions of the debate more in detail:

– First, the product or service is hardly ever described in the contract or user manual enabling consumers to glean a reliable idea of its value. This is prevalently due to the mass of information the documents contain. Only a minute number of

[5] For the European market, see Helleringer and Sibony [6]. *For the American market, see* Sunstein [7].

people ever read their contents. Especially in Europe the wealth of information in a contract is normally justified in the name of consumer defense. It is justified in the name of having to give more detailed information to defend the consumer offering all the explanations to improve their knowledge of the product or service being purchased. Research on the readability of documents for the purchase of a license and user manuals show that the longer the document and the time to extract useful information, the less legible and accessible the information is. The European Community agrees on the need to simplify documents and reduce the information overload, personalizing and contextualizing information in the appropriate manner.[6]

– The second important point is that available information is aimed prevalently at describing service and product attributes and functionality. Information on use is typically in texts (manuals or handbooks) that reveal the characteristics of the product and how it works. According to Bar-Gill,[7] producers and manufacturers have no interest in supplying information on use and tend not to make use patterns of their services and products clear. Underlying this reluctance is the fact that use patterns cannot be presented in such a way that they are valid for all consumers due to the variety of users and the different levels of knowledge and ability. Typically benchmark analyses on use experience underline differences in terms of effectiveness, efficiency, and satisfaction in product use.

In a comparative usability study performed with a team of colleagues on a global scale for fast-moving consumer goods (FMCG) manufacturers for 2005 and 2006,[8] we were able to ascertain that revealing knowledge on the real value of the comparative usability of own products constitutes for the producer a factor of potential disadvantage in the competition. Revealing this knowledge could reduce possible advantages over the competition, as others would have the information to reduce the gap. A different reason is also true, as knowledge on product use value could also inform consumers in a possible lower quality compared to the competition. This would lead to say that in open and competing markets, there is an advantage in not being transparent on use patterns and quality of use experience and in maintaining an information asymmetry between manufacturers and consumers as happens in closed and monopoly markets.

Lastly, examining user manuals and the information therein, it is noticeable that their main aim is to protect the producer in the event of the product or service being used in ways other than the interactive process envisaged by the producer/manufacturer. We observed that such information is designed bearing in mind an average consumer's profile, thus distorting actual consumers and denying the influence of the context where the service is being used and reducing the value of the information supplied.

---

[6] See EC reports.

[7] Ibid.

[8] Confidential report not published.

As a result, product and service producers and salespeople stress functions not revealing the value of use experience and use patterns. Contractual forms typically used to reveal value are not enough to improve the autonomy in choosing, and consumers' ability to judge is left to simplification. The wealth of information on the features of the product/service supplied is not enough either: consumers' freedom of choice is reduced to the freedom to make inadequately informed choices. As clearly illustrated in research on behavioral law, the possibility of trade law offering a correct description of service and product value—and therefore correctly influencing consumer behavior—is quite limited. Behavioral law is a framework to gain a better understanding of consumption behavior underlining the information asymmetry between producers, salespeople, and consumers, the imperfection of information available to consumers, and the market inability to correct errors due these causes. It is no longer able to significantly influence consumer behavior.[9]

European and Anglo-Saxon experts have a slightly different angle in interpreting what behavioral law can lawfully pursue. Europeans tend to say that the objections Anglo-Saxon cultures raise on *libertarian paternalism*[10] with reference to the influence that laws, regulations, and policies can have on behavior basically do not exist in Europe.[11] As a result, and according to their interpretation, regulations and rules tend to evolve according to the evidence that consumer models and market faults regulate consumer models and behavior according to post hoc approach. This observation is benevolent and possibly fails to address the urgency of the sustainable innovation challenges all countries are dealing with. Maybe, we should accept that the system of rules and regulations would be more forceful in promoting sustainable innovation, favoring, and promoting actions to improve consumer decisional competence and cooperative collective agentivity ex ante. Favoring correct trade and contractual relations using laws and policies is an undisputed means to promote a greater awareness of the value of the service and to develop a reputation following a win-win approach. Consistently with this approach, some European countries are establishing centers for policy-making with experts in psychology, economics, and behavioral law. The United States displays a strong tendency to balance service and product producers' and traders' economic power, offering consumers the opportunity to revert decisions and purchases according to a *soft and hard paternalism.*

We can usefully distinguish between systems which *protect* from errors due to bounded rationality and systems which *prevent* and *correct* errors due to bounded rationality. In the former, we act with systems of legal protection using laws and policies; in the latter we act through design practice. In fact, the first and foremost aim of intentional design is to prevent unwelcome consequences caused by the inability to control one's behavior. This relative *inability* refers both to *bounded*

[9] Longo [8].

[10] For instance, see Glaeser [9].

[11] See Helleringer and Sibony, ibid.

willpower and to the limited ability to consistently pursue one's personal interests, *bounded self-interest*.[12]

As mentioned earlier in the chapter, the main aim of behavioral design is to favor individual and cultural agentivity to favor the relevance of responsible behavior for oneself and collaborative behavior with others, which can be attained designing systems that highlight the intentionality of aims and the real value of the service for that particular user. From this point of view, revealing value means firstly reducing the gap between the narrative of the service and actual documented situation.

When analyzed, currently dominating digital services clearly indicate that the great majority of these services fundamentally prejudiced the tenets which underpinned them at the start: let us take the examples of Facebook and Google that are at the center of attention due to their dominant position and because of the many legal, juridical, and professional controversies generated by the business model they followed. Advertising is known to produce perceptive distortions.[13] However, although Facebook and Google acquired their dominant positions in digital economy precisely because of the advertising-based business model, the algorithms produced by these companies are being accused today.

In time these algorithms have become a powerful means for a governance leading to a brutal shift to satisfy economic interests regardless of the real value generated for the consumer. The value systems stated by these giants of the digital economy no longer corresponds to reality and basically deviate from the aims these technological companies presented themselves with to consumers. For instance, Google describes the value it generates with a generic self-evident sentence which cannot be easily disputed: *to organize the world's information and make it universally accessible and useful*. The intentions that founders, Page and Brin, stated were a free service, open to all, and unlike other platforms such as *Yahoo!* or *Altavista*: the information organized according to a directory that users could then use to refer to specialized service providers. By navigating these hypertextual directories, users could progressively get an idea of what they were looking for and where it could be found. According to *Google*'s creators, these platforms had a conflict of interest as they were pre-organized according to debatable criteria answering internal portal rules generated by the commercial policies they pursued. They said *Their search engine doesn't necessarily provide the best results; it provides the portal's results. Google conscientiously tries to stay away from that. We want to get you out of Google and to the right place as fast as possible. It's a very different model.* Just over 15 years after this statement issued in 2004 when the company was being officially floated,[14] they have strayed far from their intentions: in the overwhelming majority of cases on when googling, you cannot tell paying links from those who are not following advertising strategies. I would like to add that the so-called organic

[12] Mullainathan and Thaler [10].

[13] *See*: McChesney [11].

[14] https://pandodaily.com/2012/01/23/google-do-yourself-a-favor-and-just-come-clean-already/ (last visited on December 2021).

results are buried beneath many pages—in some cases 20 or more—that paid for their position with the search engines. What can one say about the fact that over 50% of searches on Google land on pages of services offered by the same Google?

Facebook's case is even more obvious in this respect: when the interests of IT companies do not match the interests of the end users, proprietary algorithms have no doubts as to which should prevail. Facebook's values are simple and generic, but assessable and rebuttable *to give people the power to build a community and bring the world closer together*. After just over 15 years since it was created, evidence, statements, legal disputes, parliamentary questions, colossal fines, and the like have shown us that Facebook always promotes and defends the sponsors' and clients' points of view as opposed to the consumers'—except when occasionally it has to retreat under the pressure of public authorities. The idea of the founders that Facebook consumers and users would have created or strengthened social bonds is undermined by their governance that has not monitored nor avoided the manipulation of data and information. Since the service makes its profit thanks to micro-activities a page generates, there is no distinction between true or fake information, between misleading and genuine descriptions, between hate speech and debate. Even after the Cambridge Analytica scandal, Facebook users can be easily manipulated, and one should notice the absence of convincing systems to prevent all this happening.

Behavioral design makes it possible to unveil the gap between consumer influencing narration and the real world when it reveals the role the service performs for the consumer. We could agree that attained desired results overstated ones is the value of the service. The main way to understand the mismatch between narrative and reality is to seek and convey evidence on service use and the value it generates, to understand which consumers the mismatch is strongest for, and what could be done to correct trends when necessary. Evidence is different from information: it is the result of meanings that shape in a defined context with real people. All this might seem obvious if not naive, but we cannot escape this logic that underlies the scientific approach behavioral design necessarily refers to and draws from. Reference to contexts and to behavioral differences is what is needed to design sustainable innovation, preventing and correcting nonsustainable trends and behavior.

The tension that develops between preventing and correcting nonsustainable individual and collective behavior reveals the value of the service and generates opportunities of continuous innovation. This form of behavioral design is the most advanced result of *human-centered design*.

As the next two chapters will discuss, the agenda develops in two macro-areas to re-imagine the economy:

(a) To facilitate the definition and the participation in programs of individual and collective sustainable innovation and change,
(b) To facilitate the formation of cooperative ecosystems to meet the collective challenges,

In the digital economy, content personalization is definitely an added value compared to other quality services that can be offered. According to behavioral design, personalization means organizing and offering service models that react appropriately to a person's variables and to their context. This can be obtained by defining reference models to base the architectures of choice, developed according to the characterizing differences. Personalization makes it possible to deal with and reduce the undesirable effects of bias due to judgment and to motor perceptual automatisms. If de-biasing is neither realistic nor desirable, one can bear it in mind by adopting methods to correct short-sighted behavior.

Behavioral reference models define personal aims in all spheres. Furthermore, reference models also help to reduce the incremental value of negative experiences, to the point it eliminates them. Where possible, these models also contribute to define programs and enhance the cumulative effect of positive experiences.[15] A case in point is the invitation to re-imagine the economy promoting what 33 authors of a key paper call *brain economy* creating *brain capital*.[16] According to these researchers that belong to 41 centers of excellence, *Brain capital can be developed, strengthened, and empowered, as well as deteriorate or be impoverished depending on the stimulation and dynamics between the person and the social context.* By revealing the value of services for the different types of users and by contributing to attaining personal and collective objectives of change, behavioral design is a key and necessary trigger to move toward a new economy based on sustainable models of innovation.

The other sphere concerns the creation of collaborative ecosystems. Behavioral design acts on context power and the strength of cooperation to solve collective challenges triggered by an unbalance caused by the mismatch between technological narrative and the real world. We have to develop systemic cooperation to rise to the challenge: we cannot act counting on traditional research cooperation and action for change. Progressively we are developing the idea that it is necessary to have swift experiments with a common goal, in the context of connected geopolitical situations.[17] Many economists are supporting the notion of dealing with common problems using innovative means: Mazzucato stands out as one of those who suggests traditional issues should be seen through new lenses. She also believes efforts and resources should be pooled in *mission-oriented projects and policies*.[18] Other economists refer to *climate change* and also the aims of sustainable development including some of the devastating issues for subsistence economies, as well as for those based on farming or fishing.

These are the problems that will have to be managed in the coming decade: if we wish to succeed, there will have to be an alliance between and among nations

[15] At last digital services like https://www.stickk.com/ and https://www.dacadoo.com/ and many others are being developed with the aim of promoting mental well-being through educational tools and behavioural aims and the creation of positive habits.

[16] Smith et al. [12].

[17] See Seppälä [13].

[18] Mazzucato [14, 15].

(states) and government powers to use new tenets of political economics to establish a new economy. It calls for a systemic point of view involving a host of players and will have to be extended to all the private sectors that rise to the challenge of sustainable innovation and to the idea of revealing the real value of transactions.

Part III discusses the topic of behavioral models and how to plan viable paths to facilitate individual and collective changes and reshape the evolution of cultures. Part IV discusses how to deal with these challenges in spheres such as health, and energy consumption, key sectors for development not just in advanced economies. Systems for value creation and assessment have to be established and be proportional to the attainment of desired results. Lastly, I shall endeavor to highlight and make explicit an intuition often implicitly found in behavioral economy: the social costs of an economy based on the implicit or explicit exploitation of bounded rationality exceed the costs required to design solutions that prevent or correct bounded rationality.

Highlights

- In real life, design can facilitate two types of awareness: evidence-based awareness and action-based awareness.
- Evidence-based awareness means to provide a more comprehensive and adequate knowledge operating on content architectures (the architecture of choices).
- Action-based awareness means to provide a better sense of control on own actions, facilitating a balance between autonomy and heteronomy.
- In the consumer vs. service control, heteronomy means that the consumers can transfer part of the control of their behaviors to the service system.
- When behavioral design is based on modeling, it becomes intentional.
- The central value of behavioral design is to favor individual literacy and cultural agentivity.
- Another fundamental role of behavioral design is to reduce the unbalance of information and the resulting errors of judgment.
- Behavioral acceptability and desirability is the third important value of behavioral design.
- Participation and involvement of consumers and service users is facilitated through evidence on design constraints to satisfy.
- Behavioral design accelerates progression defining desired impact in terms of usability and sustainability.
- Both user-centered design and behavioral law disciplines are practiced to safeguarding consumers rights.
- Usage patterns are typically not designed in such a way that are fit to the heterogeneity of users, their different levels of knowledge, and skills.
- In competing markets, there is an advantage in not being transparent on usage patterns and on the quality of user experiences.
- A feature-based description of the value of the product or service is preferred in a typical contract.
- The capability to influence people behaviors on the basis of the existing framework of value disclosure is quite limited.

- The systems of rules and regulations would be more forceful in promoting sustainable innovation, promoting actions that can improve consumer competence and collaborative agentivity.
- The system of laws and regulations are good to protect from errors.
- The intentional behavioral design is fit to prevent and correct errors, augmenting self-control, reducing the effects due to bounded willpower and bounded self-interest.
- To reveal the value of services it is necessary to reduce the gap between the narrative of the value of the service and the actual documented situation.
- Providing evidence is not like providing information.
- Behavioral design personalizes experiences through the definition of reference models.
- Behavioral reference models define distinguishing behavioral traits and aims in all spheres.
- Behavioral design aims to build "brain capital" helping to develop and strengthen personal and collective objectives of change.
- Behavioral design promotes systemic cooperation and swift experiments with a common goal across connected geopolitical situations.
- The social costs of an economy which grows based on the implicit or explicit exploitation of bounded rationality exceeds the costs required to design solutions that prevent or correct bounded rationality.

References

1. Zamir, E., & Teichman, D. (Eds.). (2014). *The Oxford handbook of behavioural law*. Oxford University Press.
2. European Commission. (2019). *Behavioural study on the digitalisation of the marketing and distance selling of retail financial services*. European Commission., EB-04-19-332-EN-N.
3. European Commission. (2018). *Behavioural study on the transparency of online platforms*. European Commission., EB-02-18-417-EN-N.
4. Bar-Gill, O. (2012). *Seduction by contract. Law, economics and psychology in consumer markets*. Oxford University Press.
5. Bjerknes, E. P., & Kyng, M. (Eds.). (1987). *Computers and Democracy*. Avebury.
6. Helleringer, G., & Sibony, A. (2017, May 16). European consumer protection through the behavioral lense. *Columbia Journal of European Law, 23*, 607–646.
7. Sunstein, C. (2014). Chap. 23: Nudge.gov. Behaviorally informed regulations. In E. Zamir & D. Teichman (Eds.), *The Oxford handbook of behavioral economics and law*. The Oxford University Press.
8. Longo, E. (2017). Beyond the power of constraints: The contribution of cognitive science to law-making. In E. Calzolaio & P. Serrand (Eds.), *The constraint in law*. Lit Verlag.
9. Glaeser, E. L. (2006). Paternalism and psychology. *University of Chicago Law Review, 73*, 133.
10. Mullainathan, S., & Thaler, R. H. (2000). *Behavioral economics* (NBER Working Papers 7948). National Bureau of Economic Research.
11. McChesney, R. W. (2008, May 1). *The political economy of media: Enduring issues, emerging dilemmas*. Monthly Review Press.

12. Smith, E., et al. (2021). A brain capital grand strategy: Toward economic reimagination. *Molecular Psychiatry, 26*, 3–22. https://doi.org/10.1038/s41380-020-00918-w
13. Seppälä, M. (2021). Radical uncertainty requires radical collaboration. In *Memorandum*. Published by the Finnish Innovation Fund Sitra. https://www.sitra.fi/en/publications/radical-uncertainty-requires-radical-collaboration
14. Mazzucato, M. (2018, October). Mission-oriented innovation policies: Challenges and opportunities. *Industrial and Corporate Change, 27*(5), 803–815. https://academic.oup.com/icc/article/27/5/803/5127692
15. Mazzucato, M. (2021). *Mission economy: A moonshot guide to changing capitalism.* Allen Lain.

Part III
Shaping Change

Abstract What does change imply in relation to sustainable innovation (SI)? Can lasting and sustainable changes be determined through design and behavioral science? How can one support individual and cultural agency? To what extent can behavioral design generate and reveal value? In answering these questions, I will dwell on a more in-depth description of behavioral models. My aim is to maintain that behavioral models are a key tool in guiding SI and implementing it. I shall offer practical examples of how behavioral models and their planning artifacts can play a key role in describing SI aims. I will show how they can be traced and monitored for scale and impact assessment. I shall also describe common features of the theories of cultural and behavioral change to highlight the convergence with the evolutionary theory of change, the latter currently being the most comprehensive in describing the forms of behavioral and cultural transformation.

"Everything Must Change So That Everything Can Stay the Same"[1]

Tancredi utters the famous sentence to his uncle, the Prince of Salina, to explain the underlying reason for some of his choices: the same words are often used to indicate the will to apparently yield to the pressure of change while intending to maintain stability. The case described in the famous masterpiece of Italian and world literature sees Tancredi referring to his joining the struggles of the Risorgimento[2] as the new bourgeois middle class emerges. The newly emerged class wants to manage Sicily's financial resources and politics, rearing to replace the aristocracy Tancredi belongs to. In the wider context of the plot by the Sicilian novelist Tomasi di Lampedusa, the words enshrine many nuances linked to the reflections by the Prince of Salina. His thoughts resignedly linger on the passing, ephemeral nature of change and its inability to last. The many invasions and dominations have not changed the nature of the people of Sicily who adapted to the new laws and innovations relatively unscathed. The acceptance of the conservative noble Sicilian refers to the

---

[1] Tomasi di Lampedusa, Giuseppe, *Il Gattopardo*. Italian: Feltrinelli, Milan. 1958, English Vintage Classics, London, Sept. 2010.

[2] Literally the *Resurgence*, a term used to indicate the struggle for the unification of Italy.

unchangeable nature of Sicilians' behavior, shaped by the nature of the island and its "excessive" weather 6 months a year. Young Tancredi's sentence echoes an active propensity to accommodate change, a hallmark of his and of his friends' attitude, rather than resisting change, as clearly transpires from some of the remarks and thoughts of the Prince of Salina.

The characters—Tancredi and the Prince of Salina—fully mirror the two archetypes at the center of the theory of change. Their distinct points of view illustrate the tension that ensues between trying to maintain a balance and changing it, true to most theories of change. The contrast between these points of view outlines some of the key questions we will address in the present part of the book. What does change imply in relation to sustainable innovation? Can one determine lasting and sustainable changes through design and behavioral science? Can one introduce *prescriptive* behavior addressing the logic of sustainable innovation? How can one support individual literacy and cultural agency? When is this useful and necessary? How far can behavioral design go in generating and revealing value? In answering these questions, I will dwell on a more in-depth description of behavioral models referred to at length in the two previous chapters. My aim is to maintain that behavioral models are a key tool in guiding sustainable innovation and enacting it.

I will describe the tools or instruments of sustainable innovation programs in Part IV, while in this section (Part III) I shall offer practical examples of how behavioral models and their planning artifacts can play a key role in describing the aims of sustainable innovation. I will try and indicate how they can be traced and monitored for scale and impact assessment. I shall also describe some features shared by the theories of cultural and behavioral change: my aim is to highlight the convergence with the evolutionary theory of change, the latter currently being the most comprehensive in describing the forms of behavioral and cultural transformation. It makes it possible to identify a common ground for the complex phenomena psychological, anthropological, sociological, and biological research described in Part I. As we will see, individual, community, and societal behavior is constantly changing. They can evolve or involve. Technological innovation, new norms, and policies are ongoing challenges to behavioral balance and to human and biological cultures. Behavioral models offer a prospective vision to better understand the opportunities to develop, not just to shape transformational potential but also to guarantee a good management of well-managed pressure to change, offering desirable perspectives for both the individual and for society as a whole.

Behavioral models are qualitative holistic representations based on qualitative data. They are analogous representations of observed phenomena for intermediate descriptive aims: models offer insight, explanations as well as new perspectives and ways of telling stories. They are design artifacts that inform design processes. However, since they are explicative, their narration is versatile; it can take many forms and including predictive and above all prescriptive forms.

In the course of the Part III, I shall deal specifically with two forms that carry out a key role in design processes for sustainable innovation:

(a) *normed* reference models and
(b) homogenous clusters referring to distinctive features.

Both forms offer a qualitative description of a prospective view of change. In the first case they are complex representations of a journey's facets. *Journeys* represent the aims of change and are so called *normed* models as they contain the knowledge of the practice and policies that govern processes, decisions, and behavior. In the second case, they are adjacency maps of behavioral models used to describe potential/possible evolutions and involutions characterizing given behavioral traits, routines, and mental heuristics. Representations can also be aimed at identifying behavioral patterns required to characterize clusters, needed when prescribing innovative services to promote change. If the distinctive features of a cluster are documented, they can subsequently undergo quantitative validation. Qualitative model validation gives merit to the versatility of the tools providing evidence and pilot experimentation scalability. Public and private institutions can use qualitative and quantitative behavioral models to act on individual and collective behavior to create (generate) and pursue opportunities of sustainable innovation. Unlike narrative that emphasizes big data's power, qualitative and quantitative models do not require enormous amounts of data. Models can be based on data gathered ad hoc for innovation: unlike models that big data generate, individuals and communities can actively participate to make data available for shared aims. Sustainable innovation paradigm marks shift from vertically organized organizations to cooperative ecosystem.

Chapter 6
Change and Innovation

Traditional views underlying the debate on innovation see the two vectors of technical and normative innovation as the drivers of societal and thus behavioral change. In the present chapter, I would like to offer an alternative thesis purporting that neither normative nor technological innovations include transparent and intentional—that is explicit—models of individual and collective change, especially where behavior is concerned. There are no data nor theories on the relationship between innovation and the change of individual and organizational behaviors. An objective needs to gain a better understanding of the rhetoric of innovation and, in the event, to be able to criticize and compare it to another, new, rhetoric of change. I believe that gaining a better insight into this sphere is called for to understand what we need to do to shape behavior change through sustainable innovation.

Research on nudging has led to a major debate on behavior change on a large social scale, following the introduction of new norms and policies [1]. Unquestionably, new norms and different rules and policies will lead to innovations in society, although one needs to query what type of innovation they are going to trigger. Normative innovations are mainly aimed at establishing the conditions to regulate social relations: in other words, they lead people to cooperate to reach common aims [2]. In fact, normative innovations lag one or two steps behind the ones triggered by the introduction of new inventions, new technologies, and the many other disturbances that are the hallmark of the so-called Anthropocene. Normative innovations may offset the inability to anticipate the previous lawmakers' indecipherable consequences of choices and decisions and also mirror the dominant ideologies. In democratic countries, norms are intended to safeguard and improve the ethics of interests and different positions cohabitating in society. In other terms, norms and policies put pressure to standardize choices, behaviors, and decisions with the aim of

[1] Sunstein [1].

[2] Akerlof & Snower [2].

M. Visciola, *Sustainable Innovation*,
https://doi.org/10.1007/978-3-031-18751-3_6

promoting inclusion, reducing inequalities and redressing the unbalance caused by conflicts between interests expressed by social partners. Lastly, throughout history, norms and politics act as mediators offering points of reference to negotiate social instances of innovation.

I shall not dwell extensively on the relationship between norms, policies, and change. For the purposes of this book, readers are referred to Part II where I informed the position whereby laws and norms are not typically used to determine the comprehensive value of a product or service. I believe that in democratic societies, one cannot merely count on norms to determine the paths to promote change in individual and collective behavior. Technological innovation, the other engine of change, is discussed below.

6.1 Technological Innovations and Disruptive Technological Innovations

I ended Part II of the book by saying that innovation is *sustainable* if and when it fulfills the basic aim of preventing and correcting the social consequences of bounded rationality. As mentioned above, we can avail ourselves of the technical instruments of design and behavioral models for this purpose. This will help us understand why currently available innovation models do not match the aims of sustainable innovation. In economics, innovation often coincides with the entrepreneur's aim: this means value and well-being creation by either improving or upgrading existing products or services, creating new ones, or opening new plants. They aim to change the conditions of the pre-existing market offer. From Shumpeter to Drucker, innovation is the creative and destructive aim achieved by modifying the existing situation. However, the most common interpretations suggest innovation is also the means to generate value. In Peter Drucker's words "Innovation is the specific tool of entrepreneurs, the means by which they exploit change as an opportunity for a different business or a different service".[3] It might be unnecessary to recall that academics' innovation theories are the ones most often selected by large companies. In fact, there is a substantial symmetry and continuity between the evolution of academic thinking on innovation and the development of strategies large company CEOs implement to expand their presence on the market. In this respect, Keynes is the most practical guide: as expressed in this captivating thought of his: "The ideas of economists and political philosophers, both when they are right and when they are wrong, are more powerful than is commonly understood. Indeed, the world is ruled by little else. Practical men, who believe to be quite exempt from any political influence, are usually slaves of some defunct economist".[4]

[3] Drucker [3].

[4] Keynes [4].

Clayton Christensen, one of the best-known productive academics on these matters greatly influenced company innovation strategy. His authority is unquestionable in the narration on how to resolve the innovator's dilemma, described in a widely known text of his.[5] For companies operating in consolidated markets, innovation *poses* a serious dilemma as the introduction of new products could "cannibalize" their existing market(s) and lead them to neglect their established clientele. According to Christensen, a company might divert the resources required for innovation from the resources required to develop the market where they were already established. Furthermore, the new product or service requires time and a host of interactions to succeed. In the light of these remarks, the management of a large company would pursue incremental innovation models. However, the presence of small enterprises on the market, aiming to follow in the wake of the large companies through disruptive innovations, is a real challenge for those who pursue incremental growth. Hence the innovation dilemma, which Christensen proposed in 1997 for the first time: just 6 years later, in the wake of the long-awaited beginnings of digital economy and of the acritical diffusion of Silicon Valley innovation model, but also because of the load of counter-evidence other researchers had produced referring to tenets of his demonstration, Christensen gave the solution of the dilemma. In a later book, with some adjustments to the first version, he re-launched the theory of the "disruptive innovation".[6]

The solution suggested is to incubate innovative ideas and technologies in other "enterprises or adventures" concentrating on markets and types of clients other than the traditional goods and service ones. The rationale for this approach is to create rupture and disruption in a manner so as not to be pushed out of the market. This time the demonstration is based on an econometric model represented by a sigmoid curve aka an S-curve. Companies mostly aspire to profits from products close to maturity: well-established products with a large public yield a bigger profit, when incremental innovation is close to peaking in its cycle of interaction. Following the S-curve profits are lowest at its two extremes at the beginning and at the end of the cycle of product cycle, when the product's perceived value is at its lowest. This illustrates how disruptive innovation fits in; the term was suggested and used by Christensen and his school but clearly goes back to the idea commonly attributed to Shumpeter whereby innovation is equivalent to following the market's gale of creative destruction and pre-existing offers. The story suggests that start-ups and new ideas also intercept large enterprises' unanswered demand by established customers when they generate new value for new customers. Old customers are also ready to accept ideas and technologies with a higher degree of innovation, but when ongoing improvement cycles have come to an end, there is space for other solutions incorporating new technological innovation. This gives rise to a sigmoid curve that yields new value and new profits rising from the products' ashes of the previous products.

[5] Christensen [5].

[6] Christensen [6].

The disruptive innovation theory is at times ambiguously presented as a theory of behavior change: as well as modifying both the supply and the markets, according to the theory, successful technological innovation introduces radical behavior changes which everyone will adapt to sooner or later. The narrative speaks to the ambitions of the investment capitals looking for new business as well as fast and safe ROIs. However, the actual situation appears to offer evidence contrary to the picture outlined: the engine of behavior change is not limited to enterprises implementing disruptive innovation. The history of technological innovation shows that moments of disruption and innovation coexist with the tendency to continuity and may require the slow pace of incremental innovation.[7] An innovation cycle may start quietly and develop forcefully only after 50 years or more, which has been the case of digital technology and one of its offshoots, the Internet. About 80 years after the invention of digital machines, and 50 years after the first computerized office workstations,[8] we are still speaking about *digital transformation*, when we refer to a wider use of digital machines, or to them being applied to a wider range of applications. Furthermore, incremental innovation yields a greater overall social value because it can count on investment capitals that can wait patiently and is very inclusive. As the historian Jill Lepore suggests, the theory of disruptive innovation is basically a theory on the why companies fail or go bankrupt and on management's decisional errors when faced with innovation investments.

Christensen's theory and all the set of narratives on disruptive innovation fail to account for the prevalence and the success of incremental innovation models on the market and do so to emphasize the rewarding of disruptive innovation investments. Funding disruptive innovations is a deceptive approach in interpreting conditions that favor the success of an innovative product and do not seriously assess the consequences such innovation may have on individuals, communities, and society as a whole. In an article published in 2009, I referred to the fact that technological innovation theories, including that of disruptive innovation and of the diffusion of innovation (see further in the text), offer no clear understanding of the forms behavior innovation and cultural evolution may have.[9] As a result, they are unable to indicate how to develop models that will have the desired effects such as the reduction of fossil fuel energy consumption, improving eating habits, and reducing chronic diseases—and therefore do not concern themselves with it. Eighty percent of innovation ideas fail at the beginning of the sigmoid curve, in the very first years of the path leading to the market. Of the remaining 20% that make it to the market, the amount of technology that has immediate disruptive effects is a minimal, even laughable, amount.

These cases of failure or lack of success prove that it is very rare to guess which technology or which idea will have a disruptive effect. In the overwhelming majority of cases, technological innovation is not seen as an engine of behavior change

[7] See Lepore [7].

[8] See Part I of the present book and specifically, page 10.

[9] Visciola [8].

and is unable to foresee how preferences will breakdown and which behavior can be modified. At times it may solve issues generated by previous technological solutions and possibly extend the number and type of users. However, it is beyond the remit of this book to offer hard evidence to prove that technologies obtaining swift changes in society only to gain a better and quicker ROI and could be put to a better use if targeted to sustainable and social investments. That said, clearly no one can deny that in the past decade, a strong unbalance in investments has led to increasing inequality and a strong polarization of wealth. There is an obvious systemic correlation between the race for disruptive innovation and an increase in the concentration of capitals and in the number issues that require strong reaction by entire communities often without adequate resources to be able to act.

A pondered conclusion is that if we had more adequate theories of change, we could hope to identify the direction of sustainable innovation programs. In this case, the aim is to identify which technologies and which innovative ideas are best suited to solve critical issues requiring a full adoption of behavior innovation models.

Everett Rogers's theory on the diffusion of technological innovation includes a theory of user adoption of the relevant innovation.[10] It is probably the most popular theory on how to assess potential success of new ideas and technologies. The theory also presents major suggestions on the appropriate communication strategy to attract the various user categories. The idea that technologies and innovative ideas must be adopted by individuals and communities within their social systems, such as networks and organizations, to be successful is the core of the theory. If innovations fail to reach a critical mass and support themselves, they tend to disappear and not to become part of society's connective tissue. As you can see in Fig. 6.1, the adoption curve is bell shaped and includes five adoption categories. The theory is made up using these adoption profiles.

According to the parametric analyses performed in several areas by Rogers, the sociologist of innovation,[11] the diffusion of innovation follows a cumulative propagation pattern and can peak after several decades. Propagation patterns are based on the principle of diffusion through explicit or implicit communication. More specifically, according to the model, each profile corresponds to a different level of readiness to accept the innovation and hence to a different potential of influenceability. The propagation model is based on the principle of diffusion through explicit or implicit communication and more specifically that each profile corresponds to a different level of readiness in accepting innovation and as a result has its corresponding influenceability potential. The potential is highest at center of the curve, where more people are concentrated—*early majority, late majority*, and *laggards* as a result of the maturity reached in the technology's life cycle. Furthermore, according to the theory, *innovators* and *early adopters* are a minority available to accept the

[10] Rogers [9].

[11] Sociological research was carried out in rural and medical settings, marketing of widely consumed products, organizational studies, and the field of health. See Rogers [10].

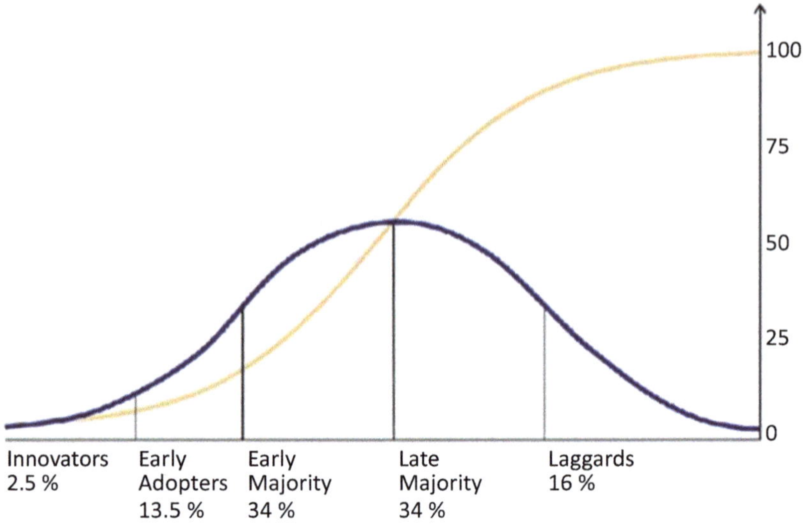

Fig. 6.1 The innovation diffusion curve according to Everett Rogers

costs of adopting an immature technology (*the innovators*) and in terms of learning costs and associated frustrations (*early adopters*).

Although the propagation model is evocative and implicitly suggests the need to use diversified communication strategies for each innovation adoption profile, the model does not actually use sufficient explanatory categories to explain the difference in innovation adoption times or to justify the percentages with which innovation spreads. The idea that innovation diffusion follows a standard deviation from the norm, according to an estimate of the variability of population with reference to a variable, is what we might term a *reasonable* representation. Probably it allows fugues and counter-fugues in interpreting the heterogeneity of behaviors toward innovation. The main weakness of this model is the somewhat lacking representation of agency in innovation diffusion: Rogers's model is at times associated with the actor-network theory (ANT) by Bruno Latour et al. [12] and with the theory of organizational networks,[13] because it foresees the spread of innovation through relational political, corporate, associative, and communication networks. In fact, unlike the latter, diffusion theory describes innovation as diffusion with a single (univocal) meaning. It also fails to register the transformations an innovative idea may undergo in individual and collective adaptations. It does not consider that an idea, just like an innovative technology, undergoes transformation that must be incorporated in the existing social tissue and the technological infrastructures, to the point it can change its initial features and meaning. Innovative technologies and ideas become aids (prostheses) and artifacts when individuals and organizations can embed them in the

[12] Latour [11].

[13] Barabasi [12].

connective infrastructure which is the hallmark of a culture and relevant social systems. In other words, these are intentional constructs that can be influenced and can be subjected to existing and budding interests. The constructs need to be narrated and ideologies to establish themselves: this is echoed clearly in the income that enterprises and markets can produce. Facts and evidence are often only a by-product which cannot easily emerge without a clear will and a critical intention.

Kevin Kelly's[14] *Technium* theory is one of Silicon Valley's most carefully listened. *Technium* suggests that technology has developed to the point and at such a great speed of change that it has incorporated the ability to evolve as a biological system, mutating and adapting autonomously. The *Technium* is a techno-social system able to defend, control, improve, and carry out maintenance on its own accord. Although at present there are no techno-social systems that have all these features, Kelly believes that even if they have just a few of them, it proves that the technological systems have the tendency to express an autonomous and independent *will*. Systems have no self, nor awareness, but include programs and objectives that make them increasingly self-reliant (autonomous) and independent, no longer needing programmers, designers, and final users. As a result, Kelly's theory suggests it is useless to try and neutralize this trend using precautions: it would be best to test the prototypes of emerging technologies to validate which ones are convivial and compatible with human and biological life. In this sense in spite of the title of his book and the rhetoric that promotes the inevitability of a threatening autonomy of machines against humans, Kelly imagines a sort of artificial selection to correct and tame the autonomous trend and the unwanted aims of technological innovation.

Starting from observations similar to Kelly's, Brian Arthur, an engineer and economist, reaches a slightly different conclusion[15] and stresses the analogy between technology and biological systems even more marked. He developed a theory of technological evolution whereby technologies have the ability to self-reproduce thanks to the combined evolution of paradigms and stratified technologies. He maintains techno-autopoiesis is a sort of natural selection whereby all technologies conserve their ecological niche even if they are surpassed by more advanced technologies, and this will make them useful for other developments and aims. Every technology has an expressive versatility and the ability to combine with other technologies: their integration is creative and virtually inexhaustible in terms of the effects it determines in society. Although Arthur does not rule out the extinction of some technological components, he believes technology evolves according to descending and combinatory processes determining a comprehensive integrated technological complex. In this combinatorial process, Arthur sees an important role for human ability in imagining new technologies, even before they are built. However, I believe he is disappointing when he reduced the role of humans and of society on the identification of needs to be satisfied: "Without the presence of unmet needs, no new technology would emerge." And continuing rather academically, he

[14] Kelly [13].

[15] Arthur [14].

states that economy *arose from the productive methods and legal and organizational arrangements that we use to satisfy our needs.*[16] Economy is the expression of technologies and consequently evolves with them inheriting "autopoietic characteristics of perpetual openness and innovation"[17] . From this ability to self-(re)produce, economy generates new problems and opportunities that in turn require new behaviors, roles, and professional figures in a process which is "fractal and inexorable.[18]" Well beyond accounting laws and truisms whereby sale and purchase transactions are a zero-sum game, economy is constantly evolving mirroring the complexity of the societies in which this is expressed.

Clearly these theories and the relative narratives have an inherent difficulty in identifying the genesis of change: narrations are vague in identifying intentions, aims, interests, and responsibilities of the direction of innovation. I believe it is very short sighted to maintain that technology evolves and develops following autonomous paths considering that technologies are resources available in innovation labs where there are people, technicians, and decision-makers working. Furthermore, it is unnecessary cover for people who hold political positions or are lawmakers and decide the norms and who issue permits to exploit these resources. Lastly, I believe it to be an oversimplification to decode the driving force of innovation as a generic need to "satisfy society's needs". Surely there is no invisible hand nor plotters who need to gain from the lack of governance of technological innovation. Quite the opposite, I believe there are reasons to suggest that the economic interests of the established capitals ecosystems play a major role in determining the courses and paths a technological innovation can take. For instance, let us take the investment indexes on a global scale for the past 5 years: there is an uninterrupted growth in investments, peaking in 2021. In the second quarter, investments have tripled compared to the second quarter of 2020, increasing from 60.7 to 156.2 billion US$. Unquestionable the most significant index compared to the previous 5 years is growing ability of capitals to channel investments in the start-ups ready to enter the market with new technologies and thus new products or services. Despite speculative investments in initial start-ups accounting for nearly 50% of all investments, financing start-ups ready to market new products is increasing at a faster rate.[19] Capitals seek new opportunities and constantly improve their learning curve to identify the new directions of technological innovation.

In conclusion, I believe technological innovation theories, like the abovementioned ones, definitely lack a comprehensive understanding of the drivers of behavioral change. Unfortunately, this translates into the lack of meaningful policies to govern technological innovation which leaves space and total freedom to the

[16] Arthur, op. cit. Page 4

[17] Arthur, op. cit. Page 59

[18] Arthur, op. cit, page 60

[19] *https://www.cbinsights.com/research/report/venture-trends-q2-2021/?utm_source=CB+Insights+Newsletter&utm_campaign=dbe42c8d58-newsletter_general_Wed_20210714&utm_medium=emailandandutm_term=0_9dc0513989-dbe42c8d58-87586053)*

organized forces with more "firing power" to influence the innovation vision that will prevail.

6.2 Visions and Narratives Guide Technological Innovation

Unlike the belief whereby technology will inevitably overrun human interests thanks to itself regulatory capacity, human visions and narratives spin an invisible web through which the weft of technological innovation grows. These are mental processes, constructs that guide choices and decisions and orient the value chain, including the final segment for the consumer. The common thread of these narrations is the funding or rewarding of the ability to generate new funds and manage the entrepreneurial or business risk. The question on the final aim is usually not mentioned or avoided. Even after the loud and subscribable statements by the CEO of BlackRock, the largest investment company, in 2018 and repeated every year, appealing to all other CEOs[20], reports on company responsibility and liability, as well as that on the impact technological innovation investments can generate, are generally empty words.[21] Needless to say, these statements say nothing about the impact innovations may have had in improving behavior and cooperation in dealing with shared challenges.

In terms of sustainable innovation, the situation is quite the opposite, and the purpose of narration is to highlight the role of improved individual literacy and cultural agency using all available levers to prevent and redress any unwanted social consequences of bounded rationality. As we will see further in the text, behavioral models show how to pursue agency strategies. Before developing the subject any further, I would like to point out why theories of behavior and cultural change play a major role in directing innovation strategies.

I intend to prove that there are key advantages in rewarding (and funding) innovation strategies based on theories of behavior and cultural change. The main advantage is the possibility of creating the conditions for experiments to be replicated in scale that may generate (and spread) psychological and economic well-being. As mentioned in the introduction to the present chapter, the theory of the evolution of the human species is the one that best explains cultural and behavior changes. The theory of evolution is a theory of change: as well as Darwin and Wallace who developed the basis of biological evolution, several present-day researchers have also contributed, agreeing on the observation that by analogy the cultural evolution of humans can be compared (or assimilated) to biological evolution,[22] despite them clearly being two separate and distinct processes. They do

[20] Larry Fink. Since 2019 his annual letters to CEOs have changed tone and shifted to the need to invest profits in activities safeguarding all interested parties, and not just owners and shareholders.

[21] Schrempf-Stirling et al. [15].

[22] Cavalli Sforza and Feldman [16]; Dawkins [17]; Mesoudi et al. [18].

share the forms and drivers triggering change. Furthermore, it has to be said that evolution and progress are not the same nor do they overlap. In no way does cultural evolution imply a greater well-being, more equality, and a better ability to manage cultural variations. Above all, even when there are greater benefits, cultural evolution has associated costs that are not always foreseeable.

6.3 Biological Evolution and Cultural Innovations

The theory of cultural evolution offers some useful explanations substantiated by how behaviors change and how such effects are transmitted. The two key concepts are *selective pressure* and *mutation*, whose explanatory matrix is the result of original observations in biology as well as *migration* and *drift*. Natural selection is the driver of the biological evolution of species: for Darwin natural selection is the mechanism used by a biological organism to adapt to environmental conditions. Adaptation is a necessary condition for survival. The human genome—that is, the cells and genes making up the organism—undergoes variations due to environmental pressure and to the hereditary transmission of genetic traits. Genetic diversity among populations accounts for only 11% of overall diversity, while 89% is individual diversity within the same population. A phenotype is an individual's makeup, that is to say the features ensuing from an individual's development in their environment in which means phenotypical variability is greater than genetic variability.[23] Natural selection acts on the phenotype and not directly on genes that are only indirectly influenced by selection; such influence depends on the limits of and according to the phenotype. Variations are the result of mutations although very few mutations actually become new genetic traits. All biological mutations are spontaneous and random and could be seen as mistakes in cell reproduction or as reaction to environmental stimuli. Natural selection determines whether a mutation is advantageous: in other words, there is no will in the selection of the mutating trait. Since adaptation is the ability to reproduce, only mutations that enable an organism to reproduce resist. These are Darwin's and Wallace's evolutionary theories for biological systems and specifically the human species.

Biological and cultural co-evolution explains the presence of both evolutionary modes in some animal species, including humans.[24] Thanks to the transmission of the mutating gene, the individual develops persistent lactase production, the enzyme required to digest sugars in breast milk (lactose) making it one of the most interesting and convincing examples of the gene-culture co-evolution. Normally, the gene ceases to be active in newborns once their nutrition varies and is no longer based on the mother's milk. The mutation of this particular gene was triggered when domestic animal milk was introduced in human diet about 6000 years ago. At that time,

[23] Diseases are a phenotypical trait, a combination of disposition and situations (see Chap. 11).

[24] Cavalli-Sforza et al. [19].

cattle farming (dairy farming) flourished. It is a clear example of how a change of habits that spread through the adoption of the new approach became a cultural innovation that in turn facilitated a genetic mutation that proved adaptive. Milk has unquestionable nutritional qualities and offers a differential value to people with persistent lactase as opposed to the members of populations that lack the mutated gene in its genome. For instance, with the exception of small migrant tribes, Asian populations have a very low frequency of lactase persistence because the population did not develop dairy farming and thus lacked the cultural mutations preceding the genetic mutation.[25] Furthermore, the case of persistent lactase highlights how a cultural mutation and its corresponding genetic mutation do not move at the same speed. The greater spread of the genetic mutation in the Northern areas compared to the South, and the mottled geographic distribution of where dairy farming, shows that genetic transmission required thousands of years.[26]

As Cavalli Sforza would say, cultural transmission is "protean," that is, it may be limited to a few local communities but can also undergo very swift and widely spread variations. Migration and drift are other characteristic common forms of genetic-cultural evolution. These two forms of evolution act as regulators, whereby genetic variability (but not phenotypical variation) tends to disappear. Migration is very common in neighboring populations and in any case tends to level off differences while drift tends to lead to the total disappearance of genetic differences. According to the theory of biological evolution, this form of transmission is especially strong in small populations, while its impact is limited in large populations.

As said, evolution is driven auto-reproduction, a regular transmission of a clearly defined unit. In a debate among researchers and academics, started many years ago, the question arose as to which was the single gene correspondent in cultural evolution. According to Luigi Cavalli Sforza,[27] cultural trait such as "ideas" are transferred through cultural evolution, the human makeup of knowledge and habits. Anglo-Saxons, starting with Richard Dawkins, prefer the word *meme*[28] which Daniel Dennet extended to the notion of the self, the basis for the development of consciousness and ethics sense in *Homo sapiens*.[29] Although the two words bear different connotations, they describe cultural traits in the same way, harmful according to Dawkins, beneficial for Dennet, and both according to Cavalli Sforza, found and identifiable through anthropological analyses. Beliefs, values, routines, and more generally the mental construct we use in attributing meaning to things around us appear to have been transferred into anthropology and cultural psychology. As can be inferred, the boundaries of transmissible units through cultural selection are less defined and not so clearly established as genes, natural selection.

---

[25] Heyer et al. [20].

[26] Feldman and Cavalli-Sforza [21]

[27] Cavalli-Sforza, et al. op. cit. 1994

[28] Dawkins [22].

[29] Dennett [23].

If—for the purposes of the present text[30]—we were to speculate on an intellectual level, we could allege that evolution transmits motor-perceptive automatisms and judgments and could reasonably presume that transmission is genetic. System 1 acts according to automatisms that make it possible to limit the risks associated with choices and to ensure a personal ecological advantage and an evolutionary advantage for the species. In the end, the automatisms discussed in Chap. 1 are cerebral circuits and neuronal networks developed in the course of embryonic development that offer an adaptation to the range of environmental conditions. In this sense they resemble language neuronal circuits.

Higher-order cognitive constructs are transmitted culturally: they refer to beliefs, values, mental routines, and habits. Higher-order cognitive constructs are a cultural endowment of the human species that impart willfulness (intentionality) to human action and to favor collective well-being and rationality. They are not automatic mechanisms and need time and consistency to fully develop. Nowadays it is widely accepted that the pre-frontal cerebral cortex reaches full development only in older people.[31] In our societies, the function is performed by the institutions in charge of controlling moral evolution that have to manage the instability of selective pressure due to the divergent interests of the societies that produce them. Since intentional systems are reflexive and thus by definition unstable,[32] sustainable innovations need special agents of change to assert itself.[33]

Continuing with the analogy, cultural selection is the decision to accept or refuse an innovation. We could thus say that unlike genetic evolution, cultural evolution bears the hallmarks of Lamarck: the selection of higher-order traits undergoes careful scrutiny. This is inherent in individual behavior despite several *agents* in the political, organizational, and social layers that make up modern societies. Selection acts on transmissible differences, and, according to Cavalli Sforza, cultural innovations are mutations accepted within a variable size social nucleus. Social groups (or nuclei) can also select by subtraction when a specific cultural construct is lost or disappears.

We might wonder whether migrations and drifts are also part of cultural evolution and facilitate some of the innovative features requiring cultural selection as effectively. One could reasonably maintain that both spontaneous variations, that is, cultural mutations, operate as a spark triggering the engine of change, and voluntary variations, that is, migrations and cultural drifts, require drivers some of which organized to transmit innovation. Unlike gene mutations which are always random, every cultural innovation is a voluntary response to grasp an opportunity or solve a problem and has associated costs. For instance, the opening of trade borders between

---

[30] Experimental research on the transmission of cultural innovation is in its early days. Observations in this text are drawn from ethnographic research and the numerous analyses of cognitive processes carried out with my team in various areas over the past 15 years.

[31] *A Bozo of a Baboon - A Talk with Robert Sapolsky (2003)* https://www.edge.org/conversation/robert_sapolsky-a-bozo-of-a-baboon. Also Greene [24].

[32] Damasio A., op cit note Chap. 5

[33] See Part IV of the present book.

and among countries was one of the first effects of globalization: it favored the exchange of goods, technologies, and the flow of enormous sums of money, but also enabled the transfer of immaterial capital and the so-called brain drain toward more aggressively competitive companies and countries. The youngsters who left their countries to complete their studies or for work enjoyed a material advantage which translated into a loss of knowledge and social capital in the countries of origin they left. Furthermore, these youngsters have to bear the psychological weight caused by them separating from their cultural and emotional systems and to the lack of stable reference systems able to facilitate transition. As a result, the demand for online psychological services offered by their country of origin has increased and has been made possible thanks to the great flexibility of the Internet technology. The search for psychological support services for the young has become extremely widespread among students, an unprecedented trend.[34]

6.4 Cultural Selection Underpins Sustainable Innovation

I have often said that it is not always possible to assess the costs of innovation, especially future ones. Unquestionably modern society maintains—unfortunately only implicitly nowadays—that the advantages of innovation always exceed its costs, especially if future costs are artfully masked. The prevailing innovation narratives rarely question why cost analysis is procrastinated, developing a cognitive bias. Given you can discuss future benefits and advantages, a discussion on future costs also should be included.[35] In a good number of cases, innovations are in fact attempts to redress unbalances caused by previous innovations. Once activated, cultural selection leads to transmission which follows a range of paths: activation could be thus defined as sanctioning selection legitimization. Researchers repeatedly describe transmission models as vertical, that is, from higher authorities such as parents or tutors, or horizontal, from peers or strangers such as friends, colleagues, and the media.[36] The transmission and diffusion of cultural innovation are more complex than some simplified popularization suggests.

It might be useful to retrace the previous chapters of this book and refer to the role of System 2 in the dual cognitive theory to gain a better understanding of cultural selection. Cultural selection's role in society resembles the one which System 2 has in the human brain: it allows perceptive-motor biases of automatism and judgments or readjusts them especially when there is time to get feedback, and this calls for adjustments. Just as if adaptive, genetic mutations need time to spread as genomic wealth, innovations need good evidence and reasons to assert themselves

[34] *Unobravo*, an online service for young Italians abroad that is spreading to China and other European countries.

[35] See Chap. 7 for and analysis of "externalities and internalities" of innovation

[36] Cavalli Sforza, op. cit. Note Chap. 5

in diffused cognition. Feedback and the time needed to receive it are key resources both for natural and cultural selection: although in the case of natural selection mutations are random and nature lacks the forecasting skills needed to correct mistakes before they fully develop all their effects, cultural selection can act differently. Once again, the comparison with System 2 (S2) can prove useful: S2 includes reasoning, thought, and meta-cognition, all needed to accumulate evidence, learning, to infer and deduct. Inference is the property that draws the biggest cognitive advantages from cognitive automatisms and makes it possible to integrate bias so as to carry out feedforward tests (i.e., anticipations) and introduce the necessary corrections.[37] Conversely, cultural selection forecasts, corrects errors and the unwanted effects of innovation, and gathers the required evidence through diffused cognitive systems. Inference is the property for feedforwards, and it is one of the hallmarks of cultural selection.

Unlike natural selection, learning from the evidence of results can lead to compromises in cultural life, which would be an unviable solution in nature where selective pressure blocks the transmission of nonsustainable solutions. Cultural innovations can be transmitted and kept alive when cultural selective pressure is not corrected by narrative or the more so when it is distorted by dominant rhetoric and ideologies. To say it more explicitly, correction mechanisms require special conditions to exercise the required selective pressure, just as in the brain learning and special forms of education are needed to correct biases to the advantage (benefit) of one's well-being.[38] The same is true for society with special forms of learning and cooperation including those between diffused cognition systems so that cultural selection may have widespread and sustainable advantages. I believe this to be a very important issue for a theory of behavior change and evolution of cultures leading to sustainability.

One of the most recent EC reports on the effects of globalization includes a passage (see below) that I believe clearly shows the cultural challenge Europe has decided to address:

> Many Europeans, particularly younger ones, see how being connected to people in other countries and continents can better their lives. They are right to do so – around a third of our national income comes from trade with the rest of the world. But many Europeans are also apprehensive. They see globalisation as synonymous to job losses, social injustice or low environmental, health and privacy standards. They consider it to be a factor in the erosion of traditions and identities. These concerns need to be addressed. And it is only by confronting these issues openly that we can do so. The debate will make us stronger and better equipped to deliver sustainable and fair responses that meet the aspirations of Europeans. Today, more than ever, local issues go global, and global issues become local. While globalisation affects nearly every aspect of our lives, our citizens and regions experience these developments very differently.[39]

---

[37] Rizzo et al. [25].

[38] System 2 needs special conditions to correct System 1 automatisms.

[39] *EC 2017—Documento di Riflessione sulla Gestione della Globalizzazione https://eur-lex.europa.eu/legal-content/EN/TXT/PDF/?uri=CELEX:52017DC0240&from=EN)*

In spite of the overall advantages of globalization, the management of disparity and the cultural transformation it implies call for targeted corrective actions that need shared processing to be implemented. Along the lines of the above-suggested analogy, natural and cultural selection are both answers to ecological instability. In anthropological and biological research, ecological stability can be defined in two apparently opposite ways: a natural ecosystem is stable when it has a low degree of biological, low species variability, and cultural, low behavioral differences (heterogeneity), variability due to limited environmental stimulations. A stable ecosystem not subject to changes tends to decline to the point it ends by turning into an *abionic* system. This leads to the loss of biomass and to the decline in the population [26].[40] Resilience is another trait when defining a stable ecosystem, if it (the ecosystem) is able to revert to its original state after the disruption defined as random stimulation caused by environmental changes and other destabilizing factors[41]; they may be challenges to both natural and cultural ecosystems. According to the stability hypothesis, variability in nature generates a greater overall productivity thanks to the selective pressure on the species.[42] Selective pressure produces irregularities in natural systems, thus producing more opportunities for change. If ecological collaboration mechanisms develop, they can lead to the creation of collaborative ecosystems.

Both the above-described notions of stability are essential in trying to understand cultural selection. Environmental stimuli and selective pressure can trigger a tendency either to close or to open: how can one forget the dynamic balance between conservation and progress between the two generations of the Sicilian aristocratic family described by Tomasi di Lampedusa? Stability and variability are both present and required in cultural ecosystems, and more varied (heterogenous) a cultural system is, the more stable and productive it is. The reason for the greater productivity can be sought (and found) in the hypothesis that collaborative ecosystems use available resources in the best possible manner. It is interesting to observe that the balance between spending and saving energy resources is dynamic and not static: in fact, a living system is never the same; it is ever changing whatever stability it may attain.[43] In the event of a plurality of stable states, selective pressure finds a route to follow, and the new balance stabilizes stopping it from reverting to the previous one, as is the case of migrations and drift perform in cultural selection. These are the two selective mechanisms and operating regulators: specifically, migration describes the phenomenon, whereby a cultural system absorbs external traits and drift the tendency to exclude external traits. Although the results may be one the opposite of the other, in both cases it is the consequence of selective pressure. I believe it is useful to remark that in social and cultural systems, these modes are lessons learnt.

---

[40] Huston [26].

[41] Nowak, op. cit. Note Chap. 3

[42] Huston M, op cit.

[43] According to preliminary research, homeostasis is in fact part of homodynamics, Lloyd [27].

Learning can clearly also happen spontaneously and also because agents of change can actively promote cultural innovations.

Spontaneous learning is unquestionably one of the most important traits, and ongoing research may clarify the unclear features that remain. I am referring to the role of emulation and mirror neurons have played in biological evolution and still have in cultural evolution.[44] Bandura uses a very evocative sentence in one of his works on social learning: he maintains that by observing others and noticing how successful they are in attaining their aims, own quest for more self-efficacy grows: "If people of widely differing characteristics can succeed, then observers have a reasonable basis for increasing their own sense of self-efficacy".[45] Spontaneous learning is a form of vicarious learning through which ideas are transferred (see also Chap. 9): in fact, it is a migration of constructs favored by the presence of collaborative ecosystems. Transferred constructs are a cultural capital that an individual can count on using the many networks and relationships producing energy and expertise that improve their individual and community ability to reach their goals.

Research carried out in the United States in open and international educational systems shows that the members of a community who can count on a wide cultural capital and a range of social networks also progress more in terms of educational and professional targets. These people are also open to reciprocate, offering other relational advantages or using the ones they counted on and are open to get involved in educational and work systems to make them more accessible and egalitarian.[46] The opportunities offered by collaborative ecosystems to pursue their aims also favor social mobility such as *homodynamic* that human ecosystems need to survive and thrive.

In conclusion of these remarks and thoughts, I think it is possible to say that *migration* is one of the most important forms of transmission of innovation to be used in carrying our experiments to change behavior and introduce cultural innovation.[47] Variations transmitted within a community, networks, and social nuclei are as or even more important than spontaneous variations that develop because of the novelty value: this is of great importance for a theory of change and sustainable innovation. This is true because of the homodynamic value they convey to the ecosystem. The theory of innovation I am presenting herein suggests that migration can follow *acceleration paths* that make it possible for the innovation to assert itself and spread in the social tissue. On the other hand, disruptive innovations (mutations) require a greater latency period so that the conditions and opportunities where innovation developed can be reproduced and relocated elsewhere. In the event of this slower process, one can implement all the measures needed for a targeted experimentation thus favoring the cultural selection for the development of sustainable innovation. Lastly, since cultural innovation favors homodynamic exchanges, it

[44] Ramachandran [28].

[45] Bandura [29].

[46] Busette [30].

[47] Part IV of the present book

underlies it produces cultural and ethnic diversity. Cultural sustainable innovation nurtures resilience whose effect is to disseminate diversity.

Highlights

- Innovation is *sustainable* if and when it fulfills the basic aim of preventing and correcting the social consequences of bounded rationality.
- Technological innovation theories offer no clear understanding of the forms behavior innovation and cultural evolution may have.
- The disruptive innovation theory is at times ambiguously presented as a theory of behavior change.
- Incremental innovation yields a greater overall social value because it can count on investment capitals that can wait patiently and is very inclusive.
- The propagation model of innovation does not use sufficient explanatory categories to explain the difference in innovation adoption times or to justify the percentages with which innovation spreads.
- Innovative technologies and ideas become aids (prostheses) and artifacts when individuals and organizations can embed them in the connective infrastructure which is the hallmark of a culture and relevant social systems.
- Innovative technologies are intentional constructs that can be influenced and can be subjected to existing and budding interests.
- Facts and evidence are often only a by-product which cannot easily emerge without a clear will and a critical intention.
- Technological innovation lacks a comprehensive understanding of the drivers of behavioral change. This translates into the lack of meaningful policies to govern technological innovation which leaves space and total freedom to the organized forces with more "firing power" to influence the innovation vision that will prevail.
- The main advantage in rewarding (and funding) innovation strategies based on theories of behavior and cultural change is the possibility of creating the conditions for experiments to be replicated in scale that may generate (and spread) psychological and economic well-being.
- Evolution transmits motor-perceptive and judgments automatisms and could reasonably presume that transmission is genetic.
- System 1 acts according to automatisms that make it possible to limit the risks associated with choices and to ensure a personal ecological advantage and an evolutionary advantage for the species.
- Ecological stability can be defined in two apparently opposite ways: a natural ecosystem is stable when it has a low degree of biological, low species variability, and cultural, low behavioral differences (heterogeneity), variability due to limited environmental stimulations.
- Stability and variability are both present and required in cultural ecosystems, and more varied (heterogenous) a cultural system is, the more stable and productive it is.

References

1. Sunstein, C. R. (2019). *How change happens*. Massachusetts.
2. Akerlof, G., & Snower, D. (2016). Bread and bullets. *Journal of Economic Behaviors and Organization, 126*, 58–71.
3. Drucker, P. F. (2006). *Innovation and entrepreneurship*. Harper and Collins.
4. Keynes, J. M. (1936). *The general theory of employment, interest and money*. Palgrave Macmillan.
5. Christensen, C. (1997). *The innovator's dilemma. When new technologies cause great firms to fail*. Harvard Business Review Press.
6. Christensen, C. (2003). *The innovator's solution. Creating and sustaining successful growth*. Harvard Business Review Press.
7. Lepore, J. (2014). The disruption machine. In *The New Yorker*. https://www.newyorker.com/magazine/2014/06/23/the-disruption-machine. Last access July 2021. Disruptive innovation is a theory about why businesses fail. It's not more than that. It doesn't explain change. It's not a law of nature. It's an artifact of history, an idea, forged in time; it's the manufacture of a moment of upsetting and edgy uncertainty. Transfixed by change, it's blind to continuity. It makes a very poor prophet"
8. Visciola, M. (2009). People-centered innovation or cultural evolution? *Interactions*.
9. Rogers, E. M. (1995). *Diffusion of innovations*. The Free Press.
10. Rogers, E. (2003). *Diffusion of innovations* (5th ed.). Simon and Schuster.
11. Latour, B. (2005). *Reassembling the social. An introduction to actor-network theory*. Oxford University Press.
12. Barabasi, A.-L. (2013). Network science. *Philosophical Transactions of The Royal Society, 371*, 1–3.
13. Kelly, K. (2010). *What technology wants*. Penguin Books.
14. Arthur, W. B. (2009). *The nature of technology. What it is and how it evolves*. Penguin.
15. Schrempf-Stirling, J., Guido Palazzo, G., & Phillips, R. A. (2016). Historic corporate social responsibility. *Academy of Management Review, 41*(4).
16. Cavalli Sforza, L., & Feldman, M. (1981). *Cultural transmission and evolution*. Princeton University Press.
17. Dawkins, R. (1976). *The selfish gene*. Oxford University Press.
18. Mesoudi, A., Whiten, A., & Laland, K. (2006). Towards a unified science of cultural evolution. *Behavioral and Brain Sciences, 29*(4), 329–347. discussion 347–383.
19. Cavalli-Sforza, L., Menozzi, P., & Piazza, A. (1994). *The history and geography of human genes*. Princeton University Press.
20. Heyer, E., Brazier, L., Ségurel, L., Hegay, T., Austerlitz, F., Quintana-Murci, L., Georges, M., Pasquet, P., & Veuille, M. (2011). Lactase - persistence in central Asia: Phenotype, genotype, and evolution. *Human Biology, 83*(3), 379–392.
21. Feldman, M., & Cavalli-Sforza, L. (1976). Cultural and biological evolutionary processes, selection for a trait under complex transmission. *Theoretical Population Biology, 9*, 238–259.
22. Dawkins, R. (1982). *The extended phenotype*. Oxford University Press.
23. Dennett, D. (1991). *Consciousness explained*. Penguin.
24. Greene, J. D. (2007). The secret joke of Kant's soul. In *Moral psychology: The neuroscience of morality: Emotion, disease, and development* (Vol. 3rd, pp. 35–117). MIT Press.
25. Rizzo, A., Bagnara, S., & Visciola, M. (1987). Human error detection processes. *International Journal of Man-Machine Studies, 27*, 555–570.
26. Huston, M. (1994). *Biological diversity: The coexistence of species on changing landscape*. Cambridge University Press.
27. Lloyd, D., Aon, M., & Cortassa, S. (2001). Why homeodynamics, not homeostasis? *The Scientific World, 1*, 133–145.

28. Ramachandran, V. S. (2000). Mirror neurons and imitation learning as the driving force behind the great leap forward in human evolution. *Edge*. https://www.edge.org/conversation/mirror-neurons-and-imitation-learning-as-the-driving-force-behind-the-great-leap-forward-in-human-evolution. Last accessed in July 2021
29. Bandura, A. (1977). *Social learning theory*. Prentice-Hall.
30. Busette, C. (2021). In W. I. Racine (Ed.), *How we rise: How social networks impact economic mobility*. Brookings Inst. Washington. https://www.brookings.edu/wp-content/uploads/2021/01/rpi_20210112_howwerise_racine_sanfran_dc_fullreport.pdf. Last access July 2021

Chapter 7
Change, Perspective, and Proximity

The general public and not just specialists have recently developed an interest in behavioral change although research outside the typical academic settings is still in its early stages. Unfortunately, academic results are not such that they can offer crosscutting guidelines and address the most important features of sustainable innovation. Ambitious research programs based on common intentions on a large scale are needed.

The next 5 years will be crucial in determining the major orientation of experimental programs able to impact environmental and social policies—including health, but not only. They will also influence government policies in view of the 2030 appointment. A semantic shift would welcome in the coming years. Research on behavioral change in human life will have to openly promote it in the framework of sustainability culture or stop its involution. Projects will have to cover a range of individual or community levels of maturity in all spheres, from economics to social life. At times, by changing the expressions, you can also re-interpret prospects which develop some key notions. If behavioral change is limited to the individual sphere, we will lose sight of actions able to promote or favor lasting and sustainable social changes. In fact, change requires piecing together contributions from several disciplines to build the evidence to redefine people's lifestyles. This approach will help overcome ethical objections on the limitations of self-determination in overall everyday life consumer choices.[1]

Basic classical studies on the theories of psychological and social change prevalently refer to learning and adapting. In the past decade, several behavior modification techniques have developed covering various spheres. However, they have mainly been medical and clinical methodological proposals due to the growth of mental health social problems and how they crosscut sustainable development

[1] See Part I and specifically Chap. 3.

M. Visciola, *Sustainable Innovation*,
https://doi.org/10.1007/978-3-031-18751-3_7

targets (SDTs).[2] Luckily, new solutions being proposed are not limited to the treatment of mental illness: the need for analytical and practical tools is increasingly obvious so as to avoid the social causes of mental illness thanks to prevention and mental well-being. As we will see, there are a number of available tools ranging from social pressure and related constraints to the point that they modify how life circumstances are perceived implementing positive interventions.

Part IV will discuss the techniques and the tools to boost behavior change. It will also discuss how behavior can be adapted and located in experimental programs focused on the social aspects of sustainable development.[3] In the present chapter, I shall dwell on the mental processes and the conditions needed to favor the evolution of consumer choices and lifestyles. The idea is that the objective should be attained in a non-manipulative manner, favoring the natural evolution and the progressive improvement of an expertise (competence) and cooperation culture. The basic premise discussed in Part I and further elaborated in Chap. 6 is that individual and community agentivity are transferrable across cultures.

Part I of the book discusses the dual theory of mental processes that has acquired a prevailing role among knowledge (cognition) theories. Part II mentions the role of homeostasis as used by the Damasios to explain the regulation of physiological mechanisms and psychological states. As we saw, cognitive and homeostatic automatisms govern most of our behavior and are characterized as a heuristic and perceptual-motor routine of judgment. However, at this point, the time has come to see how effectiveness and relevance of these automatisms react to learning opportunities, selective pressures, and the need for change determined by life cycles.

In a nutshell, we could use Thaler and Shrefin[4] and say that behavior control constantly swings between being a *doer* and a *planner* and that control mostly shifts uninterruptedly. However, we don't know much more. We still lack a theory of conscience to fully understand what happens when automatisms of the automatic control system are interrupted and when the voluntary control system intervenes in deliberate processes.

One could refer to Edelman's effective metaphor: consciousness is *wider than the sky* above us, in that it encompasses self-awareness and an awareness of what is outside the self.[5] It is reasonable to suggest that opportunities for change develop in the gap between the automatic and the deliberate systems: it is the experience of habit discontinuity. Behavior discontinuity can be spontaneous or deliberately

---

[2] Eaton et al. [1] and Patel and Saxena [2].

[3] Anyone interested in further reading may find interesting ideas in recent publications by a UK center with a good synthesis by researchers in a range of disciplines and training to define a taxonomy or classification of behavior types; Michie et al. [3].

[4] Thaler and Shrefin [4].

[5] See Edelman [5].

triggered, and likewise opportunities for change can be explicit or implicit. They can be obvious or hidden.[6]

According to the homeostasis hypothesis, we can shed light on behavior control mechanisms in processes of spontaneous change. Spontaneous change occurs as functional learning in view of the aims the person is pursuing. When the change occurs spontaneously, it is not associated with the sense of need due to force majeure that can be useful to exercise coercion on possible choices. As a result, it is easier for that change to stabilize in time and find its place in a routine, although there is no one single outcome and the new behavior does not necessarily replace the previous one.[7] Behavior and routine habits are not inevitably substituted by spontaneously acquired new behavior and habits: intentionality and an ongoing internal or external reinforcement are required, for new habits to replace old ones, becoming dominant automatisms and overriding the former.

Cognitive automatisms make it possible for us to maintain stability and regularity with a degree of efficiency. Conditions for change appear when cognitive automatisms are no longer able to guarantee a balance or when existing equilibriums can no longer easily adapt positively to change.[8] As discussed at length in Part I, potential and accessible cognitive automatism patterns are determined by context and reference models. This means they are extremely variable and can be influenced (aka *lability of reference outcomes*).[9]

Our observations suggest a propensity to change and resilience are both present in the automatisms that regulate perceptual-judgment processes.[10] An overview of these features indicates that it is best to distinguish between a spontaneous and a voluntary change. Unlike the former (spontaneous), the latter (voluntary) is a slow process proceeding by trial and error required only under special conditions that call for a systematic overhaul of one's behavior and life. Life cycles are a case in point: switching from adolescence to adulthood, a pregnancy, and a new professional role. A voluntary and deliberate change usually starts with a separation in our identity, distancing one's self from what we were and shedding some distinctive behavioral traits.

Typically, it is reasonable to maintain that automatisms are put to the test of the deliberate system if and when conditions call for a new balance because the old one is no longer sustainable. The deliberate system intervenes with supervision,

---

[6] For instance, UK research into the effectiveness of behavioral change programs following a move. The tested hypothesis is whether a change in habits determines a window where one can establish new habits. See Verplanken and Roy [6].

[7] Bouton [7].

[8] Pressures, such as factors of change, are not only external. The well-known distinction between regulating external and internal factors is not quite as clear cut as it used to be. Gut bacteria—biome and microbiome—greatly influence the regulation of cognitive automatisms. See Martin et al. [8]. As we will see in the next chapter, the variability of the conditions in which the possibility of change occurs produces a variability of change effects on people.

[9] See Chap. 1, pp. 16–20.

[10] See Chap. 1, pp. 23–24.

selecting some of the patterns (schemata) best suited to the situation, both by concentrating functions and by inhibiting inadequate patterns.[11] We resort to a deliberate system to correct mistakes and re-establish a new sequence of actions to attain an objective or to solve a problem if a known sequence is not available. In experiential terms, these are moments when we implement voluntary acts (i.e., willpower): let us try and interrupt and/or slow down what we were doing or try and focus only and totally on a task to find a new solution.

Voluntary change mechanisms require deliberate processes and precise actions that lead to a new equilibrium. We appreciate the importance of this if we stop and think of chronic stress due to lasting instability or to systemic uncertainty. Under such conditions, the brain fails to anticipate the conditions required to reduce the negative physiological consequences on the body and fails to find a new equilibrium. If such conditions persist over time, they are known to wear the body out. In other words, a negative cumulative effect develops, what McEwen and Stellar called an allostatic load followed by inflammation and leading to chronic conditions.[12] When homeostasis (the ability to regulate automatisms under normal conditions) and allostasis (the ability to modify the body's physiological parameters in abnormal conditions) interrupt their function or stop working, changes can only take place following special instructions and programs aimed at re-establishing regulatory functions in time. However, the role of deliberate processes is not merely to seek a new balance. When at last a new balance is found, we still need deliberate processes to assess the systemic consequence due to the new balance we have attained.

What said so far highlights a key feature, in fact the most important part of voluntary or deliberate change: behavior changes according to perspective. This kind of vision presumes conditions whereby reference systems emerge which in turn allow and in a certain way facilitate and enable change. Of course, one needs special lenses to tell the best-suited reference system and to acquaint oneself in all its side dimensions and sizes. As observed in Chap. 4, intentional change requires reference systems.

In a wonderful page of "The Soul of Places," James Hillman is in a dialogue, commenting on the following sentence attributed to the architect James Lloyd Wright: *Early in life I had to choose between honest arrogance and hypocritical humility. I chose honest arrogance and have seen no occasion to change*. And continued asking himself why we always think that *doing* requires an agent, a subject, someone who acts, an ego? Poesies is merely a creative activity, not needing an agent, a person, of a doer […] Things are not just built by someone, but they are "*building*" that is able to implement their own transformations. "They complete their deterioration, their own patina, they change with the wind, with reflexes".[13]

---

[11] See Norman and Shallice 1986 (Chapter 1, 15)

[12] McEwen and Stellar [9].

[13] Hillman, J. *The Sould of Places* in the Italian Edition *L'anima dei Luoghi. Conversazione con Mario Truppi*. Milano, Rizzoli. 2004.

The great psychologist and anthropologist Hillman turned his wisdom to the changing nature of things and of the places where humans are immersed and which they belong to. Their belonging gives a decisive contribution to the formation and subsequent cognitive representation of individual and cultural cognitive systems. Anthropologist Anna Tsing observed how humans have not focused enough on multi- and intra-species relations causing a tendency to disturb the ecology of places. The latter evolve "naturally" maintaining a balance which reforms after the accidental geophysically led disturbance. A forest destroyed by a hurricane or by a fire resurrects a few years later creating new ecologies. Disturbances created by humans who in the Anthropocene control the environment make such resurgence unlikely.[14] In a subsequent interview, Anna Tsing says that one of the features determining what we call "modern" is a blind trust in design and planning. "If promoters claim they are building a railroad, then, we believe, there will be a railroad, and only a railroad. We don't stop to think about all the effects building a railroad might entail, whether blocking the flow of rivers with embankments, thus forming stagnating, mosquito-filled ponds, or encouraging trigger-happy hunters, able to shoot whole herds of bison from the train, or, perhaps, sending out sparks that start small fires, allowing prairie grasses to survive in plains otherwise covered by crops and invasive weeds. I've purposely added one benign effect to my list of railroad consequences; there is no rule that all non-designed effects will be bad. Yet, in truth, I've barely started the list of terrifying non-designed effects of building railroads, which have destroyed Indigenous and peasant peoples and ecologies all over the world. The modern condition is made in not noticing. The Anthropocene—the world condition of human-caused environmental catastrophe—has been a wake-up call for this refusal to look around us. The non-designed effects of imperial and industrial infrastructures are the Anthropocene, in all its terrors. Tsing points out she no longer uses the terms *unintentional* because *intentional* is related to awareness (consciousness) and is not the key issue. And she continues: "Can anyone still say that the production of climate-change causing anthropogenic carbon dioxide is an 'unintentional' result of car manufacture? I don't think so; the car manufacturers know perfectly well. Whatever the intentions of designers, we have been caught up in the effects of their infrastructural designs, as these have changed the earth, air, and water. If we want to hold on to pockets of livability, that's where we need to begin.[15]"

The multi-species anthropologist's words sound harsh, but also totally authentic. In her essays and interviews, Tsing highlights the inter-species relationships and interactions and how these contribute to transform the environment. The study of these relations yields a new and unique expertise which enables us to understand the consequences of planning and design decisions. If we fail to consider consequences of the "effects" of planning and design intentions, then we break the cycle and

[14] Tsing [10, cit. p. 51].

[15] Riccardo Venturi interiews Anna Tsing *"Ecologia della Perturbazione"* https://antinomie.it/index.php/2021/06/25/ecologie-della-perturbazione-intervista-con-anna-l-tsing/#_ftnref1). Thanks to Riccardo Venturi for granting the original text of the interview.

circularity needed to safeguard systemic sustainability or what Tsing calls *livability*. We can but subscribe to this point of view.

All-encompassing points of view on systemic change like Tsing's help us avoid short cuts of the technical debate on behavior modification in complex topics such as chronic diseases, obesity, poverty, inequality, lower welfare, and global warming. As well as stating one's intentions, sustainable innovation programs also require prospective references. This will enable us to consider the many experiences and systemic inter-relations brought on by change. A systemic point of view has to be maintained and developed in the prospective framework considering all the possible precautions and implications.[16] The prospective view or framework in the event of change is discussed below.

7.1 Spontaneous and Induced Behavioral Change

We have already addressed the question of the cumulative and additive effects of behavioral choices, preferences, and experiences. The cumulative effects of choices and experiences in behavioral economics are described as "behavioral externalities." We can consider behavioral externalities as motor-perceptual and decision-making automatisms induced or spontaneously learned. These behavioral patterns are the result of the selective pressures of living in today's complex societies. We cannot say that there is no choice on the part of whoever acts. However, what characterizes these behaviors is rather their being in a context in which habits are formed by induced effects of structural changes that have occurred in the context itself. These behavioral patterns become "choices" and habits as they are legitimate expressions of the context in which the individual action is situated.

As we shall see, behavioral externalities potentially have a very important role when conceiving new solutions. By focusing on behavioral externalities, we can also flesh out the idea illustrated in Part II, that is, that the value of innovation can become apparent through design. We are mostly interested in the possibility of transforming observations on behavioral externalities in design principles and create conditions to favor change. As a result, you can appreciate behavioral externalities and internalities as effects of a perspective due to the introduction of modifications to typical behavioral traits.

I would like to point out that it is not yet common practice to identify externalities as consequences of design decisions and turn them into innovation design variables. Behavioral externalities are mostly treated as additional cost variables. Basically, in technological and traditional innovation models, externalities are considered as unexpected or negligible effects. These effects may be expected but not be the focus of the design. When a behavioral externality is negative, costs can be associated, and this integrated in the price system as an "internality." For

---

[16] See Blevis and Blevis [11].

instance, *the individual costs* of smoking (tabagism) are included in the health system's *social costs* by taxing the sale of tobacco products: the greater the tobacco use, the higher the consumer taxation. Likewise, *the environmental costs* due to fuel use are absorbed by excise duty. Amounts depend on single vehicle use. In other words, democratic societies have learnt how to tolerate potentially risky choices, ensuring that the impact of those behaviors are absorbed—at least partially and unfortunately at times only in a symbolic manner—by individual, environmental, or social protection systems. Readers will appreciate that it is protection against the consequences of risks, and they are part of the economic decisions. Cumulative and additional effects of behavioral choices clearly have been an additional external cost which a person or productive organization has to shoulder, hence the definition externality.

I am suggesting that by identifying, describing, and depicting behavioral externalities in real life, we have a better definition of the potential value that innovative solutions can implement. This is especially true in terms of prevention and innovation policy-led behavior regulation. The paradigm of sustainable innovation allows for results by reducing and containing the impact of negative cumulative effects while increasing the impact of positive cumulative effects. This is partially consistent with traditional approaches to externality management. In other terms, once one can describe and predict behavioral externalities, it is possible to assign a value to the solutions that reduce negative externalities and favor the development—and prevalence—of positive externalities. However, it is not just a matter of internalizing or absorbing the costs of negative behavioral externalities, as classical economics[17] suggests. It is more a matter of highlighting the value of positive externalities to safeguard the common good and spread programs of sustainable innovation.

For the purposes of the text and to highlight behavioral features of innovations, it is best to keep behavioral externalities and internalities apart from other types in economics, where typically we refer to technological and production externalities when assessing the legal and proprietary effects as well as hidden costs in an innovation. These assessments focus on the positive or negative fallouts innovations have on the other actors affected and interested in the innovation itself. Both the technological and production as well as the behavioral externalities focus on consumer experiences and behavior, as consumers bear a very important weight throughout the narration. Unfortunately, econometric models have not yet found a "consolidated" way to hold it in due account. They need to integrate all the factors ex ante, in a preventive manner. Analysis on externalities have homed in on the negative economic, social, and environmental effects, without putting the necessary emphasis on how to appropriately incentivize and reward innovations that produce positive externalities.

[17] See Medema S.G. and Samuel Ferey S. (eds) *Externalities in economic thought.* In Externalities in economic thought, put online on March the 27th, 2014, accessed on November the 16th, 2021. URL: http://journals.openedition.org/oeconomia/366

For instance, innovations concerning electrically powered mobility already offer a glimpse of the positive environmental impact by reducing the fossil fuel use and carbon dioxide emissions. The story goes that we are progressively replacing car fleets using hydrocarbon-based fuel with hybrid or electric cars and that the switch will reduce the overall negative impact of fossil fuels. Luckily this point of view is widely accepted by youngsters and by the general public. However, there is a lack of major programs to accelerate and promote a change in behavior when purchasing private means of transport, nor are positive behavioral externalities rewarded. Electric mobility is finding it difficult to take off which in turn suggests a strong lack of confidence in institutions and a collective feeling of powerlessness.[18]

About 15 years have gone by since Elon Musk announced he would soon launch totally electric Tesla models for wide consumption, at very competitive prices compared to traditional vehicles. However, in spite of having the most advanced technology at the time (2007), and in spite of massive funding and subsidies from the US Government, apparently the launch of cheap widely available products is no longer on the cards. Musk acted according to the traditional logic of technological innovation. He did not aim for a substantial change in consumer behavior, opting to accumulate advantages over other manufacturers concentrating nearly exclusively on the segment of consumers who can afford high costs for appealing and technologically new products. His strategy is now paying off, and for the first time in the last quarter of 2021, electric vehicle sales exceeded the sale of all other cars.

The US Government tried not to influence Tesla's decisions—for instance, by favoring a growth and spread of its technology on the domestic market. In 2008, one of the worst times for the car industry, the US Government funded the development of the S Tesla model with 365 million dollars as part of a 25-billion-dollar funding for car manufacturers. This suggests the US Government either did not raise the issue or failed to follow a strategy promoting conditions for a radical change of consumer behavior.

Classical economic theories suggest the market becomes more efficient when manufacturers take on the burden of hidden costs and negative externalities, regulating production with measures and incentives that can be partially internalized in the price system. For instance, according to these theories, tax on plastic could lead to the internalization of the externality costs due to the spread of microplastic in our waters. However, a critical reading of this narration easily shows that taxation was insufficient to limit the use of plastic and reduce the impact of plastic waste on the environment. We can therefore assume that the internalization of negative

[18] We can already envisage the environmental costs due to the difficult disposal of lithium electric batteries and zinc and manganese dioxide batteries. If we focus on the costs incurred by the community that will house the battery waste, there will be negative externalities on the population that are damaged even though they had no active part in the production of the batteries and in the decision on the use of their land for waste disposal. Current narrative solves this issue by arguing that there are very effective disposal solutions and that, for batteries using zinc, manganese, and other substances readily available in nature, the principles of the circular economy can be implemented. These would then be recycling models that re-establish nature's optimal conditions while generating jobs and the establishment of industrious social fabrics.

externality costs is not a comprehensive and effective measure. Without debating the effectiveness of internalization models in a more detailed manner, one can remark that positive behavioral externalities are normally excluded from economic models or not adequately appreciated.

Taxes and fines are levied on negative behavioral externalities to produce good results, and they partly limit undesirable effects of choices and behaviors but do not prevent them. Recent research has opened new inroads in important and complementary ways to improve the possibilities of using positive behavioral externalities and substantially (rather than palliatively) correct negative behavioral externalities.

If behavioral externalities are contextualized considering a collective perspective, it becomes easier to address them both from their social and community point of view and also refer them to individuals. Behavioral externalities become apparent when consumption in a given class of consumers has a positive (or negative) effect on other consumer groups. As the environmentalists say "there is no such thing as a free lunch".[19] The costs of some of the community's unsustainable behavior will inevitably impact on other communities and on the whole community (society).

Let us take the case of health. When analyzed in detail, traditional systems used to internalize the costs of behavioral externalities prove inadequate. In Western societies, moral hazards and behavioral hazards[20] are often the result of the above-described ineffective innovation models and their relative price policies. It might seem farfetched, but, in the end, I hope this argument will appear clear as the statement corresponds to the actual situation. I will show—and where possible document—how innovations systemically addressing behavioral change issues are more consistent and sustainable than so-called sudden disruptive technological innovations.

Rising health costs in all advanced economies are due to chronic disease treatment. It is also known that in poorer countries, mortality due to illnesses that could become chronic diseases is higher. Poorer countries cannot sustain the costs of treatment or are simply unable to guarantee an adequate standard of living to all the income brackets of the country. Health social and behavioral determinants have an impact on a person's or a community's life perspective very early on and in any economy.[21] In more affluent countries, chronic diseases such as asthma, diabetes, and high cholesterol spread because of the behavioral and moral hazards not intercepted in time to fight them successfully.

The above-described association was clearly highlighted by a study on the effectiveness of health insurance systems carried out in the United States. In a nutshell result proved an old European saying "The more you spend the less you spend" (*chi più spende, meno spende*). When applied to the health system, this old adage proves

[19] This phrase was first used by the economist Milton Friedman [12], a Nobel prize against the degeneration of the welfare society. Environmentalists, however, use the same phrase to communicate messages opposed to liberalism, to emphasize that the excesses of the rhetoric of entrepreneurial freedom have led to the overexploitation of natural resources.

[20] See Baicker et al. [13].

[21] See Chap. 11. Vineis et al. [14].

how an insurance system that fails to close the gap between naive and sophisticated behaviors leads to a double negative effect (externality) in that it increases the global use of drugs without reducing the chance of the disease becoming chronic. According to research by Wharton School of the University of Pennsylvania,[22] the lack of corrective mechanisms explaining the actual value of the insurance system in covering risks leads to two well-known hostile actions affecting systemic insurances and more in general civil society as a whole: adverse selection—that is, not purchasing an insurance policy and moral hazards.[23]

The project compared the so-called PDP (Prescription Drug Plan) and the MA-PD (Medicare Advantage-Prescription Drug) insurance plans. They are by-products or stand-alone modules of more comprehensive insurance plans and can be sold separately or as a part of a more general plan. The PDP plan provides coverage for prescription drugs and medications, with several options for excesses, price, and refunds. The MA-PD covers both prescription drug and medical cost coverage with graduated differences considering the policy price, the excess and refunds. Results shows that the MA-PD is "more generous" than the PDP and offers a greater value for the same cost, although this may vary according to the state or region and offering a greater value at the same price. Basically, and especially for people with chronic diseases, savings range between 8% and 10%. That's not all. The choice of a PDP plan entails an overall increase in drug costs up to 8%, a greater cost for society as a whole and thus a waste of resources and of opportunities to solve the problem. The global increase in use is mainly due to drugs that act on symptoms and have short-term effects.[24] Furthermore, since *low-cost* plans lead to an increase in overall health costs, insurances and health systems arrange more expensive health plans. However, the "generosity" of premium plans is underestimated by less sophisticated consumers who end up by opting for less effective products that are able to solve part of the most acute problems in the short term.

This proves that insurance companies have the essential means to incentivize and reward the insurance products that try to improve consumption behavior instead of exploiting short-sighted consumer decisions and channel them toward lower-end products. Technically this opportunity can be enacted by acting on the price system, internalizing the costs of behavioral externalities. It is a good example of how to plan innovative strategies in a series of domains. It also requires internalizing externalities due to the underutilization of available resources using product or service design. Resources may be underutilized because of an associated premium cost: we can make use of an additional tool to make the more traditional price lever more consistent. This can be done by reducing friction due to partial information and risky behavior and by revealing value through product and service designs that trigger participatory models and positive choices.

---

[22] Starc and Town [15].

[23] Starc and Town [16].

[24] Amithab et al. [17].

Behavioral internality is a notion that corresponds to the ability of absorbing the costs of behavioral externalities. Once again one has to consider it from a collective point of view to fully appreciate features of individual behavior. In a community, there are advantages in identifying specific member's behavioral profile since people don't all behave in the same way (homogenous behavior) (see Chaps. 2 and 8) and each person's living conditions are key in determining behavioral automatisms and the relative systemic trends. For instance, if most people in a given community abide by recommendations in managing the pandemic, the community will have a prevalence of positive behavioral externalities. That community will easily absorb the negative behavioral externalities due to the small number of people who fail to comply with the majority. The management of the COVID-19 pandemic is a case in point: as the gap between vaccinated and non-vaccinated shrinks, communities can more have a prevalence of positive behavioral externalities. In such a community, it will be easier to absorb the costs of negative behavioral externalities since only a minority will not follow. This is why one has to create the conditions so that even those most adverse to accept the rules for the pandemic are gradually put in a position where they cannot harm the rest of the community. In a democratic society, individual freedom of choice can be safeguarded with a range of methods designed for all circumstances considering very diverse (heterogeneous) behaviors. The logic of what has been said so far leads one to conclude that the label "libertarian paternalism" used for nudging strategies cannot be used to describe the need for biological, anthropological, sociological, and psychological preservation, before being a choice determined by the philosophy of law and thus politics. Nudging strategies and other strategies of change discussed in this book regulate individual and collective behaviors in situations where the limits of responsibility of a political class are exceeded which is why these limits do not condition them.

We can apply the notion of behavioral internality to many situations. Traditionally (positive and negative), behavioral externalities are internalized by managing health costs. Health systems can be public or private or a mixture of the two. Whatever the system, there are rules to access prevention and treatment. Without debating the differences among health system,[25] a good system must find a balance between inclusion strategies and strategies to avoid costs exceeding the ability of the system to cover them. Let's presume that a given health system's access is regulated and that it operates like an insurance. The system must avoid losses in the medium and long term and adverse or negative selection.[26] Typically an insurance system that lacks a pool of resources is at the mercy of one or both the above. Furthermore, the fact that people with a relatively low risk tend not to insure does not favor them reaching adequate resources.[27] If only people with a high-risk profile subscribe, the insurance

[25] Structural and situational differences definitely play a key role in regulating individual and collective behavior and are central to an in-depth understanding of choices and preferences difference.

[26] Rothschild & Stiglitz [18].

[27] In the case of systems with compulsory insurance, the market presents a range of competitive solutions that partially or entirely cover most cases, thus generating insurance switching that reduce the overall stability of each insurance company.

system becomes untenable. It is not enough to share profits between high- and low-risk profiles to internalize the costs of negative behavioral externalities.

Other features that make choices and relative preferences more intelligible are needed to consider different causes and incidence of diseases and their combinations. This behavioral heterogeneity is due to a different maturity of people in selecting the right choice. And it is unintentionally supported by the lack of inclination of health systems to manage the causes of negative externalities and promote positive behavioral externalities. Investments in primary prevention are generally low whatever the modern medical system.

In conclusion, moral and behavioral hazards are substantially tackled through price and innovation policies. Because of the rhetoric on innovation costs, resources used to promote compliance and thus better behavior are underused. This is the case of US medical insurances where insured parties have to pay an excess and contribute to the service. It is also true for alternative energies and premium products for any consumer category when the price of the innovative product is unacceptably high for most buyers. Consumers will then continue to buy more conveniently priced products, so cheaper although less effective or even more damaging on the medium and long term.

If the future aim is to change behavior and for cultures to evolve by internalizing the costs of positive externalities, the question could arise as to who can or should shoulder the responsibility of improving choices and with what means. How can we combine a fairer distribution of costs with a more widespread distribution of premium solutions? The questions are not in the remit of the present book since it concerns the political sphere, the reduction of inequalities, and the evolution of democracies. I believe there is an answer to the central question, that is, who has to pay for the costs to educate consumers and make them more choice-savvy. Advanced public-private cooperation is now common in democratic societies. Social responsibility has to be equally shared among the social parties (regulation and delivery of services). If consumers understand the value of choices and improve consumer behavior, they will better appreciate products containing high sustainable innovation. This is essential when wishing to internalize costs due to behavioral and moral hazards. Price and innovation policies, inaccurate information, and behavioral hazards lead to low levels of more valuable products (premium value). On the other hand, moral hazards and un-savvy consumers lead to short-sighted choices (myopic bias). One wonders how long we will be able to accept that the community (i.e., the public) has to shoulder the future costs of short-sighted choices and lack of consumer sophistication, leaving the private sector justified in benefiting from the advantages of accumulated enormous wealth.

Imagination and creativity are needed to reward the choices that correspond to the paradigm of sustainable innovation. As mentioned in Part II, design plays a key role in revealing the value of sustainable innovation services. Creative solutions to reward virtuous behavior and new habits have started to surface in recent years. For instance, in the *European Green Deal on Climate Change*, new ideas accelerating the transition toward sustainable mobility have emerged. One of them is to reward externalities when abandoning private means running on fossil fuels, using virtual and cryptocurrencies. Some such currencies can be exchanged on a platform devoted to the ecological exchange of services. They can be purchased by local companies that wish to compensate their locally produced carbon emissions with advantages for local communities. Incomes managed by a fund (the EU Social Climate Fund) are used to fund other green projects such as carbon sequestration. The AYR Platform also records the creation, the attribution, the transactions, and the registration of carbon credits from the market.[28] Easy transmission (transmissibility) is the driving force of these ideas. These initiatives can spread swiftly if implemented with the appropriate prominence by the European Community and indicated as positive reference models. New solutions are appearing in the field of energy consumption management: they will eliminate the choice between low-cost high-impact sources and the more expensive with little or no environmental impact. Consumers should be given the option of low impact energy consumption with choice automatisms that include the awareness of energy consumption effects with the necessary visualizations. Lastly, the interaction designer's community is starting to work on facilitating mental automatisms favoring immediate feedback on the environmental consequences of consumer choices.[29]

7.2 Proximity and Voluntary Change

Positive reference models underlying voluntary change must have an emotional impact and significanc*e* so as to be recognized as compatible and accessible reference models. All this is not new: it is part of the digital economy's main rules and of practical marketing. Consumers or users of a service are positively attracted if the service is socially acceptable, if it generates competence and mastery. Furthermore, if the new service entails new habits, users expect to be involved in a reassuring path that will encourage and enable them to overcome the concerns due to inexperience and the unknown. This means that it is not enough to trigger the awareness of the need for change to favor voluntary changes. For instance, although awareness encourages behavior consistent with the defense of the environment, it involves a minority of people. Even if most people are generically aware of and sensitive to the environmental impact of consumption, in practice they fail to focus on the impact of their personal choices. Valid and carefully considered arguments tailored to the person's characteristics have to be offered, so that the exchange value between immediate costs and future advantages of behavioral rationality appear clearly.

While future advantages are a useful information that must be included in any model of sustainable innovation, it could be difficult to identify immediate advantages. In fact, the main objections to be addressed concern the difficulty in making acceptable the immediate change-related behavioral costs. At times, the behavioral costs of subscribing to change can be insurmountable. The hiatus or gap between

[28] See the project at http://weayr.com/#/home

[29] Wiberg et al. [19].

the intention of following a plan and the actual ability to carry it through requires a mitigating strategy.

Compared to others, proximity strategies are the ones that so far have yielding the first successes. There are three basic types of proximity strategies: proximity in time, space, and culture. One might add a fourth, psychological proximity but it is the least understood and known. Let us take it a step at a time.

7.3 Proximity in Time

A case in point is global warming and its increasingly disastrous effects for all the populations and nations of the planet. The growing number of catastrophic events due to the acceleration of climate change—now close to the point of no return—is considered a fact by all climate experts despite a sizeable percentage of climate change deniers. One might wonder how and when the actual size of the phenomenon will give rise to systemic changes in the community's behavior. More importantly for the purposes of this chapter: when will the time come to be personally and individually concerned about the effects of climate change? In other words, what is the subjective threshold that will trigger action and voluntarily modify individual consumer behavior?

When objectives are distant in time and space, it generally elicits inconsistent individual behavior. Furthermore, it is difficult for anyone to assess the actual impact of one person's behavior on climate change. Our cognitive biases range from procrastinating practical actions that could be carried out here and now to the lack of trust in the future effects of individual virtuous behaviors. We also tend to belittle the negative impact of today's unsustainable behavior on the future.[30] Both appear to be subscribed by the political action following the world leaders' summits. For many, especially for the younger generations, the change is too slow and not great enough to introduce systemic behavioral changes. The timeframe of urgency to act and change the environment crosses personal specificity which complicates the picture: for instance, the generational differences in consumption and how they interface with the types of economy.

Timewise, 2030 and 2050 are considered the thresholds to limit temperature raise below 1.5° C and for fossil free energy but consider how different they sound for the young Millennials or Generations Z and Alpha compared to Baby Boomers just as Generation X.[31] Older generations naturally tend to consider climate change as an event that will fully express its impact in the distant future and will therefore mainly concern future generations. The practical solutions available now are not so important because they are not timely enough. To close the gap between individual intentions and collective actions, this twofold time perspective has to change.

[30] Frederick et al. [20].

[31] Baby Boomers and Generation X precede generations Z and Alpha in the order.

If we consider the impact each country has on climate change and make a projection for the two-time proximity thresholds used to measure political decisions and international agreements to reduce emissions, carbon dioxide sequestration, and storage, then the individual vs collective dimensions become even more complex. How can we ask people who have not benefited from the wealth of consumer societies to reduce their expectations of achieving a more affluent lifestyle? Once again, in this case we have to close the gap between some communities that are already accruing and feeling negative externalities as the result of consumption models and those individual and collective behaviors of communities that already perceive the effects of other country/communities' negative externalities.[32]

We are in a position where we have to mediate among generational lifestyles and among parts of the planet that experience differently time and the objective urgency to deal with climate change in a consistent manner. Realistically how can one manage such a complex picture? Behavioral science offers a "modest" proposal: acting on the perception of time by manipulating the perception of time proximity. These actions are practical and thus reduce the level of abstraction in the intentions to modify behaviors. The practical nature of these actions will reduce the generational and spatial mismatch in perception of relevance and urgency of the threat thus reducing the gap. However, we have to bring the timeframe we can act in closer, so as to realize actions to be carried out.

Research carried out in the United States echoes president Obama's 2011 observations when, considering future risks, he condemned the lack of action. Experimental research like this one showed that significant effects can be obtained by accentuating pessimism on climate change trends while encouraging new habits with specific programs to follow with individual commitments, for example, no longer buying plastic bottles and containers, recycling and separated or differentiated waste collection, fewer combustion engine local transportation, and other pro environmental behaviors which a research team and participants can agree on.[33] One of the positive outcomes of the experiment is that the new habits' latency extends at least in the short term, as researchers checked on participant involvement in the projects, continuing past the end of the research. One can reasonably expect for the "contracts" with specific rewards to extend the duration of experimental condition so that new habits will take hold and become part of the people's lifestyles.

[32] Societies that came later to Western consumption patterns are in fact already outpacing the West in the percentages of fossil emissions produced. For example, China and India plan to increase coal production through 2030 and at the same time have made commitments to overall emission reductions: https://www.climate-transparency.org/wp-content/uploads/2021/10/CT2021-Highlights-Report.pdf

[33] Bashir et al. [21].

7.4 Space Proximity

Spatial or geo-referential proximity is another way to make objectives of voluntary change appear more attainable. Closeness to a place where positive change takes place has a great influence. Successful experiences are more likely to be replicated close by. Despite that COVID-19 containment measures have shown how professional communities can adapt to new conditions of distance working and that teams can operate and influence each other at great distances, pre-COVID research had shown that spatial proximity plays a key role in changing behavior in most of the population whatever their level of education.

For instance, an Italian geostatistical research highlighted a substantial proxemics consistence among communities from small towns in the provinces.[34] Researchers observed that the whole differentiated or separated waste collection is strongly influenced by proximity. The provinces with good levels of environmental pro-sociability have a positive influence on neighboring communities that adopt similar norms in a short time. Likewise, local authorities who are unable to act consistently and make pro-environment choices whatever their official position and statements are on environmental sustainability and waste control appear to resemble neighboring authorities. In other words, proximity tends to produce assimilated behaviors in either case.

The research's most interesting result shows how in the long run where pro-environmental innovation is favored there are more clusters of separated waste collection compared to other localities. Results prove how good social pro-environment actions require time and constancy so that communities can adapt and implement new habits and responsible behavior. Once such habits have consolidated, they last over time. Habit formation can be faster if information on differentiated or separated waste collection is made available adding easily understandable signs and signals that resident can remember. In other words, looking for information on how to recycle must be as easy and short as possible by incorporating the service in the social fabric of everyday life. This might mean supplying households with boxes or bags in the same place as where the waste is produced and opening special waste collection centers in every district, to increase control on each resident's behavior.[35]

Similar research ought to be carried out systemically on many topics, such as tending to the landscape, caring for the elderly and the disabled, and other community resources to identify strategies to spread behavioral innovation on a wider scale. System acceleration of habit formation can be favored by an alliance between best practices of behavioral research and behavioral design practice (see Part IV).

Lastly, facilities or infrastructures being created in Europe to favor the dissemination of social innovation experiments to promote sustainable business and entrepreneurship, usable throughout on different scales, are of great interest. The initiative started in 2021 offering social innovators financial backing and capacity

---

[34] Govino et al. [22].

[35] Rosenthal [23].

building, to develop practical solutions and ideas to promote a new European culture of social innovation and social entrepreneurship. Two thirds of the EU contribution are earmarked for pre-market demonstration projects that can rapidly be disseminated throughout.[36] The success of innovation clusters is probably the most significant effect of the infrastructures built to house innovation communities and start-ups. In fact, they can become structured cooperation ecosystems, a driving force for innovation and to trigger innovation processes. However, for innovation clusters to disseminate and promote systemic changes, the 2030 and 2050 appointments cannot be missed. This will require implementing sustainable innovation structural systems based on appropriate strategies to facilitate a pervasive local acquisition of new habits. Consistently and constantly supported local communities can play a key role in the transition toward sustainable behavior and cultural models. The main objective—that is, guaranteeing lasting sustainable innovation—falls to local communities, as they have the greatest perseverance especially when they are objectives with deferred gratification.

7.5 Social and Cultural Proximity

The groups and communities have the potential to direct and correct individuals to establish (stabilize) behaviors to attain social aims and especially deferred benefit programs. Their potential is related to the fact that groups and communities can develop behavioral norms and models that become a proximal point of reference for individuals. This means it is not enough to set norms: one must create the conditions whereby such norms are followed. This aspect is often disregarded as it requires consistency and constancy. In other words, during the transition periods, tools, instruments, and services have to be identified so that individuals can absorb cultural innovations a little at a time. Research on these topics has greatly developed in time in several specialist spheres such as organizational psychology, environmental, and ecological psychology.

Social proximity is one of the distinctive traits of the present research. Social proximity is a watershed between adherence and indifference to behavioral and cultural models of reference. Reference models to promote and facilitate cultural changes must represent cultural proximity, and specifically positive proximal social references are natural candidates for success. Social proximity develops on sharing and following norms, but it is consolidated especially on the basis of the observations that a person can make when comparing themselves to others. The identification of behavior deviating from the expected norm can contribute to the failure of cultural innovations and of the strategies disseminating new behaviors. Identification and belonging to a community are not favored by abstract and idealized reference models. Social comparison with neighbors and with people with similar social

[36] https://ec.europa.eu/info/funding-tenders/opportunities/portal/screen/opportunities/topic-details/horizon-cl4-2021-resilience-01-31

characteristics favors compliance to virtuous behavior: norms are more respected—such as using less energy at peak times—and no additional incentives are needed when norms are close to the prevalent behaviors in the social reference group.

Compliance to the expected behavioral model improves with feedback when one's behavior deviates from that of the other members of the reference group. Vice versa, data referring to standards outside the proximal reference models does not lead to the expected behavioral and cultural compliance. The most important feature in cultural transitions is to supply people with the information of other people's behavior. According to a recent research project carried out in the United States and four European countries, this essential expedient is enough to stop the erosion of complying with norms.[37]

Communication strategies based on awareness to favor a transition toward models of sustainable innovation are more likely to succeed if they are based on a contextual understanding of behaviors and on how to deal with social proximity. The community's perception on energy consumption behavior has been proved to be a very important variable in transitioning toward sustainable consumption models. Adapting to global warming due to climate change will require a collective action aimed at creating a greater resilience. A Canadian study highlighted how resilient communities have also a greater understanding of the social norms associated with the awareness of the risks climate change entails. These communities also display a specific will to undertake pro-environment behaviors and also to comply with the taxation required to manage farsighted environmental policies. As a result, they have a greater degree of activism that feeds into identification with community culture, norms, and leadership.[38]

In another controlled randomized study carried out in several communities in California, residents in comparable residential units were studied to examine the effectiveness of social norms on energy saving. Participants received feedback on their behavior compared to reference models close or more distant from their lifestyles. The hypothesis being tested was those participants with consumption models closer to the norm had a better compliance with the energy saving models recommended by the experiment. Proximity to the social norm proved to be a significant predictor of behavioral response. The experiment specifically confirmed that regular and contextualized feedback to consumer groups improved their compliance to the expected consumption norms—when compared to groups that received no feedback. The role of feedback in regulating consumer behavior is well-known. Adding information that makes it possible for participants to compare their behavior to the social cluster they identify with (declare they belong to) leads to a stronger compliance with new recommended standards.

The results of this project showed that individuals comply more strongly to expected social norms when they receive relevant recommendations and suggestions referring to the specific circumstances (context) of consumption behavior. Targeted standards aimed to favor transition behavior modifications can improve the

---

[37] Bicchieri et al. [24].

[38] Smith et al. [25].

environmental management and the attainment of energy policy objectives. Solutions stemming from targeted observations of energy saving individual behavior in a given context can play an important role in the design phase. They can also lead to optimal implementations of behavioral actions improving environmental management thus reaching energy policy targets.[39]

Lastly, as we will see in more detail in the next chapter, individual behavior can be best described and understood by observing deviance from the reference models. If social and cultural proximity models are used as references, we can observe behavioral clusters diverging from the reference model (taken to be normal) to different degrees.

Divergence is not necessarily voluntary deviance from social norms. In many cases divergence indicates a difficulty in understanding the rationality of expected behavior. In many cases it could signal a difficulty to understand the rationality of expected behavior or a lack of information or shortcomings in the mental models caused by underestimating the environmental impact of individual and collective consumption can generate. During transition toward pro-environmental models of behavior and basically in the transition toward models of sustainable innovation, one has to consider what is the possible behavioral deviancy, monitor it, and understand the underlying reasons to overcome it. An Australian study proved that groups could play an explicit educational role on a person, correcting incomplete mental models where possible, for instance, through specifically organized public debates involving local and national daily papers.[40]

Highlights

- Opportunities for change develop in the gap between the automatic and the deliberate systems: it is the experience of habit discontinuity.
- Behavior discontinuity can be spontaneous or deliberately triggered, and likewise opportunities for change can be explicit or implicit.
- Cognitive automatisms make it possible for us to maintain stability and regularity with a degree of efficiency.
- It is useful to distinguish between a spontaneous and a voluntary change. Voluntary is a slow process proceeding by trial and error required only under special conditions that call for a systematic overhaul of one's behavior and life.
- Voluntary change mechanisms require deliberate processes and precise actions that lead to a new equilibrium.
- Behavior changes according to perspective.
- We can consider behavioral externalities as motor-perceptual and decision-making automatisms induced or spontaneously learned.
- The paradigm of sustainable innovation allows for results by reducing and containing the impact of negative cumulative effects while increasing the impact of positive cumulative effects.

---

[39] Callery et al. [26].

[40] Belinda et al. [27].

- By identifying, describing, and depicting behavioral externalities in real life, we have a better definition of the potential value that innovative solutions can implement.
- Resources may be underutilized because of an associated premium cost: we can make use of an additional tool to make the more traditional price lever more consistent.
- Consumers or users of a service are positively attracted if the service is socially acceptable, if it generates competence and mastery.
- At times, the behavioral costs of subscribing to change can be insurmountable. The hiatus or gap between the intention of following a plan and the actual ability to carry it through requires a mitigating strategy.
- When objectives are distant in time and space, it generally elicits inconsistent individual behavior.
- Closeness to a place where positive change takes place has a great influence. Successful experiences are more likely to be replicated close by.
- Proximity tends to produce assimilated behaviors.
- Good social pro-environment actions require time and constancy so that communities can adapt and implement new habits and responsible behavior. Once such habits have consolidated, they last over time.
- Consistently and constantly supported local communities can play a key role in the transition toward sustainable behavior and cultural models.
- Reference models to promote and facilitate cultural changes must represent cultural proximity and specifically positive proximal social references are natural candidates for success.
- Individual behavior can be best described and understood by observing deviance from the reference models.
- In many cases divergence indicates a difficulty in understanding the rationality of expected behavior.

References

1. Eaton, J., Qureshi, O., Salaria, N., & Ryan, G. (2018). *The Lancet Commission on Mental Health and Sustainable Development: Evidence for action on mental health and global development*. Mental Health Innovation Network, Centre for Global Mental Health, London School of Hygiene and Tropical Medicine.
2. Patel, V., & Saxena, S. (Eds.). (2018). The Lancet Commission on Global Mental Health and Sustainable Development. *The Lancet,* October 10.
3. Michie, S., Richardson, M., Johnston, M., Abraham, C., Francis, J., Hardeman, W., Eccles, M. P., Cane, J., & Wood, C. (2013). The behavior change technique taxonomy (v1) of 93 hierarchically clustered techniques: Building an international consensus for the reporting of behavior change interventions. *The Annals of Behavioral Medicine, 46*, 81–95.
4. Thaler, R., & Shrefin, C. (1981, April). An economic theory of self-control. *The Journal of Political Economy, 89*(2), 392–406.
5. Edelman, G. (2004). *Wider than the sky. The phenomenal gift of consciousness*. Yale University Press.
6. Verplanken, B., & Roy, D. (2016). Empowering interventions to promote sustainable lifestyles: Testing the habit discontinuity hypothesis in a field experiment. *Journal of Environmental Psychology, 45*, 127–134.

7. Bouton, M. E. (2014). Why behavior change is difficult to sustain. *Preventive Medicine, 68*, 29–36.
8. Martin, C. R., Osadchiy, V., Kalani, A., & Mayer, E. A. (2018). The brain-gut-microbiome axis. *Cellular and Molecular Gastroenterology and Hepatology, 6*(2), 133–148. https://doi.org/10.1016/j.jcmgh.2018.04.003
9. McEwen, B. S., & Stellar, E. (1993). Stress and individual. Mechanisms leading to disease. *Archives of Internal Medicine, 153*(18), 2093–2101.
10. Tsing, A. (2017). A threat to Holocene resurgence is a threat to livability. In M. Brightman & J. Lewis (Eds.), *The anthropology of sustainability. Beyond development and progress* (pp. 51–65). Palgrave Macmillan.
11. Blevis, E., & Blevis, S. A. (2010, September–October). Hope for the best and prepare for the worst: Interaction design and the tipping point. *Interactions, 17*(5), 26–30. https://doi.org/10.1145/1836216.1836223
12. Friedman, M. (1975). *There's no such thing as a free lunch*. Open Court.
13. Baicker, K., Mullainathan, S., & Schwartzstein, J. (2015, November). Behavioral hazard in health insurance. *The Quarterly Journal of Economics, 130*(4), 1623–1667.
14. Vineis, P., et al. (2020). Special report: The biology of inequalities in health: The lifepath consortium. *Frontiers in Public Health, 8*, 118. https://www.frontiersin.org/article/10.3389/fpubh.2020.00118
15. Starc, A., & Town, R. (2016). *Internalizing behavioral externalities: Benefit integration in health insurance*. National Bureau of Economic Research.
16. Starc, A., & Town, R. (2020, November). Externalities and benefit design in health insurance. *Review of Economic Studies, 87*(6), 2827–2858.
17. Amithab, C., Gruber, J., & McKnight, R. (2010). Patient cost sharing in low income populations. *American Economic Review, 100*(2), 303–308.
18. Rothschild, M., & Stiglitz, J. (1976). Equilibrium in competitive insurance markets: An essay on the economics of imperfect information author(s). *The Quarterly Journal of Economics, 90*(4), Nov.
19. Wiberg, M., Taylor, A., & Rosner, D. (2022, January–February). Climate Care. *Interactions, 29*(1). Association for Computing Machinery. ISSN 1072-5520.
20. Frederick, S., Loewenstein, G., & O'Donoghue, T. (2002). Time discounting and time preference: A critical review. *Journal of Economic Literature, 40*, 351–401.
21. Bashir, N., Wilson, A., Lockwood, P., Chasteen, A., & Alisat, C. (2014). Time for action is now: Subjective temporal proximity enhances pursuit of remote-future goals. *Social Cognition, 32*(1), 83–93.
22. Govino, M., Crociata, A., & Sacco, P. L. (2016). Location matters for pro-environmental behavior: A spatial Markov chains approach to proximity effects in differentiated waste collection. *The Annals of Regional Science, 56*, 295–315. https://doi.org/10.1007/s00168-015-0740-7
23. Rosenthal, S. (2018). Procedural information and behavioral control: Longitudinal analysis of the intention-behavior gap in the context of recycling. *Recycling, 3*, 5. https://doi.org/10.3390/recycling301000
24. Bicchieri, C., Dimant, E., Gachter, S., & Nosenzo, D. (2021, December 6). *Social proximity and the erosion of norm compliance*. https://ssrn.com/abstract=3355028 or https://doi.org/10.2139/ssrn.3355028.
25. Smith, C. J., Dupré, K. E., McEvoy, A., & Kenny, S. (2021). Community perceptions and pro-environmental behavior: The mediating roles of social norms and climate change risk. *Canadian Journal of Behavioral Science/Revue canadienne des sciences du comportement, 53*(2), 200–210. https://doi.org/10.1037/cbs0000229
26. Callery, P., Goodwin, C., & Moncayo, D. (2021). Norm proximity and optimal social comparisons for energy conservation behavior. *Journal of Environmental Management, 296*, 113332. https://doi.org/10.1016/j.jenvman.2021.113332
27. Belinda, X., Hurlstone, M. J., & Walker, I. (2018). Correct me if I'm wrong: Groups outperform individuals in the climate stabilization task. In. *Frontiers in Psychology, 9*, 274. https://www.frontiersin.org/article/10.3389/fpsyg.2018.02274

Chapter 8
Behavioral Change and Heterogeneity

One might wonder whether the variability of human behavior in offering an adaptive response to the same or similar conditions mirrors the inherent heterogeneity of human behavior nature. The answer is not as self-evident as might be expected. There is ample proof that a varying behavioral range is always to be found whatever the real-life context we choose. However, there is a strong mismatch between evidence based on the observations of our daily lives and evidence gathered in scientific research and laboratory contexts.

Human experimental research in laboratories is aimed at giving meaning and an explanation of the observed effects, so that they can be told from mere chance results. Methods and statistics used to tell a random result from an experimental one have led research in all the fields of knowledge, including research into the nature of human behavior.

Research has also made it possible to draw clear lines between what can be concluded or inferred from measurements in experimental contexts and what is not confirmed by statistical significance. As a result, the behavioral results obtained in laboratory contexts cannot easily be applied to real-world settings. To date the experimental paradigm has not been able to convincingly solve the puzzle of apparently randomly different answers. Indeed, the ecological validity of scientific research, and therefore the explanation of more complex real-life events, was preferred to the possibility of reproducing behavioral effects in laboratories.

As we shall see in the course of the present chapter, we are very close to a turning point: we have become more determined in dealing with the ecological validity of research carried out with targeted observation and experimental methods. Our aim is for empirical verification and real-world conditions to match in a better manner. Real-world conditions are the ones we refer to in our observations which means we could pursue both the objectives of ecological validity and the reproducibility of results. In fact, so-called replicability or replication has seriously challenged the

M. Visciola, *Sustainable Innovation*,
https://doi.org/10.1007/978-3-031-18751-3_8

experimental paradigm of human sciences.[1] The experimental paradigm and, in particular, randomized studies with control groups are also used in large-scale experimental studies. These studies have a great potential for sustainable innovation programs. The inattentiveness of sampling in empirical tests has quite clearly reduced or eliminated the possibility of widely extending their results. This situation opens the door to a new era where the heterogeneity of behavior will be the focus of experimental design in every empirical or practical verification to extend results to real-world settings. Heterogeneity or a range of answers will no longer be considered to prove the experiment has failed, but rather to be the effect of systematic methods.

In terms of sustainable innovation, this approach offers another interesting feature: the revolution of the scientific paradigm in human and social sciences will allow to give methodological importance and greater reliability to the targeted observations conducted with ethnographic techniques for design purposes, as we saw in Part I of the present book.

However, as always let's take it a step at a time. Early researchers attempting to account for individual differences started by comparing twins who had lived in the same environment. Research did not lead to much. Francis Galton's research stands out among the projects by experimental psychologists and biologists. He was Darwin's cousin and the first to introduce promising studies on variability in genetically inherited traits. His studies led him to observe how in the Victorian Era families which were at the pinnacle of success in various arts and disciplines in time regressed toward the average (*regression towards mediocrity in hereditary stature* in his words) of the population. This was his explanation for the relative stability of distinctive behavioral traits in the human species: once the top level had been reached, one can only regress. In the course of his studies, he developed the notion of linear regression, that is, the natural tendency to improve when below average and deteriorate when above average. Furthermore, Galton laid the fundamentals of other major statistical principles, with the help of mathematicians of the time. These same principles are still the basic toolkit for any science based on observation and on experiments.[2]

Recent observations on the same sample of people evidence the variability of results, both in terms of a comparison among individuals and among groups. As observed, experiments make it possible to distinguish random (determined by chance) effects from those caused by the experimental conditions. However, the experimental paradigm being followed to date in human and social sciences has been to find results shared by the average of the group, regardless of the

[1] The replicability crisis (also called the replication crisis) has greatly affected experimental research in humanities (human sciences). Unlike medical, clinical, or biological research, psychology has devoted limited attention to the definition of the experimental sample. The so-called inattentiveness of sampling makes the possibility of replicating or extending lab research results very unlikely. See McShane et al. [1]. Also see Kenny and Judd [2].

[2] As well as the notion of linear and multiple regression, Galton's early research introduced notions such as median, standard deviation, and correlation.

characteristics of the people taking part in the experiment. University students are often used in experiments and tests without making any distinction. Usually not even gender is considered as a distinguishing feature, except in particular experimental samples where gender is the object of study. Technically, experimental samples are known as haphazard samples, that is, selected without a scientific criterion of sorts. However, the general and a-specific nature of the experimental sample means that the macro-effects that can be generated in a controller setting are less probably replicated in the real world.

The absence of means to control social, experimental, and context-related determinants in the course of the experimental programs leads to other undesired effects. These include the possibility that these behavioral effects cannot be reproduced if the sample varies. In these cases, there were biases in the sample that lead to select some profiles and deselect others with no specifications in the experimental design. Lastly, and as is discussed in more detail further in the text, critical literature documents how some effects on judgment automatisms do cause the expected effects but in groups of people where the effects are harmful or not indicated.

The following are some of the factors that can lead to a great variability in reactions to identical stimuli in a range of people: social identity, beliefs and values, culture, and specific competence on a given field of knowledge or skills. These are features which count more in real-world situations to understand which buttons to push to favor rational behavior. As seen in previous chapters, context determinants and life circumstances are distinguishing reference viewpoints of people's choice and preference systems. Later in this chapter we shall also see how such features can not only be controlled but also appreciated and valorized to understand behavioral variability. It might be useful and in fact necessary to make a quick reference to biological differences and diversity among ethnic groups before branching into the major implications leading to the revolutionary perspectives on behavioral heterogeneity for sustainable innovation. We need to clear the ground from possible semantic misunderstandings on the nature of behavioral and cultural differences.

Let me go back to the question I raised at the beginning of the chapter: how can we rule out that behavioral heterogeneity or variability is due to psychological diversity attributable to biological difference?[3] More specifically the question is what relationship is there between behavioral and cultural/ethnic heterogeneity? If ethnically determined heterogenous behavior can be traced to variables that are not passed down exclusively through the genes, then we are justified in trying to concentrate on culturally transmitted variables because we can act on them.

I believe anthropology and research in the framework of the UNESCO project launched at the end of World War 2 suggest a basic thesis which is worth referring to as follows: Claude Lévi-Strauss was invited to the UNESCO General Conference with other experts in an attempt to clear the international stage from racist and

[3] In statistics, variability is not the same as variance. The latter refers to the shift from the average or mean, thus making it possible to determine the statistical distance among the individuals in a group. Variance is a statistical index to ascertain or disprove the veracity of the causal effect, while variability measures the absence of the effect.

imperialist interpretations based on presumed ethnic biological and psychological differences. Three editions of the Conference were held in 1952, 1971, and 2005. The great anthropologist developed a framework and contents enshrined in three resolutions to eradicate racial prejudices and in particular get rid of the presumed biological differences that justified the supremacy and the historical domination of certain ethnic groups.[4]

His thoughts and the evidence informing his position are summarized in one sentence spoken at the 2005 Conference: *Cultural diversity and biological diversity are phenomena of the same type*.[5,6] With this statement Lévi-Strauss pieced together the ongoing similitude made in previous contributions between anthropological, biological, and genetic lexicons. All his contributions clearly stressed the role of cultural differences as an engine of creativity and of liveliness, able to happily withstand the pressures of uniformity. However, he also showed how diversity is the fruit of cultural exchanges, of the drive toward independence and coexistence among ethnic groups, maintaining that biological differences are the by-product of cultural differences.

Lévi-Strauss had become extremely familiar with early cognitive sciences and the progress of genetic research in biology. Presumed racial differences due exclusively to biological traits was not underpinned by any scientific evidence. Lévi-Strauss was, for instance, aware of Luca Cavalli-Sforza's early studies and of the role of "genetic distance"[7] that had proved the genome of people in the same village was genetically equidistant to those living in another village. Let us not forget that the sequencing of the human genome had been completed in 2003, leading to conclusions that further proved the positions of the UNESCO Conferences from a scientific standpoint: over 99% of the human genome is shared by all humans regardless of their ethnic group. Furthermore, only 5% of this genome can be traced back to the origins of the *Homo sapiens* species. Such data proved that nature and culture evolve along similar lines living rise to mutations and migrations (also see Chap. 6).

At the UNESCO 2005 Conference, Lévi-Strauss reiterated what he had stated in previous conferences important comments: "*We no longer invoke racial characteristics in trying to explain the macroscopic differences appearing to exist between cultures,*" ...., "*but these same racial traits—which can no longer be considered as such [i.e. as racial traits] when viewed in finer detail—in combination with cultural phenomena of which they are less the cause than the result, give valuable*

[4] The UNESCO General Conference established three points: to gather scientific data on race-related issues, to circulate the said scientific data and to prepare an educational campaign based on the data. The anthropologist's work was published by UNESCO. See Lévi-Strauss C. "*Race et histoire*." The text was then modified, specified, and clarified in the subsequent one called "Race et culture". UNESCO/Albin Michel; Paris: 2001. https://openlibrary.org/works/OL11315676W/Race_et_histoire

[5] Müller-Wille [3].

[6] Lévi-Strauss [4].

[7] Ibid. Chap. 5.

information about relatively recent periods which, unlike earlier prehistory, can be corroborated by archeological, linguistic and ethnographic data."

Lévi-Strauss's words referred to and re-launched the cultural and scientific movement of the time. The prevalent intellectual movement of the time avoided any deterministic interpretation of the relationship between evolution and the fate of the human species. As an anthropologist, he offered an original interpretation of the relationship between evolution and innovation and related the many diverse directions the relationship between nature and culture had taken to the development of human history. Accordingly, progress was not seen as a linear trend. This means questioning the paradigm of the uniqueness of progress, a theory that suggested dominant cultural expressions plough a furrow that other cultural expressions will follow. In other words, the history of humanity and evolution can be represented by stochastic processes, and that developments cannot be entirely predetermined although possible outcomes can be outlined or discerned.

In conclusion and to return to the main argument, the vision which emerged from the UNESCO Conferences suggests the results of progress are determined by the type of instruments or tools, by technology, and by available data. A scientist, like an engineer (or a designer, the figure we might add to the original paradigmatic ones proposed by Lévi-Strauss), construct the useful representations for the transformation and mutual adaptation between culture and nature.[8] Learning by experimentation (aka *thinkering*) is a distinctive feature of humans. This skill has grown into a more complex agentive ability that means we are able to shape the environment using both cultural and genetic experiments. This has led to conditions for the ongoing change of cultures and behaviors, according to ever-new and ever-changing perspective which unfortunately remain within the *Homo sapiens* specificity. Lévi-Strauss identifies this distinctive feature as a universal feature, shared by all ethnic groups and society.[9]

8.1 Behavior Moderators Traits

Individual and cultural differences in the agentivity as the ability to transform culture and lifestyles are at the origin of the heterogeneity of behaviors. When we study behaviors and their evolution, how they change spontaneously, and how they can be influenced by a selective pressure until new habits are formed, we are in fact looking at how lifestyles and cultures change. The paths lifestyles and cultures can take are

---

[8] In the mentioned text, Lévi-Strauss compares cultural development and the evolution of biological traits, highlighting how some genes of the human genome have a function that regulates so as to adapt genetic traits to cultural modifications and lifestyles. For instance, in some areas, innovations following irrigation in agriculture, a product of human labor, led to malaria and in some zones to thalassemia and sickle cell anemia, a genetic mutation that has a selective advantage in that those who suffer from it are immune to malaria.

[9] Lévi-Strauss [5].

not attributable to a mere cause-effect chain. This means we have used methods, techniques, and processes that enable us to reach proven and reproducible conclusions while still remaining in a pragmatic sphere.

Observations suggest that to identify the causal links of real-world behavior determinants using scientific methods, we have to go beyond ambitiously seeking the effects on the reference sample average. We need to refer to and move toward understanding the potential range of impacts of the intended effects. The main way to attain that aim is to identify behavioral distinctive and differentiating features. It is a matter of understanding and measuring so-called moderators of behavior causal effects. In this case we are using one of the terms employed in statistical experimental research and also in carrying out the analysis of the variables interacting in machine learning and artificial intelligence algorithms. Being aware of and knowing moderators substantiates behavioral determinant analysis offering a more pragmatic value.

Technically the moderator effect is felt when a third variable intervenes in a significant manner, thus modifying the nature of the relationship between a behavioral determinant and the person's or the group's decisional behavior. For instance, let us imagine we are verifying the accuracy of a behavioral model (see further in the text) and that there are two main subgroups of neurologists, one conservative and one progressive with a weak or a favorable propensity to change standard therapeutic regime. Let us also presume the standard therapeutic regime enables the patients to survive with their chronic disease. And lastly let us presume that the innovative therapeutic regime promises the patient a better quality of life. To verify the moderator effect, we could use an interactive variable, such as the fact that the new prescription could improve and bring forward diagnosis and therefore improve the prevention protocol. We should observe a corresponding change in the decision-making process of our sample. More precisely, if this variable intervenes selectively modifying the protocol in only one of the subgroups—the progressive one in the case in point—then the variable is deemed a *moderator* or having a *moderating effect*.

Moderators play a key role in defining and validating the so-called behavioral models. Most of *moderator* analysis is intended to measure the causal link between two behavioral determinants by using a—positive or negative—regression coefficient.[10] A traditional interpretation suggests moderation leads to a weakening of the causal effect on the average of the considered population. However, a moderator may equally amplify or even corrupt that effect on either of the subgroups that have been subjected to its effect. In this sense, if we have a criterion to reliably measure the intensity of the moderator, we can verify the heterogeneity it has on each determinant. Likewise, we can measure the behavioral effect directly on the main variable. In other words, moderation makes it possible to understand and assess effect

[10] A negative coefficient indicates a weakening of the variable's causal effect on the behavior determinant; a positive coefficient indicated a stronger causal effect.

modifiers. Moderators are determinant variables where their causal effect can differ (heterogenous) according to the subgroups as defined by the variables.

Ecological validity of experimental behavioral research requires identifying effect modifiers ex ante. They must be seen as variables that precede the experimental pilot tests and must be specifically identified and taxonomically classified to assess their effects on the subgroups. However, one must not forget that moderators are not the main variables understudy. In fact, as mentioned, these are the determinants that lead to a great variability in people's answers. Each category of moderators can be manipulated when possible, at different levels of intensity and by integrating them with other categories of moderators. When probing a new innovative solution, researchers' or designers' freedom is to roam and determine the intensity of behavior moderators to verify their effectiveness in influencing specific decisions and behavior on pre-identified subgroups in a given population.

8.2 Taxonomy of Moderators and Heterogeneity of Behaviors

The moment has come to ask ourselves what are the taxonomies and categories of moderators that can be usefully applied on research on heterogenous behaviors. To measure behavior effects of moderators, we should remember that the aim is to improve our understanding of how spontaneous behavior changes take place and also how we can influence decisional behavior for shared aims. It is a matter of having to substantiate sustainable innovation programs and improve both participation and the impact of choices for the common good. By pursuing these aims, we also intend to develop innovation models that encompass an overt intention to obtain the behavioral effects we wish to attain.

Sampling according to ethnographic research principles and resulting from ethnographic studies can be very reliable to support experimental studies. This approach enables a clear definition of the distinctive qualitative traits of the sample chosen for the experiments. As a result, experimental studies can be carried out with a clear identification of the sample, of the variables we intend to assess and the moderations to be considered. This goes beyond the moderation sources typically selected in marketing, such as population data (demographics) and domicile (geography). The latter are easy to measure, but likely to be wide-ranging proximity factors not focused on the most important latent variables that actually moderate most determinants.

The identification of moderator effects can be traced back to three main categories or determinants: structural, situational, and dispositional (see Chap. 11). Behavioral traits of behavior models stem from these variables. Structural variables are factors which at a given time in the history of a society's civilization or in a collaborative ecosystem typify coexistence policies and the balance of the ecosystems. Policies refer to specific domains such as health, nutrition, energy consumption, transport, and mobility as well as to the ecosystems' socioeconomic and environmental features. Policies affect the understanding and perception of the conditions where the action takes place. Situational variables refer to the variables of the context where the action takes place and include features of the reference communities; links with reference communities and people; and aspects of space and time that mediate individual and collective values, beliefs, and opinions. Lastly, dispositional variables are defined as a person's inner factors and concern the motor perceptual and decisional automatisms, biases, and the control styles that govern a person's agentivity.

The map in Fig. 8.1 refers to the factors determining a person's health and well-being in a hypothetical heath ecosystem. Systemic holistic maps can be drawn up for other domains too, for instance, referred to food consumption, electric energy, mobility, and so forth. Once a domain has been identified, we can generate a taxonomic model so as to identify the macro-variables at play and use them to analyze how behaviors differentiate in each area or domain. This map shows the

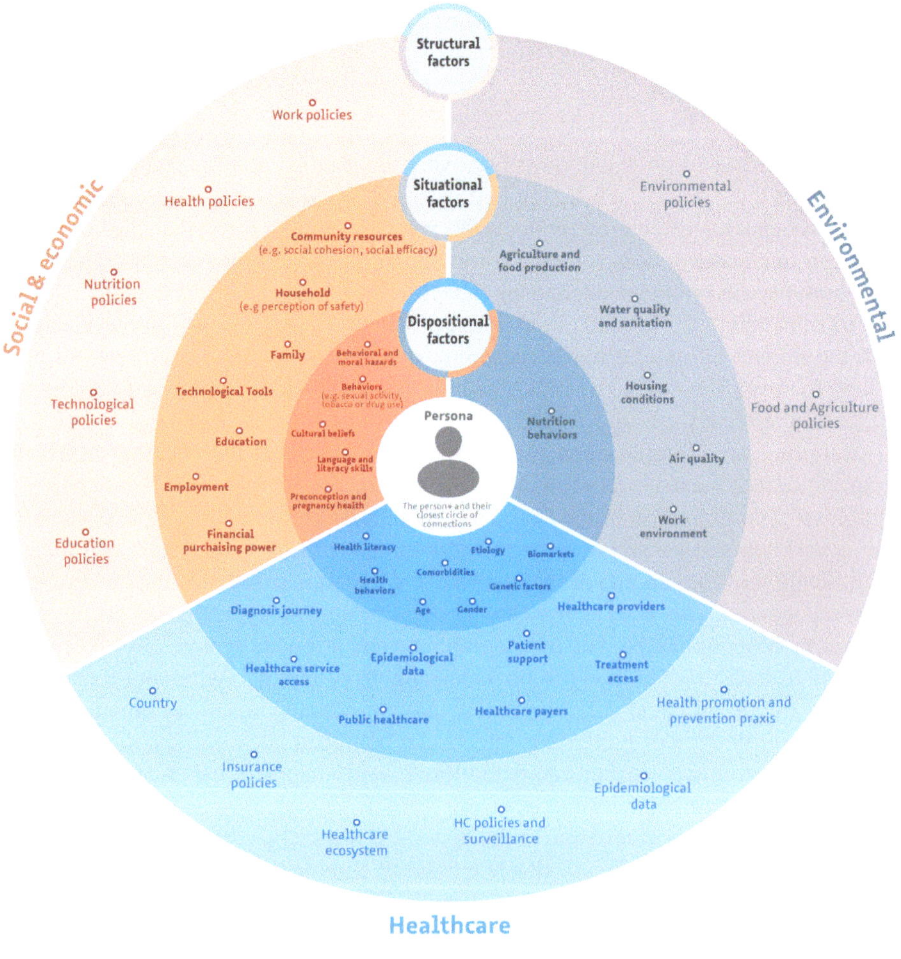

Fig. 8.1 A holistic map of the health ecosystem. (Thanks to Chiara Agamennone and Elena Messina for having identified the main health ecosystem categories in scientific literature. Thanks to Thomas Schertenleib for having designed the visual map)

complexity of the factors that directly or indirectly affect behavior. Each taxonomic category contains defining subcategories that can be used in preparing ad hoc studies and programs for a specific action, to define and understand the variables which affect the transformation of behaviors and cultures.[11]

Without going further, I think it is evident that a map and a relative taxonomy of the variables that systemically affect behavior in daily life makes the variables involved transparent. It also allows you to make the choice of moderating factors with respect to the variables that have a direct impact on shaping preferences and choices. By acting systematically, we can pursue our ambitious aim, to imagine and develop finalized intervention programs improving consumer experience and that of people in all decisional domains. This will facilitate cooperation among ecosystem functional and structural parts and promote the organized participation of interest groups. Unlike the programs that typically aim to act on the average of the population, sustainable innovation programs must consider the heterogeneity of behaviors and the complexity of moderator variables.

8.3 Distributive Effects of Behavior Influence Procedures

Research carried out in recent years have highlighted how nudging can cause the opposite effects (to those expected) in some groups of consumers or alternatively not have any effect on others. Research was carried out in the United States to verify whether reminders can increase consumer awareness on what they are spending, especially if they are made just when they are making a decision on how much to spend. Results indicated "distributed unintentional effects" spread out on three consumer groups.[12] Unlike typical research on the effects of *nudging* reminders, in this research the experimental design included three types of consumers defined a priori. They were classed as "spendthrifts," "tightwads," and "unconflicted."

Research was carried out in an Economics Lab and thus had a very low ecological validity. Consumer profile categories were defined without any objective even qualitative comparison, of the situation where consumer behaviors were defined in the experimental design. They were simplifications and hypotheses drawn from a doctoral thesis at Carnegie Mellon and were not the result of actual observations.[13] However, in spite of our reservations on the ecological validity of these profiles, research offers empirical results suggesting that the effects due to *opportunity cost reminders* or to *spending booster* are distributed unequally among the three profiles. Specifically, results show that stimuli and incentives designed in the experimental tests to reduce *overspending* only work for those who are keen not to spend.

[11] In epidemiology and prevention of syndromes with a risk of becoming chronic, researchers are starting to test how effective these taxonomies are in generating predictive models of chronic diseases and preventive models with targeted programs. For instance, see "Lifepath" a program on the elderly and chronicity funded by the EU https://www.lifepathproject.eu/

[12] Thunström et al. ([6].

[13] Zellermayer [7].

Researchers believe nudging is important only for the tightwad profile, as they feel stronger negative emotions in spending (*pain for paying*) compared to the happy-go-lucky spenders (*spendthrifts*).

Authors stated that the nudging reminders impact on feelings. By defining the prominence of the emotional value, it could be increased or decreased to verify any further effects on distribution. The test was not included in the design of the experiment. In fact, the experiment compared two types of reminders sent indifferently to all the 350 students in the experiment to those who received none. As explained below, by modifying context variables and defining the moderating variables, the experiment helps define the conditions where reminders on the opportunities to save also work on *spendthrifts* just as opportunities to spend also work on the more frugal *tightwads*.

Policies regulating widespread consumption typically target a generic consumer. There are relatively few studies to understand the effects of policies on consumer behavior.[14] There are even fewer to assess the heterogenous (or mixed) impact it has on the population. One of these rare cases focused on the effects of a provision introduced in South Korea to make it easier for consumers to trace expenses. The provision requires immediate feedback using customer digital touch points, sent as soon as the credit card purchase has been made.[15] The lawmakers' intention was to improve decisional competence and control of credit card spending with the help of the digital service. Results showed that only 12% of the population increased their ability to save as a result of the improved control system. Researchers suggested that intentional effect of the provision was felt only by the population with the greatest spending power. In the remaining 88% of the relevant population, saving levels dropped. The provision increased dependence on the digital service for most of consumers without significantly improving their saving levels.

It is well-known that in countries where pensions are linked to citizen's ability to save and where there are neither constraints nor precise obligation to ensure that a person will have savings in their old age, a good percentage of people with uncertain incomes fails to set resources aside for their pensions.

Nudging policies have been used in a large number of US and Canadian studies and projects to increase savings.[16] In one study in the effectiveness of actions aimed at increasing savings for pension, nudging strategies were compared to the traditional ones such as financial and education incentives. Results showed nudging was more effective both when comparing cost/efficiency—that is, the relative cost in implementing strategies and results—and also when looking at the absolute result, that is, the increase in savings.[17] Attempts to transfer these prevalently North American insights to Latin America failed to give the same results. For instance, Canadian researchers in Mexico highlighted a distinctive cultural variable in that

[14] See Chap. 5, Part II.

[15] Kim et al. [8].

[16] For instance, see Hershfield et al. [9]. Also, Franklin and Hochlaf [10].

[17] Benartzi et al. [11].

country: young workers living in the family house has no propensity to save. Any attempt to involve young workers and get them to subscribe to a savings plan fails until they have a family of their own.[18]

Columbia University published another ambitious lab research in 2021, carried out during the pandemic. They developed several other hypotheses on the heterogenous effects of nudging.[19] The project was developed around five experimental studies considering three types of nudging, to manipulate the selected architectures.

They took into consideration (i) default, (ii) sorting, and (iii) partitioning.

Default acts on an *opt-in/opt-out* system to present the choice as the best for the consumer—for instance, with the best (most generous) price quality. *Sorting* acts on the so-called faceting presented accordingly with the price of the product, consumer rating, total costs, sales volume, or other attributes. Lastly, *partitioning* acts by simplifying the decision-making process.

Interestingly each type could be characterized according to what it was intended for such as (*a*) advantages for the consumer and for the service provider or goods supplier (*nudges for good*), (*b*) using the service provider or goods supplier's advantage to the disadvantage of the consumer (*bad nudges*), and (*c*) no nudging strategy (*neutral nudges*). Intentions with the various nudging strategies were presented as a nudging moderating variable. Each of the five experiments concerned one nudging type only. Altogether there were 450 subjects.

One the project's main aims was to assess effect heterogeneity in relation to the characteristics of the experimental subjects who were profiles according to socio-economic status (SES), numeracy, finance literacy, and health literacy.[20] Furthermore, they wanted to test which nudging strategies were most effective. The basic assumption is that nudging has a selective effect, whereby the people in the lowest levels of each profile measurement are the most receptive. This follows a behavioral model suggesting a greater vulnerability of people with less spending power and ability to plan the future to marketing strategies. The model also presumed that these people had a lower level of numeracy, finance, and health literacy and that they had a higher level of decision-making anxiety in deciding the most appropriate choice. Nudging selective effect on motor perceptive and decision-making automatisms on more vulnerable populations has never been proved.[21] This research is an initial exploration of differential effects due to nudging types on a larger scale.

The project's noticeable idea was that both public good managers and private enterprises should take on *nudging for good* strategies to give less well-off and less sophisticated consumers advantages in decision-making. According to the results of the first of the five research experiments, moderator effects of the default choice

[18] Shah et al. [12].

[19] Mrkva et al. [13].

[20] See Mrkva, K. et al. ibid. for the scales used for each profile.

[21] Behavioral economics suggest that mental automatisms or biases concern everyone and that generally all behavior is characterized by systematic tendencies we are unaware of.

have a major effect on people with low SESs and low levels of financial and numerical literacy. The result of this experiment indicates that *nudging for good* acts as a moderator that somewhat closes the gap between profiles with high and low SES, high and low numeracy, and financial literacy.

Effects were confirmed by the following four experiments. All the considered nudging types considered had significant selective effects on low SESs and low levels of financial and numerical literacy. Since *bad nudging* was not included in the four experimental tests after the first one, the series proves that *nudging for good* improves decisional accuracy in profiles with low SES and low levels of financial and numerical literacy, in relation to their knowledge of the domain as well as pension and insurance choices. The fourth experiment on distancing during COVID-9 failed to show any selective effect of nudging strategies in low SESs.

In conclusion results were consistent with the growing research on the heterogenous (or diverse) effects on marketing and communication procedures with a view to influencing behavior. Columbia University's experimental series is the first of a new approach on intentional effects of nudging strategies. It is a new and extremely interesting perspective for the development of sustainable innovation.

8.4 Behavior Models

The innovative drive of studies on the variability of behavior effects goes well beyond the analysis of the effectiveness the actual actions may generate. As previously seen, these interventions open new doors for intentional design. In this paragraph I would like to document how these opportunities can be actually implemented. The main argument is that behavior models offer a guiding role for the development of proof-of-concept design creativity and implementation[22] so as to offer tailored or customized targeting. Tailored constraints specified in a behavioral model offer designers the insight they need to develop creative solutions.

A model is a sort of controllable theory that can be useful in developing experiments bolstering the aims of sustainable development. Chapter 7 discussed how innovation always has a cost associated with benefits in terms of behavioral internalities and externalities. Behavior models make it possible to appreciate the trade-off between costs and benefits for each considered target. Specifically, behavior models enable us to develop intentionality as it is enshrined in the idea of innovation in terms of its impact on behavior. Lastly, according to the perspective outlined in Part II (and especially in Chap. 5), we can assess the impact actions have in leading to behavior and habit modification (see Part IV).

The domain or scope of the considered issue and our design objectives have to be fully understood when generating a behavior model. In Part I at least four domains were outlined using ethnographic research. In summary they concerned (*a*)

[22] Also see Chap. 5.

planning digital services to support financial resource management skills for personal and household or family budgeting;[23] (*b*) a 5-year master plan for services for the elderly; (*c*) planning urbanization services in a neighborhood to improve the perception of nighttime security; and (*d*) identifying opportunities to develop cancer patient treatment orientation services. Over the past decade, my collaborators and I have developed behavior models to support innovative digital services in domains including investment management, health insurance, digital services to residents, and the innovation of telecommunication services.

Behavior model plays a key role in channeling design strategies for sustainable innovation. Furthermore, so-called digital transformation has reached a turning point as service personalization (tailored solutions) and automation lead us to a new frontier where behavior models can play an essential role. Let us see some of the key behavior model components.

First, let us refer to the empirical evidence behavior models are based on: they summarize a great amount of context and domain information gathered through research on documents in a scheme, offering interviews with experts and research in the field. Information is gathered and processed according to the nimble procedures shared by the creative industry and design. The aim is to develop important assumptions on the state of knowledge and on the new objectives the team of researchers will investigate with targeted observations.[24] Tipically the team of researchers tests the veracity of these assumptions thanks to a research protocol with the means to sample as part of the ethnographic research and to the guidelines to carry out research in the field. Their report is completed by visual documents, videos, minutes, and other evidence gathered with ad hoc cultural probes and instruments. Reports are summaries that disseminate evidence gathered through people's stories and direct observation. Reports are also representations and narrations of what was observed: the qualitative nature of information offers a wealth of nuances and details that the team of researchers highlights focusing on the many meanings. The core of these technical reports is typically devoted to the evolving dynamic nature of observations using ethno-methodologies.

That said, taking down detailed minutes of what has been observed requires special skills. To relate objects observed by researchers to what said by participants is one of the most appealing and demanding tasks of ethnographic research.

Ethno-methodological research techniques assure impartial views separating opinions from facts, the relative value of the fact (datum) from the complexity of the observation context, and the presence of a bias in the approach to the research. Clearly, the more informed the research brief, the more objectives are explicit and

---

[23] For a more comprehensive description of the behavior model, see Chap. 5.

[24] Ethnographic research in design uses a number of books and technical handbooks and guides, thus covering a wide range of developments and methodological depths. EPIC is still the international reference community for corporate ethnographic research professionals (see Jordan [14]). EPIC is a global community of practitioners doing ethnography for impact in businesses and organizations. Their selection of guides and bibliographies is especially rich and focused https://www.epicpeople.org/bookshelf/

the more structured research in the field. In the 15 years of ethnographic design research my colleagues and I have carried out in Europe, Africa, Asia, and the Americas, we have refined the data collection system to inform and produce creative digital solutions and proof of concept. As time has gone by, the value behavioral modeling offer design activities has become more apparent. In presenting data referred to the present, researchers contribute outlining the challenges design has had to rise to picking out opportunities to improve people's agentivity, domain literacy and expertise. The representation of data appropriately organized in models suggests how behavior may evolve in a given knowledge domain according to a perspective, such as adjacent heterogenous (diverse) behavior models (see Fig. 8.2). It also shows the effects that can be obtained through the implementation of design results (see Fig. 8.2d).

In a perspective view (see Chap. 7), targeted experience of daily behavior observed over the past few years indicates a heterogeneity of behavior in relation to individual domain literacy and cultural agentivity. This point of view introduces competence or literacy. Behavior models for a specific profile have an inner consistency: in other words, they document a sort of behavioral adaptation to the conditions of the civilization they develop in. However, they also bring to light the levels

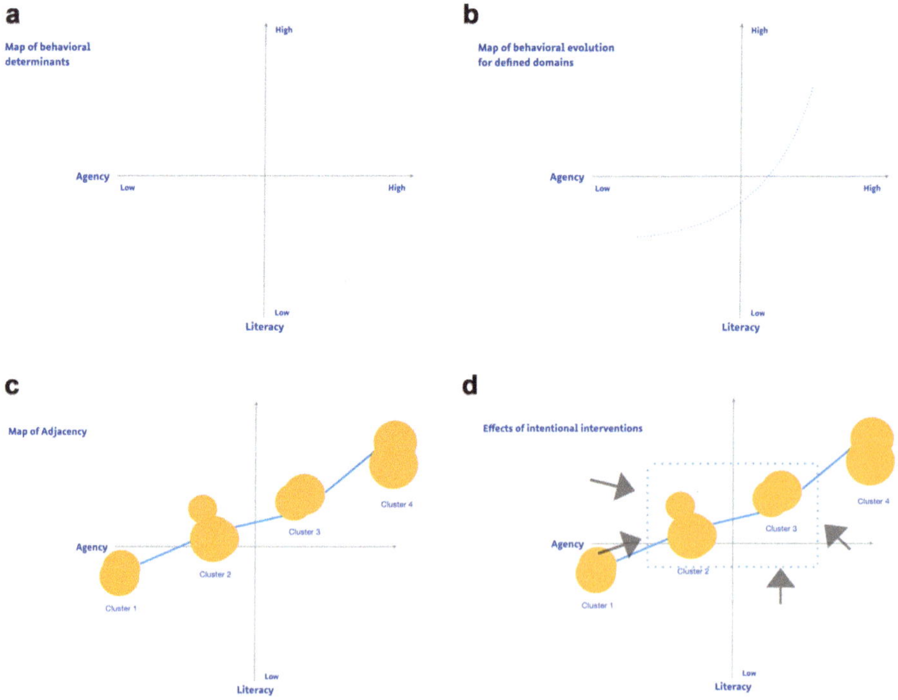

Fig. 8.2 The four phases of behavioral models' definition

of a specific competence and understanding on how to improve self-control and orientation in a given domain, which as shown in Fig. 8.2b can be plotted on a curve. Such research is finalized and aimed at identifying opportunities for new services improving the relevant populations' agentivity and ability to adapt. More specifically it is a matter of understanding how services can (*a*) improve people's sense of competence, (*b*) facilitate a cooperative relationship, and (*c*) increase people's involvement and participation in addressing challenges for sustainable innovation.

The two axes of Fig. 8.2 show the (behavior) determinants used to describe the main behavior clusters. They are termed clusters because they contain dispositional and situational variables for characterizing domain behaviors and profiles. The descriptive variables are qualitative data extracted from the observations and coded as objective elements resulting from observation and (protocol) minutes. A cluster contains a data set on people who share the same profile (homogeneity) with regard to the variables observed. The main aim of the identification and subsequent definition of clusters is to document and represent inner homogeneity and also to describe the distinctive traits and variables which characterize cluster heterogeneity. Agentivity includes people's individual domain literacy and the cultural sphere: it is the ability to control one's behavior translated into routines and habits, lifestyles, values and beliefs, and ability to cooperate and participate. Domain literacy, that is, competence of it, is the sum of the specific knowledge of a given domain and the propensity to regulate behaviors consistently to manage inner homeostasis and environmental uncertainty. As a result, when mapped, agentivity shifts toward behavior regulation on lifestyles; then the axis of competences shifts behavior regulations with respect to the knowledge domain (see Fig. 8.2a, b; also see Chaps. 1 and 2).

These maps show varying levels of agentivity and competence. Besides, it shows the existing relations in a given number of sample participants. This makes it possible to define behavior clusters by profile and their possible shift toward adjacent clusters (see Fig. 8.2c). Cluster adjacency shows the relative distance between and among the distinctive features of each cluster with reference to the behavior determinants of the map axes.[25] Furthermore, it shows the reference points within the map. Reference points in the map of cluster adjacencies offer designers and researchers an understanding of what levers (technological, contents, and services) and what moderators can be used to help behavior evolve within a given domain. The aim is to increase participation, an understanding of behavior objectives, and the growth of individual and group competence. By combining adjacency and evolution maps, you can appreciate the potentially gradual process of behavioral change programs and how it can be seconded with targeted actions. Lastly, the map of the mediator effects reliably describes how design can generate a selective pressure on the expected behavior (Fig. 8.2d).

As well as a natural shift (migration) to the adjacent cluster that can lead to an overall transformation, moderator effects generate a pressure for a systemic change of the adjacent clusters that can lead to an overall change of the evolution map. Part

[25] See further in the text for the statistical importance of distance between clusters.

IV will discuss how the moderators' effects can be generated by a range of intervention programs and/or boosting techniques. As well as pilot programs to modify behavior (i.e., actual contracts among the parties), interventions may include digital nudging programs using marketing technologies, digital services with wearable technologies, and behavior design strategies aimed at modifying the architecture of choice.

Visual maps such as these are reliable representations of observed reality if developed using sophisticated ethno-methodological tools for data gathering and analysis. The behavior models included in the maps are the result of teamwork. The team normally includes expert behavioral researchers, anthropologists, and designers. Models are subsequently critically reviewed by each team research member, the research supervisor, and the various stakeholders partaking in the participatory research process. However, consolidation undergoes two further validation steps, one in a workshop setting with domain experts and the other as a quantitative validation.

My team and I carried out both kinds of validation throughout our designing activities for public and private clients. The first type of expert validation follows principles of participatory design and thus mostly translates into formal reports for design, underwritten by the project stakeholders. The second type of validation requires the formalization of a questionnaire validated for large-scale administration. Questionnaire results can be then used for the statistical validation of the behavior model and also to finalize a map on the heterogeneity (diversity) for the domain under investigation so as to obtain the percentages for each cluster for the reference population.

As previously discussed, participant sampling for the targeted observation of session participants and the concurring research take place through screeners, that is, participant selection grids prepared in the course of the research.[26] Unlike traditional experimental protocols for lab research, research sessions in the field carried out using ethno-methods, the focus is on participant selection analyzing traits well beyond socio-demographic determinants. Dispositional and situational variables are the basic criteria for participant selection. They are used to explore individual domain literacy and cultural agentivity and domain competence in doing.

The research brief is usually the first step, and it is then enriched by an in-depth study of scientific research—if available—and by any available documentation. Behavior model validation is a very advanced standard. Although it is not part of the methods used in classic experimental research, it has enormous advantages for large-scale programs (see further in the text). Thanks to behavior model mapping techniques, these programs can take advantage of very useful additional tools not to be overcome by the degree of complexity due to heterogeneity of behavior and to avoid unreliable simplifications.

[26] Selection includes the use of questionnaires published in scientific journals on lifestyles, propensity to continued mental work, self-control, and self-effectiveness and questions on relevant expertise.

Since ethnographic research on behavior models is usually flexible, this means the relationship with the research team and participants can extend over a variable albeit limited period of time.[27] The research team optimizes information, data, and experience gathering data and experiences in the timeframe established by the completion of the project. Data gathered by the ethnographic and contextual research typically takes place according to professional ethical codes. In the case of sensitive information referred to health, medical ethics codes are also applied. Personal behavior data management is a very delicate matter. However, high standards to respect the private sphere and confidentiality have to be followed so that people's identities are preserved outside the context of the team that work on the data. That said the data collected does not refer to the person themselves.

Information gathered is paradigmatic and is used to modulate project/design and/or experimental action strategies that can give rise to targeted digital tool aimed at new personalized prevention aims and objectives to improve the lifestyles the person may wish to follow voluntarily.

8.4.1 Data and Contextualized Behavior Models

As above described, and argued in previous chapters, agentivity and domain competence are the key determinants in behavior model development. Evolution and adjacency maps on two axes and starting from the research objectives can vary according to the variables that the research team uses to capture behavior heterogeneity and their progression. Behavior models can be located and organized with great attention to (data) details.

One of the most obvious possibilities is to clearly position behavior models according to geopolitical and structural variables that define behavior policies, regulations, and frames. For instance, cultural variables pre-identified in the research project and referring to policies and regulations can act as cluster moderators, if models are intended to represent the heterogeneity of behavior referred to a given domain in a Northern European country compared to a Southern European one. As a result, the two axes of the graph that represent certain behaviors will have to be contextualized to observe differences among clusters. As illustrated in Chap. 2, another systemic and behavior artifact is recommended as a procedure to contextualize behavior models. It is the so-called journey map, a visual format of behavior models illustrating the steps of the passage from an initial to a final state of a data, events, facts, and experience. *Journey maps* (*JMs*) have become popular in representing product or brand service purchase experience, i.e., *customer journey maps*. Many of our research projects document how JMs can help visualize the various stages of information and cognitive activity processing in a given context.

[27] Research sessions may span from a few hours to days in person and from weeks to months remotely.

Chapter 2 described in detail the main stages of cognitive and behavior activity in the saving and household budget management journey map. We described in detail the activities needed to retain control over spending (output) behavior and savings planning and/or the aims of future purchases (i.e., stability and spending aspiration control). Furthermore, we identified the progression between behavior clusters (Fig. 4.6), and the five profiles we identified were distributed according to the large clusters ranging from the Northern and Southern samples, especially where the physical vs digital services were concerned. The distribution mainly concerned the different weight each cognitive-behavior activity entailed—that is, greater agentivity and ability to control. It also focused on the propensity to use more or less comprehensive banking services—that is, a greater or lesser financial expertise. The financial service model was developed bearing in mind behavior heterogeneity with the aim of offering a service through *touchpoints* favoring a gradual increase in the ability to control purchases (expenditure) and save.

The example illustrates that if behavior models are contextualized, they can lead to service innovation strategies. Their aim is to enhance behavior control by increasing awareness on how best to use service and digital support. In this case, the project team and the service provider acted on the habits and mental capacity of each user profile. Service contact points in person at the counter and digital contact points both have interactive tools and communication strategies which can usefully help habit models shift to more evolved models of activity.

Journey maps are a visual key tool to guide designers and developers produce the digital tools to implement the service blueprint. As discussed in Chap. 4, the model also foresees that the ability to save and allocate resources for precise objectives leads to an improvement in planning future expenditure or for a comfortable old age. Clearly the *savings and expenditure planning* model has also become a guide to define the data model. Specifically, the model includes information on how to gather and code data through the different service points of contact and how they can be visualized as diagrams and utility function for service user stakeholders.

Figure 8.3 shows the five service user profiles described in terms of their ability to manage savings. They are positioned in the matrix according to their propensity to focus on specific routines in the five phases of the activity model (see Table 8.1). In the last column, Table 8.1 also shows the levers which the new service uses to improve that particular profile's control. For instance, for the so-called slider, the service favors new routines to balance and stabilize income and output. As for *builders* the new service encourages the propensity to plan savings with a special focus on medium- and long-term expenditure. Since the model uses five profiles and therefore refers to different hierarchy purposes, the aim of modifying savings is based on a range of techniques offering prominence and affordances for every moment of user and service interaction.

Given the nature of the project, it has not been possible to carry out specific experiments to prove the effectiveness of the techniques for each user profile. However, one of the non-explicit results of the project is the possibility of launching intervention programs on new and existing customers. For instance, one could create programs facilitating the progressive shift from a *slider* profile to an

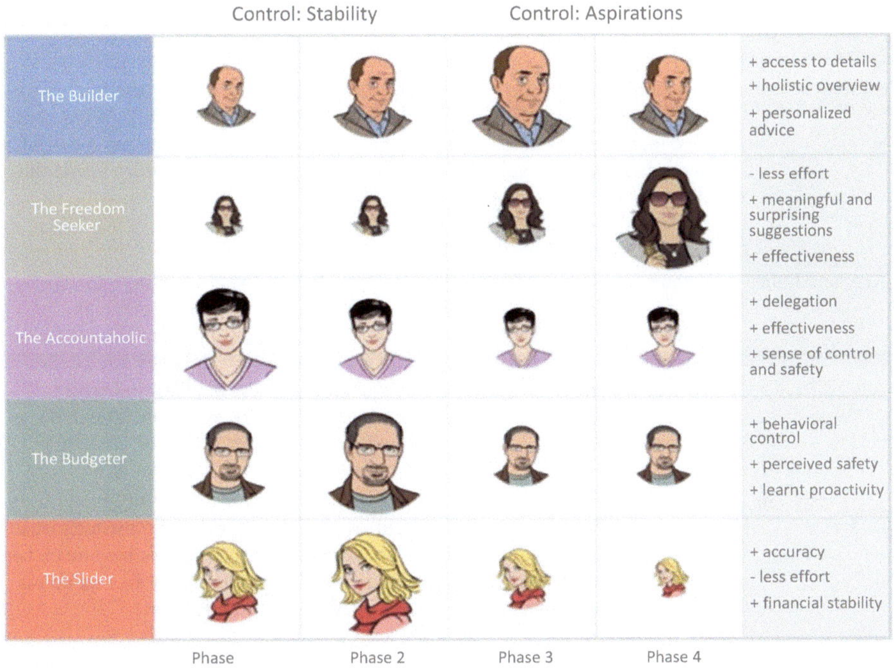

Fig. 8.3 The five saver profiles. The matrix highlights some macro details referred to the extent of the ability to satisfy in the four phases when designing the digital service for each profile. Thanks to the team who worked on the project and particularly to Laura Polazzi, Nicolas Hoffbeck, and Heiko De Simone

accountaholic or *budgeter* profile who have not yet acquired resource allocation habits, to verify which strategies are most effective.

Situating behavioral models pursuing design objectives is one of the features that calls for a greater constructive ability and creativity in behavior researchers and designers. It is a matter of defining and creating a behavior evolutionary path, establishing reference points to facilitate the progressive shift in behavior styles, moving toward a better agentivity and competence. To this aim the map of behavior determinants can be adapted to the aims of the project. In Chap. 2, we were able to illustrate the versatility of a behavior determinant map and how it can be adapted to the specific cases of services for the elderly, for security and urban regeneration, and for cancer therapies. For each of these projects, the axes of the map were as follows:

- Services for the elderly (Fig. 2.2).
  - X (agentivity): reactive vs proactive—Y social skills (competence): isolation vs community oriented.
- Services for urban re generation (Fig. 2.3).
  - X (agentivity): high vs low—Y (remit and rootedness): rootless vs roots in the community/territory.

Table 8.1 Descriptive macro traits and their routines of the five saver profiles

Name	Descriptive trait	Distinctive routine
Slider	Paola is approximate and impulsive when it comes to finance management. Her behavior is "situated": she reacts to the current situation instead of planning and forecasting consequences in advance[a]	Distinctive routine: typically, she frequently checks transactions paid with her ATM card, and if she sees she is spending too much, she impulsively decides to cut some expenditures
Accountaholic	Giovanna keeps track of all the expenses daily, regardless of whether it serves an external purpose or whether it is an end in itself as it gives her a sense of security	Giovanna has an Excel file where she keeps track of the cost of the electricity, gas, telephone, petrol, top-ups, and any other expense, even though she does not use this information to make budgets or analyze trends. Occasionally, she goes through these data to recall another period of the family life: the Excel spreadsheet provides awareness and supports reflections
Budgeter	Marco is a cautious planner and feels secured by allocating money in advance to be able to cope with budget limits and reduce waste	Marco makes a forecast of the main expenses every month, so that he knows how much he can spend on other things. He has set up his own personalized tool for that
Builder	Luca is a responsible investor, who makes financial decisions based on accurate evaluations of past behaviors and forecasting of realistic opportunities. His focus is on building a future for himself and his family	Luca is familiar with the behaviors and needs of his family and does not feel he needs to check expenses in detail. When a decision has to be made, he and his wife make calculations and simulation to estimate the impact of different options and decide accordingly
Freedom seeker	Aurora manages to keep and enjoy her financial stability and to effectively invest her money thanks to consolidated routines. Her focus is on maintaining and possibly improving her lifestyle, but with little effort and no sacrifices	Aurora focuses on the macro-situation and has no interest in tracking specific expenses. She has developed semi-automatic investing strategies for surplus management, such as moving money from her account when a given threshold is reached

[a]Situatedness: characterizes behaviors that are strongly influenced by the context of the specific situation the person is in

- Cancer treatment service orientation (Fig. 2.4).
  - X (agentivity): reactive vs proactive—Y (emotional competence in the proximity nucleus): low vs high promptness in managing the diagnosis.

For each of these projects, we selected a variable number of clusters, corresponding to the profile of a person described according to their distinctive traits that were identified according to the behavior and context determinants. Lastly, to conclude on this point, we have to observe that the coding of the traits reproduced the types of information gathered in people's stories (see Chap. 2). Careful readers will have understood that the data coding procedure is a key innovation that opens an entirely new road for data management systems and for enriching behavior data in models.

8.4.2 Large-Scale Experimental Programs

I have shown how it is possible to highlight behavior heterogeneity with regard to the ability to control one's behavior and skillfully orient one's self in each decisional domain. This is done by using observation targeted on the features and types of behavior. Behavior models are based on the full appreciation of heterogeneity (diversity) in everyday life. If the objective of appreciating behavior heterogeneity is taken seriously, then we can start from these models to inform standard sampling methods which, as a group of young researchers uphold in a recent publication, can guarantee large-scale, solid experimental results that can be replicated and generalized.[28] Ecological validity is the absolute priority for behavior design. Hence the need for large-scale experiments based on the value of the intuitions developed in the course of ethnographic research. Above all, there is a need to launch programs of behavior change that consider how to achieve targeted effects on each cluster (see Chaps. 10 and 11).

Behavior design for sustainable innovation aims to produce major effects that go beyond the average of the population. I am referring to targeted effects that can act on each cluster, increasing the ability to control and the each one's relative competence. Experimental effect moderators also have to be identified: they refer to the context variables and mediator effects making it possible to identify causation mechanisms. In every innovation domain and digital transformation, we have to develop a deep understanding of behavior heterogeneity and of its dispositional and situational matrix.

A key feature of behavior design that sets it apart from basic behavior scientific research is that effects are felt in different contexts of human lives. Defining the sustainability challenges (and not only the determinants' types) for each behavior profile is essential for a good strategy of change. For instance, if we take the issue of cancer treatment orientation, then the close environment of the sick person plays a key role in filtering information, developing precautions, and offering the necessary care in seeking diagnostic advice. A timely diagnosis of the potential manageability of some syndrome is essential for prevention. For instance, in metabolic diseases, there is often an issue of self-control, hyperbolic discount, and the difficulty in procrastinating immediate gratification: all of these are made more difficult if there is a household/family tendency to obesity. Preventive medicine programs can help act on individual responsibility just as on situational factors. Eighty people

[28] Bryan et al. [15].

out of a hundred are thought to fail in their specific prevention of manageable chronic disease programs and thus fail to reach their targets because they lack adequate models characterizing pathogenic lifestyles and behavior. How many of people at risk of developing chronic diseases are aware of their mental representations of the scientific knowledge referred to their physical conditions? Which strategies are the authorities implementing beyond generic communication on primary prevention? What are the strategies of good eating and having an active life in each cluster? Are such strategies effective and do they reach all the segments of the population? How can we see that the objectives of a program of systemic change of lifestyles will reach all potential targets? What are the variable parts of a message that have a single meaning and one alone? How can we differentiate and articulate the message?

Large-scale experimental programs are the new frontier of fundamental or basic experimental research.[29] Because of their relatively low cost, for a time, they have been the ambition of the design teams for innovation policies. In conclusion large-scale programs must focus on the intentional design of change, considering the heterogenous effects and the possibility of also proportioning the differential impact it can have. As illustrated in more detail in Part IV, currently there are many ways and means with a range of cost-benefit options. Coded behavior models on a qualitative scale offer unique features (characteristics) and potential to inform large-scale experimental strategies and to adequately calibrate the use of resources for sustainable innovation.

To facilitate change by removing the obstacles to results may make incentive-based measures more effective, for instance, by reducing undesired effects. A differential analysis of situational or structural factors that define the makeup of dispositional determinants is essential to understand the reasons for the ineffectiveness of innovation policies as well as the limited capacity to foresee any possible individual or collective sources of resistance. Furthermore, a clearer definition of the research sampling using behavior models, including descriptive traits, distinctive habits, and structural and contextual determinants will increase the possibility to replicate the research pilot programs on a large scale. By eliciting personal (subjective) experiences and validating behavior models, we can hope to prepare large-scale pilot programs in several cultural contexts. We are dealing with global issues, so we have to develop the same design intentions acting on variables and mediators that have a contextual validity, with control groups and objective measurements. We could establish where (in which domains) sustainable innovation programs should be implemented and which behavior changes can be obtained, with which aims and main players.

[29] See Daniel Kahneman's interview in Edge on so-called adversarial collaboration https://www.edge.org/adversarial-collaboration-daniel-kahneman. March 2022.

Highlights

- Unlike the programs that typically aim to act on the average of the population, sustainable innovation programs must consider the heterogeneity of behaviors and the complexity of moderator variables.
- The general and a-specific nature of the experimental sample means that the macro-effects that can be generated in a controller setting are less probably replicated in the real world.
- Heterogeneity or a range of answers will no longer be considered to prove the experiment has failed, but rather to be the effect of systematic methods.
- Individual and cultural differences in the agentivity as the ability to transform culture and lifestyles is at the origin of the heterogeneity of behaviors.
- Sampling according to ethnographic research principles and resulting from ethnographic studies can be very reliable to support experimental studies.
- Nudging for good improves decisional accuracy in profiles with low SES and low levels of financial and numerical literacy, in relation to their knowledge of the domain as well as pension and insurance choices.
- Behavior models play a key role in channeling design strategies for sustainable innovation.
- The representation of data appropriately organized in models suggest how behavior may evolve in a given knowledge domain according to a perspective.
- Contextualized behavior models can lead to service innovation strategies. Their aim is to enhance behavior control by increasing awareness on how best to use service and digital support.
- Behavior design for sustainable innovation aims to produce major effects that go beyond the average of the population.
- In every innovation domain and digital transformation, a deep understanding of behavior heterogeneity and of its dispositional and situational matrix is to be developed.
- A differential analysis of situational or structural factors that define the makeup of dispositional determinants is essential to understand the reasons for the ineffectiveness of innovation policies as well as the limited capacity to foresee any possible individual or collective sources of resistance.
- A clearer definition of the research sampling using behavior models, including descriptive traits, distinctive habits, and structural and contextual determinants will increase the possibility to replicate the research pilot programs on a large scale.

References

1. McShane, B. B., Tackett, J. L., Böckenholt, U., & Gelman, A. (2019). Large-scale replication projects in contemporary psychological research. *The American Statistician, 73*, 99–105.
2. Kenny, D. A., & Judd, C. M. (2019). The unappreciated heterogeneity of effect sizes: Implications for power, precision, planning of research, and replication. *Psychological Methods, 24*, 578–589.

3. Müller-Wille, S. (2010). Claude Lévi-Strauss on race, history, and genetics. *BioSocieties, 5*(3), 330–347. https://doi.org/10.1057/biosoc.2010.17
4. Lévi-Strauss, C. (2007). Refléxion. In *60 ans d'histoire de l'UNESCO. Actes du colloque international.* UNESCO, 2005 November 16–18 .
5. Lévi-Strauss, C. (1966). *The savage mind.* Weidenfeld and Nicholson.
6. Thunström, L., Gilbert, B., & Ritten, C. J. (2018). Nudges that hurt those already hurting – Distributional and unintended effects of salience nudges. *Journal of Economic Behavior and Organization, 153*(C), 267–282.
7. Zellermayer, O. (1996). *The pain of paying* (Doctoral dissertation). Department of Social and Decision Sciences, Carnegie Mellon University.
8. Kim, J. K., J. H. Yoon, Y. H. Choi and D. Soman (2020), Do text reminders about credit card spending help reduce spending? A quasi-experimental evaluation. Working paper.
9. Hershfield, H. E., Goldstein, D. G., Sharpe, W. F., Fox, J., Yeykelis, L., Carstensen, L. L., & Bailenson, J. N. (2001). Increasing saving behavior through age-progressed renderings of the future self. *Journal of Marketing Research, 48*(SPL), S23–S37.
10. Franklin, B., & Hochlaf, D. (2017). *The global savings gap* (Technical report). International Longevity Centre.
11. Benartzi, S., et al. (2017). Should governments invest more in nudging? *Psychological Science, 28*(8), 1041–1055.
12. Shah, A., Osborne, M., Lefkowitz, J., Fishbane, A., & Soman, D. (2020, November 12). *Can making family salient increase retirement savings? Evidence from a large-scale field experiment.* Available at SSRN: https://ssrn.com/abstract=3460722 or https://doi.org/10.2139/ssrn.3460722
13. Mrkva, K., Posner, N. A., Reeck, C., & Johnson, E. J. (2021). Do nudges reduce disparities? Choice architecture compensates for low consumer knowledge. *Journal of Marketing, 85*, 67–84.
14. Jordan, B. (2012). *Advancing ethnography in corporate environments: Challenges and emerging opportunities*. Left Coast.
15. Bryan, C. J., Tipton, E., & Yeager, D. S. (2021). Behavioral science is unlikely to change the world without a heterogeneity revolution. *Nature Human Behaviour, 5*, 980–989.

Part IV
Accelerating Sustainable Innovation

Abstract We wonder if a future without an economy of restrictions is possible, an ecology without environmentalism, a release from the sense of guilt to fully live one's life. Choices must be made, and the merits of those who are transparent about the objectives they intend to achieve by pursuing innovation strategies must be acknowledged. There is an urgent need to focus on the effectiveness of strategies for behavior change and sustainable innovation (SI). Methodologies accelerating experimental innovation and behavior change programs must support personalized change, understand and implement the heterogeneity of contexts to safeguard diversity, and promote harmony. Policymaking based on the principles of law and increasingly experimental programs are required for the pursuit of synergistic objectives. The results of these experiments can yield key indications for innovation and incentive policies that work. They are the natural fertilizer shaping design strategies aimed at facilitating the individual behaviors and collaboration systemic change.

Being interested means I'm in charge. Being fascinated means that something else is [1].

There is a regrettably large mismatch between the relevance that human, cultural, and behavioral factors have in determining the success or failure of innovation strategies, and the probability that design and behavioral sciences nowadays play a relevant role on strategies implementing innovations. In countries with a high percentage of GDP spent on innovation, trends in company RandD and other research centers' expenditure for innovation show limited capability to integrate humanistic expertise and design within product and service innovation cycles from the very beginning. This is true even in the case of matters that have an environmental and social impact. In most cases, technological expertise prevails and has the last word. The EU offers a note of hope, as nearly all its R&D-funded projects require integrating the technological side of the project with the social science side. Regardless of how mature and standardized geopolitical conditions are in the EU and the world, we need to trace a path for a comprehensive integration of the disciplines of change and innovation, and we must show our determination in hastening the pace of change.

Communication, debates, and publications on the challenges of sustainability convey a sense of urgency that encourages us to improve our lifestyles. However, a plea for responsible behavior is not enough to deal with the urgencies human beings have to address. It is difficult to disentangle oneself without accepting the sense of disconnection and inadequacy that it generates. As we are overwhelmed by the sense of urgency, personal and collective responsibilities blur into each other, today's responsibilities will be inevitably inherited by future generations, and there is a weak boundary between possible answers and the sense of loss that such great challenges entail. As the environmentalist Timothy Morton says, we are dominated by a sense of guilt, fearing that our behavior may have caused climate change, the impoverishment of primary raw materials, and the growing social and economic gap. Morton asks a question to which we can also subscribe to, that is, whether a future free of economical restrictions is possible. Is an ecology without environmentalism possible, can we live to the full and be guilt free? Ecology pushes us beyond standard environmentalism raising the known dilemma on the responsibility of the state, of the elites that rule over us, and on the right to individual freedom.

The debate is at times limited to being in favor or against the criticism of so-called *libertarian paternalism*, a notion pertaining to Thaler and Sunstein's philosophy of law and ethics,[1] a notion that also outlines a political avenue. Libertarian paternalism is mainly for policy makers and can be defined as the responsibility that decision makers have in making up for the limitations of rationality that our daily actions are subjected to. According to the original idea and subsequent modifications, nudge policies affect the order and hierarchy of choices, offering prominence to the choice that gives the person a greater relative advantage, so that it stands out from the others.[2] As Thaler and Sunstein note, libertarian paternalism proposes low-cost interventions aimed at conditioning decisions and preferences, without damaging a person's freedom to refuse the suggested choice. Given that a person's freedom is upheld, law makers take on the responsibility to indicate choices that should generate the greatest positive impact for the individual and for society as a whole.

Those who disagree with political decision makers being entitled to influence the freedom of choice do so raising philosophical and pragmatic objections. According to these critical positions, the deliberate (voluntary) influencing of a person's choice limits the person's rights and freedom to choose their own fate. Furthermore, there is also a practical problem of defining strategies to attain the objectives intended for the person they are addressed to. In other words, we always require specific (targeted) analyses, specific skills to establish what is right, what are the means to verify what should be done, and the right ones to make sure that results are pervasive and lasting. The people upholding these critical positions, prevalent among supporters of ultraliberalism, conclude with a degree of satisfaction that law makers hardly ever have the means to implement this.[3] Hence, according to them, actions that may

[1] Ibid., 2008.

[2] Also see Chap. 4.

[3] For instance, see Pennington [2].

impact on people's behavior and choices are unlawful, arbitrary, and not easily implemented.

We have already widely proved that these criticisms stem from points of view that hardly tolerate or even ignore the evidence of the negative consequences on the societies based on unregulated freedom with no limitations. If the evidence of the limits of individual human rationality (limited willpower, limited self-efficacy, time inconsistency), the fragility of cooperation due to the social dilemma of a collective risk, the limited ability of markets to rebalance inequalities, the tragedy of common goods, and the *tyranny of freedom* have little or no impact, then the appeal not to turn one's gaze elsewhere has failed. Denying evidence is often a means of shielding and hiding well-established interests. It opens enormous gates to organized actions that end by damaging the environment and social cohabitation irreversibly. Actions such as these also undermine the basis of cooperation and participation in the management of the common good raising the question of how we can contrast this destructive tendency. Challenges of sustainability call for the redefinition of the quality of existence and coexistence. It is a major endeavor we are all urgently called to address. Widespread activism aimed at systemic change is a good alternative. It is certainly preferable to doing nothing or yielding to the convergent interests of those who uphold the principle of inalienable unfettered self-determination and consider policies and collaborative actions to improve the quality of life and existence unviable. Widespread activism generates very favorable conditions for behavior designers to be actively involved and implement the aims of sustainable innovation.

Morton, Hillman, and many other philosophers and scientists contemplate the beauty of things and how they come to be. This inevitably flows from a collective commitment contrasting the possibility of exploiting the vulnerability of cooperation and the limitations of human rationality. Although innovation policies play a key role, it is also important to understand that the task cannot solely depend on the policy makers' definitions. Cooperation aimed at favoring the sustainability of individual choices must also involve innovation dynamic forces and their players, yielding economic advantages. I suggest this contribution and the work of those who use innovative strategies should receive societal recognition and appropriate reward. Furthermore, virtuous behavior and collaboration in the defense of the interests of the common good should also be rewarded.

Those who design innovation are directly responsible for those who directly or indirectly use the technological and creative artifacts of innovation. This means there are elements of discontinuity between taking on the responsibility of innovation, favoring the growth of self-determination and cooperation, safeguarding resources and the common good, and refusing to take on such a responsibility. Choices have to be made. The authoritativeness of those who are clear about their aims with innovation strategies must be acknowledged. New methods to assess the impact of innovation need to be developed. It is vital to focus on strategies for behavior change and sustainable innovation. Lastly, thanks to these methods we will be able to test systemic change programs, which is discussed in the pages that follow.

The techniques and methods to positively influence behavior and well-being are functional and in synergy with the aims of sustainable innovation designing. This last section of the book deals with the methods and techniques that behavioral designers and agents of change have to guide service design strategies to facilitate systemic behavior changes. It will inform my underlying interpretation of the debate underway: available techniques and methods to determine a systemic impact using sustainable innovation programs; these characterize a paradigmatic switch in the design function and the synergies among the disciplines of change.

Sustainable innovation design can be best described as deliberate or intentional in its aims, systemic in its objectives, and works in synergy with those who favor policy innovation and change. It is not a mere "technically neutral" approach. One wonders and it is a real question if behavior designers should be the "special" agents of sustainable change because they activate mechanisms of participation and cooperation, as well as widespread activism, and as such they are promoters and agents of change. By facilitating the acceleration of sustainable innovation behavior, designers combine scientific method (systematicity) and design creativity, offering a new interpretation to the challenges we share.

Methods used to accelerate innovation and change experimental programs must support personalized change, understand and implement the diverse nature of contexts (heterogeneity) to safeguard diversity, and favor equality. Anyone relinquishing control over their behavior even for a short time, trusting the product, or the innovative service is not merely trusting the brand of the innovation. They are implicitly also counting on a mediation able to ensure stability and the ability to improve uncertainty and complexity management. It is a very delicate task that, as mentioned, requires a tool box for design science, behavior, and culture change. We can count on policymaking based on the principles of law, but also, increasingly, on experimental programs for synergic aims. The results of these experiments can offer important suggestions for innovation policies and incentives. Above all, they are the nourishment that will help shape design strategies to facilitate systemic change in individual behavior and cooperation. The following pages describe some of the practices and techniques that prove useful in accelerating sustainable innovation programs. Lastly, I will describe suggestions for health and primary prevention, energy consumption, lifestyle, and consumption patterns.

References

1. Morton, T. (2016). *Dark ecology. For a logic of future coexistence*. Columbia University Press.
2. Pennington, M. (2016). Paternalism, behavioral economics, irrationality and state failure. *European Journal of Political Theory*. https://doi.org/10.1177/1474885116647853

Chapter 9
Behavioral Change Design

Nowadays agents of sustainable change have many tools, methods, and techniques at their disposal and this increases the scope and implementation of actions. This chapter illustrates programs to facilitate change and how the evolution of behavior can be strategically integrated within intentional perspectives of sustainable innovation. Sustainable growth programs favor the evolution of behavior and act to improve individual agentivity and cooperation between individuals, groups, and communities.

The techniques and methods we are interested in refer to the aims discussed in the text, focusing on how they can be implemented in practice. Actually implementing is also linked to the skill and elegance, the consistency with the aims of sustainable innovation. Results, their duration, and differential values have to be highlighted. There is a hidden thread that links patterns of sustainable innovation with the patterns of change. Techniques and methods support the knowledge underlying wise actions. In shifting from theory to practice, one has to remember that actions aimed at facilitating behavioral change do not only affect individual behavior determinants as they act on the interactions between behavioral and dispositional determinants on the one hand and social, context, and structural determinants on the other. Effects vary and as a result one has to consider how these variations result in a variety of behavioral patterns.

The effectiveness of techniques and methods is the result of the direct and indirect impact they are able to generate on people's behavior. They may favor homeostatic stability, progressive change of habits and routines, and active adaptation to the circumstances of life. Healthy mental processes as well as agentive and collaborative skills are in fact closely related. These methods must offer clear perspectives references to assess the evolutionary impact of a given action and possibly offer both visualization and quantitative descriptions. The ethical implications of the effects these methods can cause are yet another facet one has to consider when defining the intervention programs' strategic guidelines.

M. Visciola, *Sustainable Innovation*,
https://doi.org/10.1007/978-3-031-18751-3_9

We are clearly interested in understanding the duration, costs and benefits, latency, and the type of effects that techniques and methods facilitating behavior and culture changes can generate. This is why we have to raise some basic questions to lead in defining and carrying out sustainable innovation programs. What results can a behavioral designer expect? How long will the effects the designer wishes to produce last? Will the effects last over time? What heterogeneous (diverse) effects can we expect? What techniques enable us to work on the short and long term? Which cognitive, behavioral, and social effects should be used to attain the aims of systemic change? What steps are required to set up a program of sustainable innovation?

9.1 Changing Behavior

There has been a vast debate on *nudging* ever since it was first described in 2008, and specifically on the political and social legitimacy of the practices that make use of it, on its efficiency, as well as its associated costs and benefits. The debate is still ongoing in the press. The popularity of the term, nudging, is certainly well deserved especially as it has brought behavioral science and economics to the forefront.[1] However, as I believe this book repeatedly proves, it would be reductive to use the definition exclusively and comprehensively every time reference is made to practices aimed at changing behavior. As mentioned, there are several available techniques and we have to make shrewd choices. A detailed description of the underlying techniques is required to better understand the variety of available techniques. The number of techniques points to the versatility of behavioral sciences and to the need to consider the complexities of real life and human culture, as well as the range of environments and experiences. Furthermore, when selecting methods and technologies, we have to have clear objectives of the change we want and defining intentions and strategies of the innovation program strategies.

Techniques can be classified into two large sets: those that act mainly on System 1 (automatic processes) more precisely nudging techniques, kept separate from the techniques that act mainly on System 2 (voluntary processes), otherwise best known as boosting techniques. Members of the Max Plank community have created the definition *boost*, without subscribing in a convinced manner to the dual architectures of behavioral sciences.[2] Despite the necessary *caveats* on the comprehensiveness of dual models,[3] it is more than guesswork to say that boosting are mostly typified by their effects on nonautomatic and voluntary processes (see Table 9.1).

We have discussed at length how nudging techniques can be used in digital applications[4] and more in general in communication practices to increase automatic

[1] See Grüne-Yanoff and Hertwig [1].

[2] See Hertwig and Grüne-Yanoff [2].

[3] See Chap. 1.

[4] See Chap. 4.

Table 9.1 Nudging vs boosting

Basic features	Nudging	Boosting
Relevant cognitive system	Motor-perceptor and decision-making automatisms	Voluntary thought and reasoning mental processes
Duration of effects	Short term	Medium and long term
Target effects	Facilitating choice and preference shaping	Growth of self-efficiency and the ability to deal with difficult and complex situations
Effect duration	Limited but with lasting consequences	Long and with possibly lasting consequences
Type of effects	Accuracy of choice Experienced as fluid Managing uncertainty Managing time pressures Overcoming heuristics and systematic trends leading to errors	Improving self-control Acquiring specific expertise Ability to update competence Ability to integrate different types of information and action
Formats and digital channels	Onboarding modules and systems Filling in online procedures All digital channels	Expert system support AI systems support
Ethical implications	Users may or may not be aware of being influences but has the freedom to refuse suggestions	Users accept support to strengthen their abilities

consent to programs. For instance, they may be modules for organ donation, or campaigns for the donation of a percentage of your tax, automatic savings, automatic registration to job-related insurance policies, or consent to a vaccination program. In all these cases the person is not required to do anything: choice is completed by inertia, without any deliberate action.

Furthermore, nudging techniques are frequently used to personalize the contents of a webpage or a digital solution. By recognizing the visitor's profile, for instance using A/B testing or thanks to registration in the digital archives to manage customer relations, page contents can change to mirror the main aims the visitor has. Alternatively, the content hierarchy can be changed highlighting the meanings and aims that the profile has accessed in that specific area of online services. In all the aforementioned cases, designers consider the mix of behavioral profiles and tailors the information architecture to the specifics of the expected profiles. By activating on the architecture of choices, the designer makes information search easier by reducing the chances of confusing or clouding the user with a host of unorganized information. Furthermore, by reducing conceptual barriers and perceptive obstacles in practice, it makes more possible to reach specific objectives. In other words, it shapes the path users take, helping them to develop intentionality and complete a task. All of this is accomplished though decision and motor-perceptor automatisms.[5] In cases of uncertainty, limited knowledge, or time pressure, the implicit

[5] See Chap. 1.

suggestion—that the designer can highlight with the appropriate signs and signals—improves the user's ability to choose.

Although nudging only acts on cognitive automatisms, nudging techniques can also have a role in education,[6] although it should be said that they are intended for people not to stop and think. At most they can evoke patters and notions the person (who is making the choice) is familiar with. Alternatively, the person may guess the adequacy of the aims and the tasks required. For instance, an "environmentally friendly" (aka ecological) note clearly shows as the person makes the choice such as asking whether one wants a printed receipt at an ATM that reduces print outs by 80% (see Fig. 9.1). A nudge can make the interaction with the interface or with the point of contact with the digital service smoother.

The experience of a particular task can change according to how information is conveyed. Visual supports supplied when a choice has to be made increase the immediate understanding. For instance, a numerical representation in absolute terms makes it easier for the less expert to understand what is needed to complete a task than say giving the figure as a percentage. Another example: if statistics are given with a natural frequency rather than an inference value expressed as a probability, doctors, patients, and students have a better understanding.[7] By simplifying the way, information is presented without prejudicing meaning can facilitate the acquisition of perceptive automatisms and thus improve the understanding of the actions required. These educational expedients are some of the basic nudging-led features.

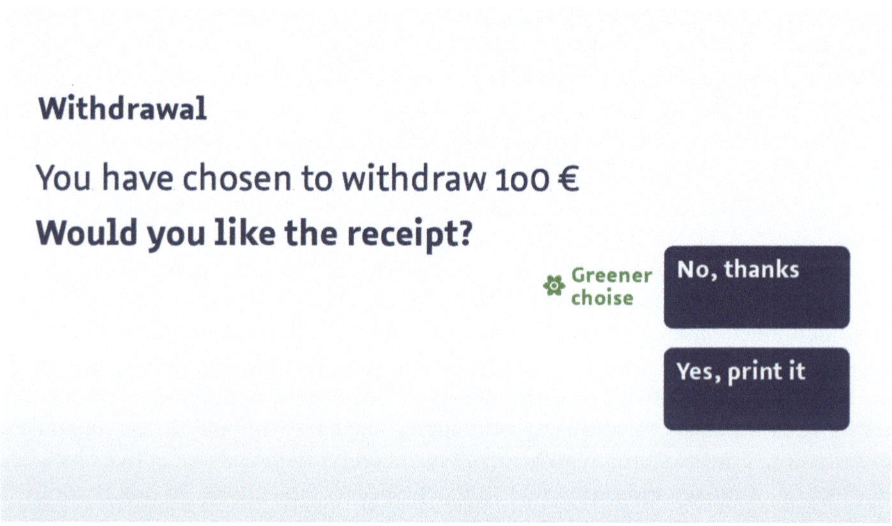

Fig. 9.1 Environmentally friendly nudge to reduce paper receipt printing

[6] Sunstein [3].

[7] Hoffrage et al. [4].

As shown in Table 9.1, booster techniques are aimed at improving voluntary mental processes. The aim is to increase people's skills by boosting their thought and reasoning processes. Even when it is a matter of improving emotional skills such as the ability to recognize one's own or other people's emotions, booster techniques address controlled mental processes. Apparently contrasting systematic trends may require booster activities that are only apparently divergent: for instance, deferring an action to keep fit, such as postponing the fitness exercises and the opposite one, which is indulging in immediate reward rather than a greater future reward, as is the case with lots of purchases for small gratification rather than saving for more gratifying future objectives. In both cases they are heuristics to boost the ability to assess and evaluate, so that the healthier or more informed choice can prevail. For instance, in the case of fitness exercises, knowing a set of exercises to be performed during the day, whether one is with or without exercise equipment, will reduce the trouble associated with going to the gym on a regular basis. Learning physical exercises and developing the habit of exercising persist even when one has not the freedom to decide all one's daily movements during the working week.

Frustration can be dealt with using "flexible" behavior: likewise to enhance saving skills, learning how to itemize one's budget allocations defining goals, and to tell fungible resources from those that are not, one can progressively learn to manage impulse buying. Emotional fulfillment extends as an effect of a better "self"-control. In both cases, acquired heuristics are internalized as action patterns to the point they can be implemented voluntarily without the need for a facilitating external trigger.

Techniques to boost self-control and skills are based on the acquisition of "simple" heuristics or practical advice. These heuristics lead to learning if presented in a practical context that can offer stable points of reference and facilitate the acquisition of appropriate mental models or patterns. Boosting not only facilitates the acquisition of specific skills but also influences the development of subsequent cycles of virtuous learning. For instance, the ability of a person to update their heuristic baggage independently and possibly extend the number of applications is part of a lifestyle that includes gains greater than the ones pursued with the acquisition of heuristics. Learning how to recycle glass, plastic, and paper using a system that makes it possible to allocate each one in its bin improves the household's ability to have more awareness in purchases. A lifestyle consistent with basic choices helps to strengthen the development of healthy and positive habits. In psychology, behavioral economics, and sustainability theories, it is known as the spillover effect.[8] The fall out of results obtained with boosting increases self-efficiency potential and the ability to coordinate one's choices consistently with what initially learnt. By extending it to new abilities and skills, they become habits. Boosting cognitive skills leads to persevering in new habits, updating them, and integrating more complex action and thought cycles. It is the most advanced system we can hope for and follow with

[8] Geiger [5].

behavior modification programs.[9] The duration of the effects is especially important for booster techniques. Unlike techniques aiming at changing behavior that use motor-perceptor and judgment automatisms, techniques to boost voluntary mental processes, thought, and reasoning target pervasive and lasting effects. Furthermore, the aim of these techniques is to produce effects that last beyond boosting, and this is a key difference with nudging (see Table 9.1). While the latter influences choices guiding and possibly correcting an action underway as it develops, boosting impacts on people's ability to develop a description in their minds. These images then turn into habits that make it possible to change choices and preferences, as well as the conditions of a specific context and situation. In other words, nudging manipulates information hierarchies and the architectures of choice. Boosting affects a person's ability to change the image they have of the environment in their minds. It also strengthens their skill in seeking evidence and identifying the relationship among the various pieces of information that lead to choices consistent with their value system.

In a digital context, boosting techniques have a great potential in applications: they can increase a person's skills in managing choices, risks, and decisional uncertainty in everyday life. Since boosting requires the person to cooperate and to be actively involved in implementing an action plan, digital booster technologies are seen as cognitive prostheses that improve the understanding of the action domain. Thanks to automation techniques information and the data underlying behavioral models that include information on the person's profile. As a result, booster techniques can offer a dynamic support to improve behavior control.

As discussed below, these new options raise ethical questions for behavior innovation and change strategies. However, unlike digital environment design that uses nudging, designing competence, or skill, booster aids clearly favor agentivity and responsibility for choices made.

These ideas are further developed in the remaining chapters, which focus on actions aimed at changing behavior in health and energy consumption. The following is a description of the main techniques used in innovation programs for stronger control and cooperation skills.

9.2 Taxonomy of Booster Techniques

Following the approach I used in the first part of this book, I have classified techniques to increase self-control and the resulting agentive and cooperative skills through competence into three categories. These are methods to strengthen change: (a) individual and group behavioral change, (b) proximal or situational context, and (c) environmental or structural context.

---

[9] See Chaps. 10 and 11.

Table 9.2 Methods to boost behavioral changes in individuals and groups

Type	Technique	Goals
Participatory	Engagement and orientation Cooperative learning and group building	Facilitate orientation skills Promote cooperation
Goal oriented	Self-determination assessment Motivational assessment Selecting values and beliefs Self-monitoring	Assessing propensity for agentivity Understanding the will to change Identifying objectives and hierarchies of aims Consolidating results
Skill oriented	Selection and planning of skills Learning journey Selection and planning aims Tailoring aim levels	Define and select hierarchies of skills Identify learning paths Planning progression of aims Defining relative importance of aims according to need
Booster	Personalized cycles of analytical reporting	Promoting a continuous improvement and internalization of habits

As shown in Table 9.2, there are four types of actions to enhance individual or group or community changes. The *Participatory* category includes techniques to progressively favor the ability to find one's way (orientation) in the community, and more generally in civil society, to understand the values, goals, incentives, its members, operational potential, and obligations or duties. Participation has to be defined whatever the action program to facilitate and promote a change of behavior in individuals or the community needs, for instance taking part in a workshop for participated design, webinar, attending specialized subgroups, and the strategies to foster individual and group goals.

The main use of engagement and orientation techniques is to help participants understand the mix of community members, to promote and coordinate their ability, and to cooperate in groups and communities. Participants must feel in control, which facilitates participation considering potential differences of special interests and preferences. In communities of purpose such as energy or patient communities, digital solutions allowing ongoing participation and spontaneous or guided networks are coming into their own.[10]

Goal-oriented actions mainly refer to monitoring and assessment techniques to establish the person's or the group's level of skill, ability to establish relationship openness to change, and relative will to engage in change. This is why indicators able to identify obstacles, resources, incentives, and encouragement must be identified. For instance, health wearables for *augmented* or *quantified self* are known and used to monitor and use the appropriate sensors to asses vital signs such as weight, body volume, heartbeat, quality of sleep, calory consumption, nutrients, relative age of tissues, and so on. It has become possible to monitor and assess hundreds of parameters selected for the purpose and integrated in dashboards for their visualization and subsequent identification of corrective solutions. Programs can be guided

[10] *Patient Like Me*: https://www.patientslikeme.com/. Also see Chaps. 10 and 11.

in defining goals and purpose hierarchies, thanks to technologies for sign monitoring. In later steps of program development, they can also be used to consolidate results. As for the *skill-oriented* type, one must differentiate between (a) selecting and planning skills, (b) identifying learning trajectories, and (c) selecting and personalizing goals.

For instance, health literacy is one of the most demanding challenges regardless of the country's GDP. With customized technologies, it is possible to catch up after years of limited information and increase health literacy. There are promising opportunities to define and plan pathways to help members of the community to become active and improve lifestyles and health conditions.

The same can be said for energy communities: better skills in understanding and managing energy consumption is but the beginning of a path to literacy and to mastering the production, storage, and manage renewable energy produced in a building. Potentially digital technologies can easily facilitate actions aimed at accruing the technological and social skills that are usually in the hands of centralized energy service managers. The values that solutions can offer to increase the level of awareness in end users' actions is the biggest novelty in sustainable energy programs. Technologies aimed at customizing are based on simulations using ontologies and analysis to identify deviations from reference models. Furthermore, simulation makes it possible to design systems that use *digital twin*[11] technologies so as to use data models and their projections to assess some consequences of consumer behavior.

Lastly, boosters (see Table 9.2) can offer personalized cycles of personalized analytical reporting to explain the results of action programs, assess their effectiveness, and point to any advice to: (a) correct the program, (b) modify objectives if possible, (c) reward constancy in following the program. As in the case of attitude changing boosters, potentially digital solutions are very promising in promoting ongoing improvement and the progressive internalization of new positive habits by boosting.

Table 9.3 lists the main techniques aimed at empowering context changing activities where individual and collective actions take place. There are four types of situational change techniques. Techniques based on *simulations* are now possible, thanks to current investments on behavioral data gathering. These techniques make risk assessment possible, and specifically proximity risks refer to how proximal spatial distance and risky events influence the perception of risk. The better the person or the community perceive the spatial proximity of a risk factor—for instance, the possibility of being affected by decisions on no longer using fossil fuels is the increase in fossil fuel prices—the more they are open to adopt decisions to switch to alternative energy sources. These techniques raise awareness on the risk factors with a view to facilitate resulting actions and decisions.

[11] These are systems that emulate the overall processes of a physical entity, even a complex one, using a software system. This can refer to an industrial complex, or even a plant. The black box of a plane or fly-by-wire is an example of a digital twin.

Table 9.3 Methods to boost proximal context (situational) changes

Type	Technique	Goals
Simulation	Assessing proximity risks Role models of proximity	Understanding risk factors Understanding and learning proximity roles
Deconditioning	Altering proximity trigger factors Plans/cycles to replace habits and routines	Learning what has to be changed in the context Learning new habits
Community centered	Proximal similarity analysis Analyzing cultural and community assets Analyzing proximal contact points developing communities and models of social participation	Understanding reference models Facilitate access to resources Facilitate access to communities of purpose
Social support	Economic support models Proximity services	Support transition phases

Inside a community, proximity roles enable behavioral change and evolution toward sustainable models. With the help of decision support technologies contribute to simulation techniques to gain a better grasp of the community's opportunities in managing shared resources and to improve cooperation within and among communities. As we will see in Chap. 10, federated energy communities are emerging, making it possible to finetune proximity roles in connected communities, with major effects on the spread of new behavioral and decisional standards.

Deconditioning techniques are used to identify variables that have the greatest negative impact on people and communities and enable them to take on an active and collaborative role, eliminating or reducing the impact. Deconditioning techniques are especially important in ensuring ecosystem resilience and improve their stability. For instance, the absence of fresh food or low-calory nutrients, or the absence of proximity services can have a marked negative impact on some strata of the population with lasting negative effects and possible passive maladaptive behavior. Targeted context analysis plays a major relevant role in transforming the environment with creative solutions, enabling the establishment of new habits.

Community-centered actions are aimed at facilitating: (a) the access to resources, (b) the growth of the community, and (c) the understanding of reference behavior models. Techniques used to analyze cultural and community assets consolidate and develop community values, favoring inclusion and participation. The analysis of the points of proximal contact makes it possible to determine innovation opportunities and increase the level of participation in managing the values and assets of the community. The innovative management of common environments and spaces reduces the sense of neglect and improves the perception of security of the space. Community sustainable innovation support programs are aimed at improving the understanding of reference models and the creation of specific purpose and interest groups using techniques for community development.

Lastly, sustainable innovation programs must nearly always have *social support* techniques with funding to support the transition phases.

Table 9.4 Methods to boost the change of an environmental (structural) context

Type	Technique	Goals
Systemic	Analyzing barriers and points of conflict using the social norms approach (SNA)	Solutions and overcoming barriers Critical overview of norms and policies
Participatory	Problem-solving workshop Mobilizing social networks Developing alternatives with diverging outcomes Self-disclosure	Involvement in problem-solving programs Developing capacities and impact Developing new solutions Identifying intentions and community (territorial) goals
Scenario-based evidence	Codeveloping scenarios Supplying evidence and awareness	Develop scenarios of systemic change Promote widespread awareness

Table 9.4 shows methods to boost environmental or structural context changes. The structural level refers to the possibility of acting in a *systemic* manner with barrier and conflict point analysis. One of the preferred paths for systemic barrier analysis is an ethnographic research conducted systematically within communities (see Chap. 2). Analysis methods may require work groups to develop critical thinking and facilitate *parallel* thinking as happens in role simulations and as happens for example in the *Six Thinking Hats*.[12] One of the aims of systemic analysis is a critical overview of standards and policies, both to identify (frequent) community members' false perceptions on standards[13] and to facilitate a critical understanding of standards and policies with the help of experts. The latter have to be standards' experts and can act as facilitators if they have analytical behavioral skills.

Participative techniques are also very useful in action programs aiming to change the environmental context. In addition to the traditional participatory workshop techniques in problem solving and those to produce new ideas, such as master plans for innovative services (see Chap. 2), we should also refer to those social media use to mobilize and organize purpose networks. Lastly, participatory techniques are essential in self-determination and self-revelation when defining intentions and aims of territorial (community) transformation.

Evidence-based scenarios pursue the aim of developing: (a) scenarios of systemic behavior change and (b) action-based widespread awareness. Codesigning of scenarios with the help of drawings, photos, and parts of evidence leads to an immediate visualization of which behavioral effects are sought by introducing sustainable change acceleration programs.

[12] de Bono [6].

[13] Dempsey et al. [7].

9.3 Programs to Accelerate Sustainable Innovation Programs

The premises for ambitious transdisciplinary programs are being laid down in Europe to accelerate sustainable innovation within the next 5–10 years. We have to look beyond the segmentation generated by the thousands of public research projects granted to universities, polytechnics, research centers, companies of all shapes and sizes, institutions, and foundations on innovation. The large EU projects have a propensity for technology and a relative segmentation of programmatic objectives, despite having spread technology-based innovation and greatly promoted integration. Accelerating sustainable innovation calls to progress beyond a mere technological approach and integrating it with social and behavioral approaches in the framework of more resources earmarked for innovation. The aim is to rise to challenges of sustainable development.[14] Currently, publicly funded EU projects must clearly state how the positive effect is attained through dissemination, participation, and technological evidence. Furthermore, only projects that can prove they have fruitfully integrated humanities and social sciences (Social Sciences and Humanities—SSH) and do not cause any significant harm (Do No Significant Harm—DNSH) are considered. In view of a complete integration of sustainable development programs and of the agenda for an active protection of the environment, the EU strategic priority dictates that 25% of available resources for each of the large research programs should be earmarked for the integration of environmental matters (see the EU Green Deal). The percentage rises to about 40% for the economic recovery and resilience programs. Another positive feature is that for the first time the role of information on product sustainability and consumer awareness is highlighted. The idea is that consumers should become able to make more aware choices and play an active role in the ecological transition. The underlying idea is that if all information on services and products is reliable, comparable, and verifiable, then consumers can make more sustainable decisions. Furthermore, correct information reduces the risk of an environmentally misleading marketing, aka *green washing*.

We might wonder whether the EU approach, which I have just outlined, is enough to activate the European brain capital. Undeniably it is the right path but the next step will have to be more convincing. First of all more practical specification on how to integrate Social Sciences and Humanities within technological strategies must be outlined. Sustainable innovation as described so far calls for a change of paradigm: it will have to be at the service of human beings to favor positive agentivity. Human capability to cooperate and deal with sustainability challenges must be boosted, and DNSH must be turned into something positive. This is why funded projects should go beyond established interests and become the starting point for a cascade of other projects to replicate the positive impact documented in the course

[14] In the EU, it means a programmatic view for the energy and digital transformation in the EU Green Deal, recovery and resilience plans, see https://ec.europa.eu/info/strategy_en

of the funded project. In fact, the strategy should require supplying the evidence that the intentions to change behavioral and cultural change were actually implemented and showed a significant impact.

Bearing the above in mind, we could suggest that funding applications for R&D projects should be assessed according to the sustainable development framework, that is the *Sustainable Innovation Readiness Ladder* (SIRL). Currently, EU-funded public projects are assessed according to the technological progress the projects indicate they can introduce. EU technological innovation projects are measured according to a scale of technological readiness scale, adapted from the NASA and aerospace industry system, the so-called TRL (*Technology Readiness Level*).[15] There are nine levels and the top of the scale is reached when innovation is tested in an operation environment having had a competitive and marketable production (Table 9.5).

In terms of sustainable innovation, competition should be aimed at attaining significant progress in people's lifestyle in their ability to improve well-being and sustainability of consumption behavior, while considering the different levels of readiness to change routine and behavior. Additional questions to be answered are:

Table 9.5 Technological Readiness Level (TRL) vs Sustainable Innovation Readiness Ladder (SIRL)

TRL level	Description	SIRL level	Description
TRL 1	Basic principles observed	SIRL 1	Basic principles observed
TRL 2	Developed the notion of technology	SIRL 2	Develop innovation intentions for each cluster of clients
TRL 3	Proof of concept validated	SIRL 3	Proof of concept with personalized functions
TRL 4	Lab-validated technology	SIRL 4	Concept validation in an experimental setting
TRL 5	Technology validated in an industrially relevant areas	SIRL 5	Integrated concept in a real-life setting
TRL 6	Technology demonstrated in an industrially relevant environment	SIRL 6	Concept tested and proved in a living lab
TRL 7	System prototype testing of an operative system	SIRL 7	Advanced concept with new functions and services in a real-life environment
TRL 8	Complete and qualified system	SIRL 8	Complete validated and localized
TRL 9	Actual system tests in an operative context such as competitive production and marketing	SIRL 9	Replicable system

[15] See the Technology Readiness Levels (TRL), HORIZON 2020—WORK PROGRAMME 2018–2020 General Annexes, Extract from Part 19—Commission Decision C(2017)7124. https://ec.europa.eu/research/participants/data/ref/h2020/other/wp/2018-2020/annexes/h2020-wp1820-annex-g-trl_en.pdf

Can the projects prove they have raised the level of readiness of a community in terms of its energy footprint? What percentage of members of the community have reached maximum levels of non-sustainability? How can they progress toward adjacent proximal levels? This would lead to a system assessing the reputation of innovation programs according to the intentions stated. They would be rewarded by the market according to the successes they actually attain (see Table 9.5).

In conclusion, the assessment of TRL technological maturity is suited to measure the development and the technological capacity of an investment. It is a perspective that satisfies the business world, which is the driving force of capitalistic growth, the same one which is currently admired and imitated worldwide. A traditional user-centered design is compatible with this approach: the end-to-end experience of the digital and technological service contact points is a people-centered approach both in the front and back parts of the service. The designer's task is to study the so-called *Customer Journey*, which is the process where the interaction between service and clients takes place. Other aspects designers have to bear in mid are how it can be rethought and innovated in all touch points, solving features that lead to dissatisfaction, and taking the opportunity to offer customers more new value. Design must focus on moments that matter for the client and offer an engaging, extraordinary, and memorable solution (also see Chaps. 1 and 4). This is a business-oriented innovation.

The behavioral perspective proposes to go beyond this approach and to design experiences that allow to achieve mutual benefits ("win-win") between the consumer and the service provider. According to this perspective, the value of the service is disclosed as a function of the innovation goals. These must be adapted to the customer's level of readiness and maturity to favor their evolutionary growth. Value disclosure is symmetric to the degree of diversity (heterogeneity) expressed by clients. Designers will have to identify clusters according to level of competence (expertise) and domain maturity to design customized services and contents. This means defining fiduciary programs whereby the customer develops with the supplier and develops a greater awareness of their consumption and choices. According to this definition, clients are available to entrust their data and information to the service that becomes a sort of fiduciary to trust as a new path is sought (SIRL Level 5). If we refer to the SIRL readiness framework, we could push it to Level 7, where the initial integrated proved concept tested in a real-life context such as a living lab (Level 6) is extended to all the main expected functions.

Lastly, the social perspective is aimed at assessing the impact of innovation with the possibility to perform repeated measures over time with monitoring and localization systems. This approach offers a clear illustration of social and behavioral opportunities on a scale of innovation in a given industry or service. Research projects could intentionally favor progressive homodynamic processes so that people would have the opportunity to switch choices and preferences and migrate toward more sustainable models. It is the most advanced outlook in terms of experimenting and implementing localized and validated solutions to deal with the challenges of change according to a systemic approach. When we refer to the SIRL framework, we could reach readiness Level 9 in terms of the social impact, since we have reference systems that set the guidelines to replicate on a wider scale the results of experimental action programs for sustainable innovation.

Social impact of sustainable innovation takes onboard social differences and the gaps that need to be closed with adequate resources and strategies. In fact, low-cost strategies of change are no longer enough to meet sustainability challenges. More generous strategies are called for. The large public and private investments will have to be used in a more appropriate manner in the coming years. It will also be essential to find new forms of funding to carry out courageous pilot experiments with a view to changing risk behaviors. Pilot schemes will have to be performed over time, and in several geopolitical spheres to create the basis to replicate them on a large scale. Sustainable innovation strategies based on intervention programs with nudging and more so boosting must enable us to internalize innovation costs and especially the costs of positive externalities. Finally, digital transformation programs can be significantly guided to the difficult task of changing our consumer behavior and culture in terms of using resources for our well-being.

Highlights

- Techniques can be classified into two large sets: those that act mainly on System 1 (automatic processes) more precisely nudging techniques, kept separate from the techniques that act mainly on System 2 (voluntary processes), otherwise best known as boosting techniques.
- Techniques to boost self-control and skills are based on the acquisition of "simple" heuristics or practical advice.
- Boosting affects a person's ability to change the image they have of themselves as well as of the environment in their minds.
- Methods to strengthen change involve (a) individual and group behavioral change, (b) proximal or situational context, and (c) environmental or structural context.
- More practical specification on how to integrate Social Sciences and Humanities within technological strategies must be outlined.
- Funding applications for R&D projects should be assessed according to the sustainable development scale, that is the *Sustainable Innovation Readiness Ladder* (SIRL).
- The value of the service is disclosed as a function of the innovation goals. These must be adapted to the customer's level of readiness and maturity to favor their evolutionary growth.
- Value disclosure is symmetric to the degree of diversity (heterogeneity) expressed by clients.
- Social impact of sustainable innovation takes onboard social differences and the gaps that need to be closed with adequate resources and strategies.
- Sustainable innovation strategies based on intervention programs with nudging and more so boosting must enable us to internalize innovation costs and especially the costs of positive externalities.

References

1. Grüne-Yanoff, T., & Hertwig, R. (2016). Nudge versus boost: How coherent are policy and theory? *Minds and Machines, 26*(1–2), 149–183.
2. Hertwig, R., & Grüne-Yanoff, T. (2017). Nudging and boosting: Steering or empowering good decisions. *Perspectives on Psychological Science, 12*(6), 973–986. https://doi.org/10.1177/1745691617702496
3. Sunstein, C. (2021). *Sludge: What stops us from getting things done and what to do about it.* MIT Press.
4. Hoffrage, U., Lindsey, S., Hertwig, R., & Gigerenzer, G. (2000). Communicating statistical information. *Science, 290*(5500), 2261–2262. https://doi.org/10.1126/science.290.5500.2261
5. Geiger, S. J. (2022). Pro-environmental behavior spill over. *Nature Review Psychology, 1*, 191. https://doi.org/10.1038/s44159-022-00043-1
6. de Bono, E. (1985). *Six thinking hats: An essential approach to business management.* Little, Brown, and Company.
7. Dempsey, R. C., McAlaney, J., & Bewick, B. M. (2018). A critical appraisal of the social norms approach as an interventional strategy for health-related behavior and attitude change. *Frontiers in Psychology, 9*, 2180.

Chapter 10
Energy Consumption and Sustainable Innovation

Recently, a committee of 20 experts selected by a network of the most authoritative European energy research institutes released a report, which has become a point of reference for the scientific community and policy makers.[1] For the first time in the history of innovation, a meeting of technical experts agreed that the variable *energy consumption behavior* is comparable to technical innovation in controlling the complex issue of the energy consumption environmental footprint. The informative report states that "… *the potential emissions reductions to be achieved by targeting behaviour can be very large. Policies should not view households as passive recipients loosely connected to climate change, but as active participants whose lifestyles play a central (and disruptive) role in contributing to energy and climate problems* …. And in the last pages of the report … *Therefore, behaviour can be just as important as new technologies and would deserve a much stronger role in the policy framework of the Green Deal*."[2]

The statement is a remarkable step forward in itself. However, it could prove a mere rhetorical exercise unless there are clear policy lines on how to facilitate the energy transition, leading to sustainable consumption forms. As we shall see, despite their good intentions, incentive-based policies can at times be short sighted: the absence of guiding principles and monitoring systems channeling behavioral changes greatly curtails the potential impact of technological innovation. It would be clearer if innovation policies flowed from calculable aims to assess the breadth and duration of behavioral changes that technological innovation can generate. This is true for any strategy promoting the energy transition throughout the economy.

Any fossil fuel reduction strategy adopted entails substantial costs for society when plentiful energy resources are discontinued, as is the case of coal and gas. In the next phase of globalization, switching to renewable energy resources

[1] Science Advice for Policy by European Academies (SAPEA) [1].

[2] Op. Cit. pp. 20 and 132.

M. Visciola, *Sustainable Innovation*,
https://doi.org/10.1007/978-3-031-18751-3_10

necessarily calls for mitigating measures such as sharing investment costs. In other words, the international community should share the burden of costs and the positive externalities ensuing following the discontinuation of resources that severely impact on the ecological footprint. In general, this holds true regardless of the incentive policy. When considering the positive effects of a systemic change, one has to opt for choices with a good chance (potential) of success even when pursuing gradual change. There will inevitably be reactions and consequences that could jeopardize success if policies are aimed at optimizing effects without mitigating the negative consequences for some or all of the geopolitical ecosystems and sharing the rewards from the overall positive consequences. Furthermore, these policies have to be governed. The EU's recent choice to not allow new gasoline and diesel cars on the market after 2035 is consistent with this approach. Unlike the past, it means massive investments in sustainable means of transport, thus facilitating mechanisms of choice in the market focusing on models and brands that are more consistent with an ecological vision of a progressive energy change for the transport system.

The chances of a positive impact on behavior are limited in the absence of system tactics able to place formal or substantial barriers to (directly or indirectly) limit bounded rationality. An indirect manner to exploit bounded rationality is to use narratives that focus on individuals and on individual responsibilities in choosing and pursuing a status quo in innovation policies. Global lobbies and multinationals have always worked on what Charter and Lowenstein have named them the "*i-Frame*" (individual-frame) superimposing it on the "*s-Frame*" (system-frame).[3]

By focusing on solutions that entrust individual responsibility with the ability to make coherent and sustainable choices, we become accomplices with those who have an interest in maintaining the status quo and distance themselves from policies and solutions that safeguard the interest and the common good over that of few. As the two researchers highlighted, there is a widespread feeling to blame individual choices rather than the system-based origins of the choices among behavioral experts who lean toward individually based solutions.

In the case of energy transformation, the chance of accelerating an improvement in consumption inevitably calls for strict policies acting at the one time on prices and incentives, so as to make fossil fuels more expensive. Regulations also have to be used as a lever to limit the distorted use of limited resources, as well as energy production and stocking efficiency. The present book strongly supports this point of view. However, relying merely on the free will of people to focus more on consumption models is ineffective, a mere exercise, and an end unto itself.

The conclusions reached by studies to prove the adaptability of people show that simple actions, such as the choice of a low-consumption light bulb (such as LEDs), driving slowly, lowering house temperature in winter, can lead to a 20% or more reduction in individual consumption levels.[4] Furthermore, *Horizon Technological*

[3] Chater and Loewenstein [2].

[4] Laitner et al. [3].

Innovation Programme research indicates behavior adaptability following heating patterns in offices, an example using the appropriate contract clauses[5] or by changing the building's regulations.[6,7] However, the drive for technological innovation often ends up with policy recommendations that refer to people's spontaneous ability to adapt. In brief, whatever angle you look at it from, energy saving and efficiency lack directions on how to promote people's will to develop expertise, their active monitoring, and a better system control.

10.1 Behavioral Change Programs for Efficiency and Energy Saving

Technological investments for the digitalization of the energy sector have also led to the tendency to solve energy efficiency issues with complete automation. This enables buildings to maintain steady levels of energy consumption by adopting policy-managed steady supplies, which are based on local and national laws and policy recommendations. However, neither policy experts nor engineers nor developers seriously pushed for a critical assessment of advanced automation until it became clear that solutions were circumvented: behavior was not consistent with recommendations and left the dwellers of highly automated buildings displeased, paradoxically increasing energy waste. The results of the research are eye-opening: the project compares a trade-off between temperature settings changed at the residents' request and those they could generate locally in the hot and cold seasons using their thermostats.[8] Requests for set temperature variations increased 24-fold when residents had the chance to reset their thermostats compared to the situation where they had to formally apply to the building team in charge of controlling the automated building. Surprisingly, the temperature regulations by the building's team were higher (or lower) than the ones the residents had made with their home thermostats. In other words, the mediation of a control group failed to solve the problem of energy waste if a degree of flexibility is afforded to individuals. A growing consciousness of energy problems is generally making people more aware of the need to bring together behavior and technology-based solutions and technology requirements. As a result, energy saving and efficiency programs are in practice becoming programs to favor behavioral change. Acting on the awareness that appropriate behavior is required to produce energy savings and efficiency is only the first step on a path that will require years of research and large-scale applications.

For these programs to attain their ambitious objectives, efficiency and energy saving will have to be kept separate: efficiency objectives concern the complex

[5] For instance, CityOpt, see http://www.cityopt.eu/

[6] HOPE, see https://hope-project.net/?page_id=2andlang=en

[7] Dubois et al. [4].

[8] Gunay et al. [5].

regulation of supplies, planning, production, stocking, distribution, and sale of energy for each energy source, and then manage all the sources. Energy requirements fluctuate throughout the year and according to the time of day which means suppliers have to see to it that demand never exceeds supply capacity. Energy efficiency, with an aim to progressively replace fossil energy sources with renewable ones, has to address special political and geopolitical issues, as the Eastern European war has highlighted, as well as strategic problems in order to maintain the independence of a nation state and the principles of democratic freedom. Energy saving aims instead focus on the need to reduce waste in a systematic and selective manner.

By reducing overall energy needs, the transition toward low-impact renewable energy is swifter. Efficiency targets do not include the actual possibility of end customers to deliberately influence the choices energy suppliers make.[9] On the other hand, consumers can work with energy-saving targets. The question is therefore how we can facilitate the transition to a greater awareness, which is the necessary trigger for behavior to shift toward consistent choices, that is, *active awareness* (see also Chap. 5).

Let us see what active awareness means for energy: it is the actual possibility for consumers to act consistently with the awareness on the use of energy and therefore developing habits that lead to energy saving. A documented case in point is how active awareness is facilitated when the user is not billed directly. This is the case for students' houses, holiday residences, public and private accommodation, and private buildings used for work where the consumer does not pay according to actual consumption levels. In this case it is difficult to use price incentives to facilitate energy-saving behavior. However, a study by a group of Australian researchers shows that in-the-context reproaches referring to trust and the generosity of these establishments were enough. Measures were enough to reduce consumption at peak times.[10]

The path from a state of awareness to active awareness behavior is strewn with hurdles as it requires consistent information supports to monitor consumption in real time.

Smart meters have become so common that it is now technically possible to retrofit accommodation and connect to the interfaces of the suppliers' meters. Real time consumption of (mobile) devices is a last-mile operation. However, barriers stopping the Do It Yourself solutions have to be removed: for instance, a low-cost tool kit should be made available and installed automatically. If well thought out, these devices can process software to make the information visually accessible with data navigation function. Lastly, the data gathering technological infrastructure for ongoing consumption monitoring can be another obstacle. It has to be optimal to encourage residents to start and keep monitoring consumption and saving. Once the

[9] While wanting to choose the energy supplier that best matches the green energy efficiency vision with care, clean energy feeds into the undifferentiated energy grid and thus no supplier is able to facilitate the consumer's pondered choice of energy source.

[10] Jorgensen et al. [6].

above-described barriers have been removed, then most difficult albeit more amusing part of the active awareness programs begins, that is getting people engaged.

10.2 Strategies to Engage Consumers in Behavior Changing Programs

Over the past decade, Horizon 2020, known as *Horizon Europe* since 2021, an innovation framework program has funded a host of projects aimed at promoting consumption awareness to favoring energy-saving behaviors. For instance, GAIA (Green Awareness in Action)[11] aimed to cut energy consumption in schools by 15% in three countries—Sweden, Greece, and Italy—by promoting energy efficiency culture in educational buildings and getting schools to compete. The GreenSoul project (Persuasive Eco-awareness for User Engagement through Networked Data Devices)[12] pursues energy saving in public buildings using persuasive technologies.

Underlying the projects, the idea that automation can always make up for users' carelessness. If and when users "forget" to follow the advice to reduce energy consumption, then the automatic systems are alerted and act in the event of identified energy waste.

There are another two projects that share the same premises: *Socialpower*,[13] a Swiss project intended to establish competition among communities in managing energy saving, and *Tribe*[14] with a platform to encourage *serious* social games, promoting energy-saving culture.

The above and other similar projects developed in Europe and elsewhere until 2020 were considered first-generation programs both in terms of the change it inspires and in terms of its aims. They were projects attempting to probe how people reacted to energy-saving awareness on public spaces, presuming that games such as competitions among communities could help engagement in these practices.

Making citizens more involved in the ongoing correct management of energy resources is one of the main, if not the most, awkward problems of energy transformation. I believe the EU-funded "enCOMPASS" project is one of the most promising steps forward after the first generation.[15] Unlike other projects, this one clearly separates the technical aims from the scientific and social ones. Furthermore, it combines energy saving with energy comfort, modulating behavioral requirements according to incentives and other factors of the context organized in data

[11] http://gaia-project.eu/index.php/it/gli-obiettivi-di-gaia/

[12] Casado-Mansilla et al. [7].

[13] http://www.socialpower.ch/index.php/toolbox-de/

[14] www.tribe-h2020.eu

[15] https://www.encompass-project.eu/

gathering.[16] The project can be considered a good beginning and a point of reference for the new generation projects. Some of the naive premises of the first-generation project have to be abandoned: we have to act on the human factor in the complex sphere of energy consumption. Clearly, education and awareness, which were the foci of the interventions and technological solutions, are only the premises to engage members of the community on energy-saving policies. The following ingredients have to be integrated and modulated: (a) engagement, (b) incentives, and (c) offers able to address the range and mix of behaviors. In the coming 5–10 years, projects will have to engage users in active solutions, showing that their socio-technical solutions are able to introduce stable lasting consumption patterns.

Engagement models, incentives, and the processes (dynamics) are the three enablers of change in developing sustainable patterns of energy use to ensure user compliance to behavior change programs despite the range of profiles. Since we are referring to the engagement of residents and energy users in active awareness programs,[17] engagement models must consider at least four factors:

(i) participant value systems;
(ii) behavior drivers;
(iii) engagement measuring tools; and
(iv) duration required to keep engagement going until such time as when routines and habits have not set in and stabilized energy saving aims over time.

Enabling factors must be articulated according to the features of the program of change.

The value system makes it possible to identify the language register and the priorities used to promote the energy-saving objectives that each group, individual, or community intends to pursue. The first step is to analyze the objectives, identify and suggest practical actions to enact the change processes: for instance, the perception of short- and long-term benefits, subjective and situational obstacles to attain targets, inclination and readiness to stick to objectives, the actual possibility of non-intrusive energy consumption monitoring of each power point, appliance, and device in the house such as *Non-Intrusive Appliance Load Monitoring* (NIALM).[18] All of them need to be defined and modulated according to the specific and incremental objectives agreed in the pilot project, and they will lead the large-scale programs.

Engagement factors concern the rules and conditions needed to facilitate adherence to the programs of change. We are referring to each member's readiness to accept the program and to define specific objectives for each level, and how consumers intend to achieve them. Prochaska and Di Clemente's trans-theoretical approach has been widely used to define the steps of readiness to change and were

[16] Koroleva et al. [8].

[17] Unlike typical engagement interventions that do not set energy-saving goals and ways to achieve them, here we refer exclusively to engaging consumers in programs to systematically improve their consumption habits.

[18] Hart [9].

we to adopt the method,[19] we could identify three phases: *preparation*—when the intention to participate in an active awareness program develops; *action*, which corresponds to the actual experimental phase in applying the program; and *monitoring* that is when behaviors can be measured on a scale and are therefore comparable and can be monitored.

Thanks to the behavior drivers' definition one can establish and agree on how to manage any unexpected interruptions or discontinuation of any of the program's steps. For instance, any interruptions in the *action* phase can be managed by reducing saving targets to avoid a drop in motivation and prevent participants from giving up. During *monitoring*, it might be necessary to modify consumption control tools. In *preparation*, the knowledge developed in the first-generation programs—such as practical guides, video-clips with short essays, and educational demos—and the projects mentioned in this chapter will prove useful.

Digital tools are the best suited to monitor engagement models in the context of an experimental program of active awareness as they enable monitoring of consumption and the success of the active saving program. In this context, we have to measure how useful ongoing energy consumption monitoring is for the various user types. Once identified the consumption parameters we wish to monitor, then they must be visualized in a user-friendly easy-to-use format so as to overcome the technical barriers with data navigation systems, information with trends, and deviation from targets. These functionalities are essential to stabilize behaviors. This is especially true for notifications that must be designed as recommendations, suggestions, and personalized (tailored) tips. All the cases that may constitute a management risk, caused by incidentals during the program, should be considered to overcome any impasse. This means that the monitoring tools for behavioral change programs require software *engines* and algorithms able to analyze, remind users of specific targets or establish new ones, and send personalized messages on trends. The transparency of consumption algorithms is paramount when trying to establish trust with participants and lasting participation in active awareness programs. These algorithms are mainly thought of to offer the energy supplier with flexibility in management: they need to be tailored to consumers' needs for transparency.

Lastly, the duration of the behavior modification programs has been decided empirically and according to the scope of the targets. Since we still lack yardsticks to measure active awareness programs, pilot programs have to be used as the foundations of large-scale projects. In a matter of few weeks, it may become a motor perceptive and judgement automatism. However, it may take months before completing the entire cycle, which covers all the functions and activities of the three phases—*preparation*, *action*, and *monitoring*. Pilot projects should be able to set the time range to establish energy-saving habits with a good degree of accuracy, which is why it is best to identify the type of incentives that can determine the success of the active awareness.

[19] Prochaska and DiClemente [10].

Unquestionably, active awareness incentives are the enabling factor to develop creatively. Overall, the more incentives are the result of mixing economic, cultural, and environmental features, marketing, and fidelization, the easier and more acceptable joining the programs, thus consolidating the chance of getting good results. *Economic* incentives can be modulated according to the participant readiness or may result from the objectives in the program and are especially valuable in the action and preparation phases. They play a less important role during monitoring or in any case should be part of the verification of the objectives attained. *Cultural* incentives relate to the possibility of subscribing to the basic values of preserving the environment and are a very strong lever if they translate into accurate information on the consequences of actions and changes that participants can complete. Let us look at a case in point: the choice to be informed on what growing percentage of people has joined the active awareness programs is not per se a special booster, but having accurate information on how much energy saving, which people, buildings, and public facilities have joined and succeeded in active awareness, can be a strong cultural incentive.

Repeated visualizations of the percentage of savings explaining result rationales increase program fidelity, just as the participant competence and literacy. Furthermore, incentives can be used in fidelization programs that impact on lifestyles, for instance with vouchers for electric vehicles, transport services, joining educational programs, and community social events. Lastly, since incentives may concern more than one person in a household and public or private facility, one has to accurately determine how *fidelization* strategies include socialization and participation in the management of resource and benefits ensuing from active awareness.

Let us now move on into the world of diverse behaviors: this includes *active* and *passive* dynamics in behavior change programs. A map of stakeholders is clearly a good starting point: active awareness programs are not necessarily addressed to all energy users. Also, those who have a *passive* role in managing energy resources may have an idea of the advantages of energy-saving programs despite not having special knowledge of the advantages of energy saving. As mentioned, as well as the economic advantages of energy saving, there are social advantages in belonging to an energy-saving community and ethical advantages in terms of responsibility for future generations.

If we start with the personal feelings each one has on the advantages of energy saving, it then becomes possible to develop education and awareness raising paths. This process requires identifying moments and points of contact that can lead to *a conversation*, which in turn leads to other developments. One of the practical developments is to identify the people in the household, family, building, or office who can guide and coordinate others. These are the people who have the potential to become experts in turn and may develop an interest in active awareness programs. An expert consumer is also a stakeholder we can bank on to trigger the expertise of a producer becoming a *prosumer* (producer and consumer) and entrepreneur. These roles, as well as their interaction and cooperation, give rise to the so-called energy communities, which have a great potential for energy transformation in the years to come.

10.3 Energy Communities and Evolution in Behavior

Energy communities are a relatively new phenomenon in the economy and social innovation. They first emerged in the wake of renewable energy and the generous EU financial incentives: they actively promote environmental values and lead economic and local development benefits. It is a growing and increasingly significant trend in Europe[20] and could extend to other economic and geopolitical spheres if appropriately facilitated. According to Eurostat, in 2020, the EU has reached and exceeded the target of 20% average share of renewable energy, that is wind, solar, or photovoltaic and hydroelectric with a 60% peak in Sweden, 44% in Finland, and 42% in Lithuania.[21] The consumption of renewable energy has exceeded that of coal, oil, and gas when we consider these sources one by one, which means the target can be reached. Furthermore, in Northern European countries, energy transformation and the clean sources overtaking fossil ones is a much swifter process. Interestingly, in these countries the production and sale of renewable energies has not been taken over by multinationals or large national companies. Presuming that clean energy will become a more profitable business, thanks to service buildup and the increase of the units serviced, energy communities may become a swifter means to transform energy moving toward low or zero environmental impact consumption. The target is to double the EU average share of generation and use of renewable energy, raising it from 20% to 40% by 2030, which could be an underestimation in view of the cutting-edge results of the best countries. It still remains to be seen how to promote a widespread interest for more mature economic models in each geopolitical setting. The solution illustrated in the present chapter is to carefully select pilot projects in every geopolitical area to lay the foundations for the implementation of large-scale sustainable innovation programs. The key target is to accelerate overall progressive evolution of the energy consumption market toward sustainable models.

As for the evolution and maturity of energy communities' models, sustainable innovation and active awareness ones have been suggested. The systematic model developed by Hewitt (and other researchers)[22] is based on the criteria of socioeconomic analysis and identifies shareholding as an important variable in a community's plans. The idea is that a community that owns shares but is not a majority shareholder is less advanced or mature compared to communities that own the production and sale systems. In the former, participation is symbolical and in the latter it is silent: the actual management is by administrative staff and paid managers. A more advanced approach sees a community as not only profit sharing but also contributing to define social policies and guidelines. Totally self-sufficient communities active on the market with social and technical expertise are at the top of the ladder as they not only own most of the shares but also hold executive power. The advantage

---

[20] Hewitt et al. [11].

[21] https://ec.europa.eu/eurostat/web/products-eurostat-news/-/ddn-20220119-1

[22] Ibid.

of the energy community systems (taxonomic model) is that it mirrors the makeup of society as well as each community's ability to manage. They are very common in the EU although there is still a lot of room for progress.

The actual possibility of replacing fossil fuels altogether depends on whether the interests of the widespread communities match those of the political stakeholders and technology suppliers in promoting sustainable innovation models. The following are the key elements of success: the presence of energy distribution and stocking facilities, the ownership of these networks, and the possibility to control and monitor using advanced software guaranteeing flexibility, profitability, and transparency.

Hybrid solutions—the most advanced compromise civil society has attained so far—are likely to dominate the scene in the coming years. One of the most feasible available solutions to accelerate energy transformation to sustainability calls for a growth of maturity, agentivity, readiness, and expertise of energy communities. This system (*taxonomic model*) and solutions could lead to an evolution in energy communities considering the two main axes representing agentivity and the readiness to occupy a share of the free market (see Fig. 10.1). According to this representation, which does not take into consideration the societal makeup of the energy communities, there are two types of established energy communities and one budding energy community that has not yet decided which direction it is going to take. The two communities in Europe are RECs (*Renewable Energy Communities*) and CECs

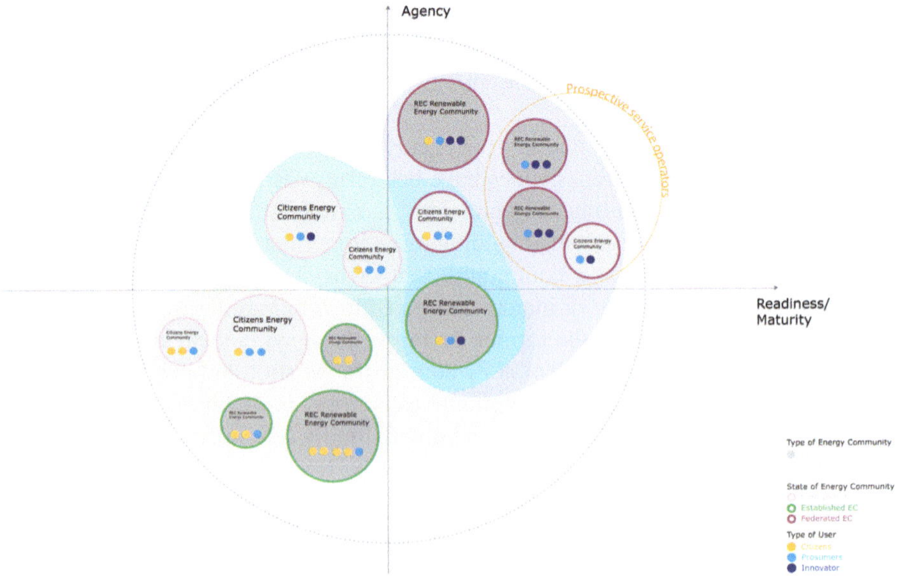

Fig. 10.1 Energy community ecosystems and their evolutions. (A special thanks to Giulia Teso for her contribution to design the visual map)

(*Citizen Energy Communities*). The difference between the two types is whether they are local and develop community and social interests—such as CECs—or grow by proximity in relation to the energy sources which they produce—such as the RECs. RECs have a greater possibility to grow counting on the ability to become a ready-made, available, and proximal reference model. CECs have a more inclusive approach counting on the relational stability of informal local networks.

The advantage of the above-simplified representation is that it offers some indications on how energy ***communities evolve*** and grow regardless of their assets and wealth, which characterize the socioeconomic model. In other words, although the company organization determines the wealth and assets of the communities, the potential of the community can be better understood focusing on its capacity to include and grow. RECs have the potential to develop preparation and readiness and occupy adjoining market niches, becoming de facto formal or informal federated networks. One wonders what RECs make available to nearby communities and what growth strategies they are pursuing.

Current studies underway[23] show these communities start with what they share, by developing existing personal relations, according to available comparable resources, prevalently wind, solar, (wood) biomasses, biogas, and water resources. These are the bases for social responsibility value systems that make conflict resolution possible without complicated intermediation. Cooperation materializes through knowledge sharing, technical skills, and sharing of software technology. Some of the most advanced RECs are nationwide enterprises that look very much the same in the various European geopolitical areas: Enercoop in France, Fermes de Figeac in France, Energy Garden in the United Kingdom, Ecostroom in the Netherlands, Beauvent in Belgium, Green Energy Community in Italy, and EWS in Germany. They have an innovative approach and offer partnerships to medium and large public or private companies or to farming communities with turnkey solutions to facilitate transition to photovoltaic or other sustainable energy solutions. They are also able to trade emission ***reduction credits***, buying and selling to lower the company's Green House Gas (GHG) emission count. Furthermore, RECs offer direct assistance to regions wishing to start up, addressing requests to the closest REC members. Only about 20% of global GHG on this planet are thought to have been taxed or traded on the market in 2020. The more the transactions, the quicker is the transition to renewable energy.[24]

The makeup of these cooperation ecosystems promotes widespread grassroots activism, which in turn can lead to experimental types of innovation. The communities' technological innovations are especially important and focus on software components for services involving consumers and helping them become producers and consumers; they also increase management transparency and promote trust and participation-based models; they upgrade managerial and technical skills in the field of energy; and lastly, they protect the ecological habitat.

---

[23] Boulanger et al. [12].

[24] IPCC (Intergovernmental Panel on Climate Change). https://www.ipcc.ch/report/ar6/wg3/

10.4 Automation Technologies and Sustainable Consumption

Technologies play an enabling role in sustainable innovation and are a key ingredient in change programs if used transparently to attain shared and inclusive targets. In the specific energy-saving cases studied and the establishment of energy communities, investments in soft technologies are experiencing an incremental growth.[25] Interestingly, the overall curve of technological energy investments has not exceeded last century's peaks, and software technology investments grow in proportion to disinvestment in traditional technologies such as nuclear and mining. Furthermore, the growth curve in technology investments indicates that an economy of scale can be reached by promoting local experiments involving activisms and dynamic ecosystems.

The role of support and local policies should not be underestimated but counterintuitively it is basically a matter of making it easier for them to join similar initiatives elsewhere. Alternatively, existing local skills could be promoted and encouraged to form cluster according to known models of maturity. It is an interesting phenomenon of migration of ideas and concepts supported by digital technologies. The wealth of experimental approaches based on experience and observations within the budding ecosystems becomes a driving force for new innovative jewels, which can then lead to new locally developed and potentially sensational solutions. According to the above-mentioned climate change report, by adopting local development, developing countries could grow exponentially using the digital technologies and their ability to spread.

The main risk of technology investments is losing sight of the potentially enabling role for behavioral change. Unless the intentions and aims of the desired cultural and behavior changes are clearly stated (see Chap. 5), the socioeconomic function of community welfare sharing is undermined, as is the opportunity to methodically reveal and develop the value of sustainable innovation in the field of energy, for instance, using the SIRL scale (see Chap. 9). As we have seen, it is a matter of building up social and environmental expertise, widespread activism, local and proximity cooperation, and communities that are self-sufficient in terms of energy requirements.

A recent survey on investments, on the methods and approaches followed to encourage environmentally friendly behavior, indicated that none of the research carried out so far has been able to assess whether investments have been able to determine lasting changes in the lifestyles of the people and communities that were involved.[26]

As mentioned in previous chapters, this is a serious shortcoming that will have to be dealt with as a priority in projects underway. I feel there is a positive note too, in that software technologies developed according to participated approaches to

[25] IPCC, ibid., p. 193.

[26] Grilli and Curtis [13].

behavior and service design may bestow sustainable intentionality on investment projects in automation technologies in the field of energy.

Digital technology enables the aggregation or clustering of new services that can be launched experimentally so that communities can receive behavior data on consumption and monitor their medium- and long-term objectives. This is why investments underway for the ontological integration of the various technologies, for the planning of infrastructure and adaptive energy grids, for digital twins, for managerial efficiency and flexibility in managing demand, for IOT (Internet of Things) technology, sensors, and AI (Artificial Intelligence) feed into the establishment and aggregation or clustering of services on a local level.

Using successful pilots, investments will have to promote acceleration on a wider scale. The question we have to ask ourselves is how, in practice, can digital technologies and automation help the establishment of energy-saving culture and the growth of energy communities. More specifically, we must ask ourselves how digital technology can foster individual active awareness behavior on a large scale to promote energy saving; and how do digital platforms need to be designed to speed up the growth of local energy communities and to develop community federative approaches.

Hopefully, the answers to these questions will be sought and developed in the coming years, and it is possible to set a few specific milestones for future experiments. Energy-saving behavior profiling and the modeling of the energy community on an evolutionary scale offers many methodological advantages for experimental research. For instance, on an individual scale, the evolution from consumer to prosumer (producer-consumer), just as that of the prosumer morphing into a service innovator, is meaningful and important for the paradigm of sustainable innovation. In communities, the evolutionary passage from a CEC to a REC community, and then into federated RECs, all have significant results to assert sustainable innovations. These shifts are unlikely to take place unless digital technologies are purposely designed to meet these behavioral requirements.

For instance, communities able to sell energy appear to develop more than those that merely focus on autonomy and self-sufficiency.[27] However, we still do not know what the mix of technologies and intervention programs for sustainable change must look like to facilitate evolution.

We can imagine a range of local experiments or pilot schemes to define global intervention models. One wonders what functions and what contents must be included, integrated in intelligent systems for new residents to automatically participate in the energy communities? What nudging mechanisms can be invented and made available to that the points of contact of the energy communities can encourage an increasing participation? What boosting mechanisms can be invented and designed to build active awareness and operative capacity? Participatory design methods are a great means of support in planning and designing new services, such as refurbishing in urban and rural areas, energy auditing, and consumption and

[27] Pena-Bello et al. [14].

energy productive flow monitoring, air quality assessment, services for the dynamic integration of the energy stored in the intelligent grids, or to integrate networks and financial services.

Federated service in federated communities may possibly give space and breathe new life into cutting-edge technologies born in specialized communities. New marketing and CRM (Customer Relationship Management) automation standards can be used to maintain participation within communities and among energy communities. Data ownership and data management acquire a new meaning in the context of innovation, aiming to modify consumer behavior and shifting to models of cultural and economic sustainability.

Result monitoring and tracing over time, made possible by sustainable innovation programs, turn data into an economic asset with an exchange value for trading (transactions) and the service ecosystem communities. Data can inform service models for community growth and for individual and collective well-being. Profiling and participation are players of the same game in that they foster the growth of skills and competence growth and managerial transparency.

The classical dilemma that opposes comfort to the protection of the environment may find new solutions in the context of sustainable innovation programs. Reciprocity between consumers and service aggregators, as well as timely, dynamic, and swift information, can also have an exchange value and lead to cooperation. In traditional innovation models, flexible supplies to address demand peaks are advantageous for the energy aggregator if they can be used to maximize utility, that is, without considering consumer preferences. Furthermore, consumers wishing to have the advantage of flexible consumption—for instance, being able to use several high consumption domestic appliances at the same time, or to exceed contract heating levels—have to pay a higher rate, regardless of the actual global load on the grid at the time of their higher demand. In other words, there is no overlap between the advantage for the aggregator and the advantage for the consumer or user. If we look at it in terms of sustainable energy, the most expert consumers could benefit from flexibility agreeing ad hoc incentives with aggregators, or for the reduction of carbon dioxide to be activated dynamically according to the loads managed by the aggregator and the day's estimated consumption.

Highlights

- Incentive-based policies would be clearer if flowed from calculable aims to assess the breadth and duration of behavioral changes that technological innovation can generate. This is true for any strategy promoting the energy transition throughout the economy.
- The chances of a positive impact on behavior are limited in the absence of system tactics able to place formal or substantial barriers to (directly or indirectly) limit bounded rationality.
- Energy efficiency, with an aim to progressively replace fossil energy sources with renewable ones, has to address special political/geopolitical issues, as well as strategic problems in order to maintain the independence of a nation state and

the principles of democratic freedom. Energy saving aims instead focus on the need to reduce waste in a systematic and selective manner.
- Active awareness is the actual possibility for consumers to act consistently with the awareness on the use of energy and therefore developing habits that lead to energy saving.
- Making citizens more involved in the ongoing correct management of energy resources is one of the main awkward problems of energy transformation.
- In the coming 5–10 years, innovation projects will have to engage users in active solutions, showing that their socio-technical solutions are able to introduce stable lasting sustainable consumption patterns.
- Engagement factors concern the rules and conditions needed to facilitate adherence to the programs of change.
- Behavioral change programs refer to each member's readiness to accept the program and to define specific objectives for each level, and how consumers intend to achieve them.
- Active awareness incentives are the enabling factor to develop creatively. Overall, the more incentives are the result of mixing economic, cultural, and environmental features, marketing, and fidelization, the easier and more acceptable joining the programs, thus consolidating the chance of getting good results.
- An expert consumer is also a stakeholder we can bank on to trigger the expertise of a producer becoming a *prosumer* (producer and consumer) and entrepreneur.
- The roles of active consumer, prosumers, and entrepreneurs, as well as their interaction and cooperation, give rise to the so-called energy communities, which have a great potential for energy transformation in the years to come.
- A careful selection of pilot projects in every geopolitical area will lay the foundations for the implementation of large-scale sustainable innovation programs. The key target is to accelerate overall progressive evolution of the energy consumption market toward sustainable models.
- Totally self-sufficient communities active on the market with social and technical expertise are at the top of the ladder as they not only own most of the shares but also hold executive power.
- One of the most feasible available solutions to accelerate energy transformation to sustainability calls for a growth of maturity, agentivity, readiness, and expertise of energy communities.
- The difference between the REC (Renewable Energy Communities) and CEC (Citizen Energy Communities) is whether they are local and develop community and social interests—such as CECs—or grow by proximity in relation to the energy sources which they produce—such as the RECs.
- RECs have a greater possibility to grow counting on the ability to become a ready-made, available, and proximal reference model. CECs have a more inclusive approach counting on the relational stability of informal local networks.
- The growth curve in technology investments of the last years indicates that an economy of scale can be reached by promoting local experiments involving activisms and dynamic ecosystems.

- Software technologies developed according to participatory approaches to behavior and service design may bestow sustainable intentionality on investment projects in automation technologies in the field of energy.
- In the coming years it will be possible to set a few specific milestones for experiments on how digital technology can favor active awareness individual behavior on a large scale to promote energy saving.
- Community federative approaches are the most advanced solutions to energy sustainability.
- Federated service in federated communities may possibly give space and breathe new life into cutting-edge technologies born in specialized communities.
- New marketing and CRM (Customer Relationship Management) automation standards can be used to maintain participation within communities and among energy communities.
- Data ownership and data management acquire a new meaning in the context of innovation, aiming to modify consumer behavior and shifting to models of cultural and economic sustainability.

References

1. Science Advice for Policy by European Academies (SAPEA). (2021). *A systemic approach to the energy transition in Europe*. SAPEA. https://doi.org/10.26356/energytransition
2. Chater, N., Loewenstein, G. F. (2022, March 1). *The i-Frame and the s-Frame: How focusing on individual-level solutions has led behavioral public policy astray*. Available at SSRN: https://ssrn.com/abstract=4046264 or https://doi.org/10.2139/ssrn.4046264
3. Laitner, J., Ehrhardt-Martinez, K., & McKinney, V. (2009, August). *Examining the scale of the behavior energy efficiency conundrum*. paper presented at the 2009 ACEEE Summer Study, Washington, DC.
4. Dubois, G., Sovacool, B., Aall, C., Nilsson, M., Barbier, C., Herrmann, A., et al. (2019). It starts at home. Climate policies targeting household consumption and behavioral decisions are key to low-carbon futures. *Energy Research and Social Science, 52*, 144–158. https://doi.org/10.1016/j.erss.2019.02.001
5. Gunay, H. B., Shen, W., Newsham, G., & Ashouri, A. (2018). Modelling and analysis of unsolicited temperature setpoint change requests in office buildings. *Building and Environment, 133*, 203–212. https://doi.org/10.1016/j.buildenv.2018.02.025
6. Jorgensen, B. S., Fumei, S., & Byrne, G. (2021). Reducing peak energy demand among residents who are not billed for their electricity consumption: Experimental evaluation of behavior change interventions in a university setting. *International Journal of Environmental Research and Public Health, 18*, 8406. https://doi.org/10.3390/ijerph18168406
7. Casado-Mansilla, D., López-de-Armentia, J., Ventura, D., et al. (2016). Embedding intelligent eco-aware systems within everyday things to increase people's energy awareness. *Soft Computing, 20*, 1695–1711. https://doi.org/10.1007/s00500-015-1751-0
8. Koroleva, K., Melenhorst, M., Novak, J., et al. (2019). Designing an integrated socio-technical behavior change system for energy saving. *Energy Informatics, 2*, 30. https://doi.org/10.1186/s42162-019-0088-9
9. Hart, G. W. (1992). Nonintrusive appliance load monitoring. *Proceedings of the IEEE, 80*(12), 1870–1891. https://doi.org/10.1109/5.192069

10. Prochaska, J. O., & DiClemente, C. C. (1984). *The trans-theoretical approach: Crossing traditional boundaries of therapy*. Dow Jones-Irwin.
11. Hewitt, R. J., Bradley, N., Baggio Compagnucci, A., Barlagne, C., Ceglarz, A., Cremades, R., McKeen, M., Otto, I. M., & Slee, B. (2019). Social innovation in community energy in Europe: A review of the evidence. *Frontiers in Energy Research, 7*, 31. https://doi.org/10.3389/fenrg.2019.00031
12. Boulanger, S. O. M., Massari, M., Longo, D., Turillazzi, B., & Nucci, C. A. (2021). Designing collaborative energy communities: A European overview. *Energies, 14*, 8226. https://doi.org/10.3390/en14248226
13. Grilli, G., & Curtis, J. (2021). Encouraging pro-environmental behaviours: A review of methods and approaches. *Renewable and Sustainable Energy Review, 135*(C), 110039.
14. Pena-Bello, A., Parra, D., Herberz, M., et al. (2022). Integration of prosumer peer-to-peer trading decisions into energy community modelling. *Nature Energy, 7*, 74–82. https://doi.org/10.1038/s41560-021-00950-2

Chapter 11
Health Services Transformation and Behavior

Perhaps never more than in this century, on a global scale, are health and care systems under pressure to change. The chronic disease trend no longer affects only countries with developed economies.[1] Interestingly, in spite of a worldwide longer life expectancy in the past 50 years, the overall picture shows a rise in premature deaths and an overall ageing of the population with bad health conditions.

WHO suggests most of the countries that subscribed to the 2030 Sustainable Development Goals (SDGs) and pledged to reduce Non-Communicable Diseases (NCD) by one-third will have to increase their work to bring numbers down in the coming years.[2] WHO believes that premature deaths and chronic diseases can be avoided in 70–95% of all cases. These are very high figures that nobody can afford to ignore. The overall understanding of chronic disease etiology has led WHO to believe the goals can be reached based on a few fundamental guidelines in at-risk areas.[3] Premature death causes are due to the use of tobacco, alcohol abuse, sedentary lifestyles, and excess sugar, salt, and saturated fats in food. These are the same factors that explain the increase in non-communicable diseases, the main ones being diabetes, cardiovascular, and respiratory diseases as well as cancer.

For a long time now, we have been aware of the direct link between lifestyle, quality of life, and life expectancy.[4] However, significant evidence on the complex interplay among biological, environmental, behavioral, and socioeconomic factors has only been accrued since 2019. A European Commission-funded longitudinal

[1] Given the distribution of the world's population as many as 80% of people with chronic diseases are estimated to be in developing countries, compared with 20% in countries with advanced economies, https://en.wikipedia.org/wiki/Non-communicable_disease

[2] https://ncdalliance.org/news-events/news/who-launches-new-ncd-progress-monitor#:~:text=Of%20194%20countries%2C%20the%202022,Progress%20Monitor%20published%20in%202,020

[3] Op. cit., p. 5.

[4] For instance, Govindaraju et al. [1].

M. Visciola, *Sustainable Innovation*,
https://doi.org/10.1007/978-3-031-18751-3_11

study looked into a cohort of 1.7 million people in Europe, the United States, and Australia. According to the research, disadvantaged socioeconomic conditions due to low or uncertain incomes, the lack of stable jobs, and low levels of education have an impact on biological system "from organs to molecules."[5] At least in the countries being considered, the *Lifepath Study*, as it is called, clearly shows that people in disadvantaged economic conditions have a greater chance of developing disabling diseases and to have a premature death.

A comparative, interdisciplinary project entirely carried out in the United States by a large number of research centers of excellence reached the same conclusions.[6] Social conditions shape environment and life circumstances,[7] which is why there is a strong association between social environment, diseases, and risk of mortality. Although we mostly focus on the relationship between socioeconomic and biological determinants, both studies offer explanations that make it possible to integrate behavioral determinants in NCD etiology. Although there is not always a close causal link between the organ, the worn-out molecule, and the type of social adversity,[8] there is a key relationship between social disadvantage and the predisposition for at-risk behaviors. This relationship is proved by behavioral science both with reference to the structural exposure to adverse factors and in terms of the accumulation of negative events. However, for the first time these two recent studies offer transdisciplinary evidence that social adversity, lack of social integration, and social status of people are precursors of the context strongly influencing behavioral options in everyday life.[9]

Results appear to confirm the conclusions that there are causal links between behavioral and biological risks to rectify by identifying corrective programs that deal with NCD reduction targets.

Other than the important identifications of the causal links, scientific research has not yet managed to comprehensively identify the right strategies to foresee and prevent the actual incidence of behavioral risk on the various diseases. Most research on behavioral risk has been aimed at analyzing causes, to come up with recommendations on prevention policies to communicate risk, and disseminate knowledge of risk factors among a wide public. In plain words, currently basic research has not yielded results that can be translated into recommendations in defining programs to implement behavioral risk prevention. Implementation programs are those that are more than mere prevention-related knowledge transmission: they are educational and corrective programs tailored to people's daily lives and systematically

[5] Vineis et al. [2].

[6] Snyder-Mackler et al. [3].

[7] Also see Part I, Chap. 2.

[8] The link is known as accumulated wear and tear or allostatic load.

[9] Comparative studies highlight that stress due to social adversity has the same impact on all mammals and cannot therefore be referred exclusively to modern societies.

integrated.[10] The lack of experimental reference frameworks becomes especially relevant when considering some of the results of the *Lifepath* epidemiological research: prevention and mitigation policies cannot be decided once and for all centrally and then merely be transferred to a specific country "*there is no single intervention model that fits all populations*".[11] Results confirm there have to be specific guidelines and recommendations validated according to their context, completed by important integrations generated by local insights. Furthermore, the most adopted political incentives and solutions, such as cash transfer and work-related tax credit, fail to act as comprehensive prevention, nor can they be considered social remedies. Experts who commented on this research suggest that the use of traditional political tools is not enough to solve the problems of behavioral and biological risk among disadvantaged groups.

The objective complexity of the obstacles to be faced, as well as the enormous collective and synergistic commitment that must be instilled, raise major issues on how to activate the suitable means and strategies to follow up on the reforms with the support of intervention programs, and thus determine a strong drive for change. Premature deaths and age-related progressive illnesses have a great social cost on families and health services, which must bear the emotional, economic, and management burden that often exceeds capacity and availability.

What can be done to trigger and guarantee continuity to the behavioral risk prevention programs? What features must these programs have to be consistent in time? What times and means should they follow? If overall health service reforms are intended to hold over time, how can the variety of local structural and individual contexts be taken on board? In deciding how to deal with these issues, I join those who say reforms are the necessary premise to start and contextualize the machine of change. At the same time, it would be unrealistic to expect reforms to be completed to attain the targets, just as in the past it proved unrealistic to think that the strategies the Behavioral Insight Teams enacted could make up for the reform's shortcomings.

Low-cost actions, such as a gentle nudge, have been shown not to have a significant impact on the transformation of health-related behavior,[12] as systematic actions based on programs translating policies into strong impact implementation strategies are needed.[13] Since the transformation of health-care systems is unavoidably based on systemic actions for sustainability, the time has come to seriously revise the practices and action strategies implemented so far. First and foremost, revisions refer to the contribution of medicine and more in general of health sciences; these areas of knowledge will have to swiftly move from the comfort area of specialist

---

[10] Translational medicine proposes similar goals by addressing biomedical and clinical research with the aim of accelerating the transfer of knowledge as soon as it is produced in scientific laboratories directly to hospital departments, and then engaging communities interested in scientific discovery for primary prevention. See: *New Horizons in Translational Medicine*. Volume 2 (Issue 3): 86–88. 11 December 2014. Doi:https://doi.org/10.1016/j.nhtm.2014.12.002

[11] Vineis et al., op cit., p. 9.

[12] For instance: Loewenstein et al. [4] and Prainsack [5].

[13] For instance: Loewenstein et al. [6].

approaches and move to transdisciplinary and experimental approaches. Furthermore, a significant revision of currently held business models and technical innovation are called for; once again a shift from short-term profit to sustainable models able to recreate necessary balances and share the positive results for a rapid spread and adoption.

Lastly, the contribution of behavior design for the sustainable innovation of health-care systems is paramount in that it determines an ecosystemic approach to prevention and change action programs. Specifically, behavioral design can offer a two-pronged approach in that it contributes to the transdisciplinary leadership in finalizing prevention strategies and targets action programs in the tailoring prevention and cure actions.

11.1 Prevention and Behavior

A first important assessment in reviewing the system is to see the relative weight of each step prevention has in our health systems. Health workers commonly use a distinction between prevention and cure as a widely accepted simplification that is also commonly used, but a distinction between the various forms of prevention can be fruitfully considered. There is a twofold advantage in extending the notion of prevention throughout life and in every interface between members of the public and the health service: it makes it possible to follow an ecosystemic approach for the management of public health[14] and, on the other, it makes it possible to take a long-term view of the prevention action programs. According to this orientation—which I believe it is useful to recall here—prevention can be divided into three macro-phases, listing the type of actions for each and their relevant targets:

(i) *Primary prevention*, individual and collective health literacy to manage risk factors and favor actions aimed at reducing the impact of diseases by promoting behavior and lifestyle for health and well-being;
(ii) *Secondary prevention*, active surveillance to diagnose and foresee any ensuing disease to act as soon as possible on the causes; and
(iii) *Tertiary prevention*, measurements aimed at managing the consequences of the full-blown disease to avoid or reduce any other consequences and illnesses.

Longitudinal and comparative studies such as the above enable us to understand and plan primary prevention to implement policies such as the ones referred to by WHO for collective prevention and public health.[15] Preventions actions and programs require a good understanding of risk factors due to the social issues among disadvantaged strata of the population. Research results suggest the highest priority

[14] Public health refers to the public good in terms of health in the community.

[15] See objective 4 referring to the prevention on non-communicable diseases in the Progress Monitor 2022 Report. https://www.who.int/publications/i/item/9789240047761. Last time accessed in July 2022.

should be given to prevention programs among school-age children and preschoolers as these are the age groups where unhealthy behaviors are developed and the NCD endogenous biological premises are laid down, such as the response to exogenous and inflammatory factors, by activating glucocorticoid and adrenergic signaling. For instance, we now know that obesogenic and inflammatory tendencies are established in the early years.[16] On the whole, primary prevention programs concern the communication of risk and risk factors addressing the population with the same standard message. This is the form of education called "functional," which contains the basic skills to understand risk factors and how to use the services of health systems.[17]

However, the mere enunciation of risk factors and conveying the appropriate information may not be sufficient to ensure a spontaneous lowering of the risk. Effective primary prevention must be adequately focused on the more at-risk groups with a greater predisposition; ad hoc programs must be drafted to favor the correct mental risk representation in families, among caregivers, and in settings that may favor them.[18] Furthermore, programs must include specific age-sensitive guidelines and recommendations to reduce risk, as well as advice on eating habits, movement and sleep, and personal and household hygiene.

The following fall under the definition of *primary prevention*: (a) the checklist of what has to be included in dealing with behavioral risks; (b) planning a communication and engagement strategy; and (c) identifying the environments that most favor behavioral risk. Finally, primary prevention also requires a critical rethinking on permanent education for medical and health staff, on evidence-based decision-making support, and on how to improve managerial and decision-making processes involving specialized staff and users. The aim is for individuals and communities to be in control and actively participate in improving prevention systems.

Secondary prevention is rife with major challenges, and policies play a key role. For instance, planned age- and risk-weighted screening programs for each specific disease mean the population, groups, and communities—such as patient associations—and individuals can be monitored regularly. Planning these interventions is a premise of great importance for prevention, although participation is a challenge in the challenge. In fact, implementation programs should clearly identify the barriers for target populations, as well as how to overcome the obstacles and facilitate a clear understanding of risk factors in each target group. In addition to functional literacy, programs should focus on "interactive" health literacy, which includes the ability to find information, process controls and meanings to be active and participate in attaining the specific targets of the prevention program in question.

---

[16] Oliveira [7].

[17] Nutbeam [8].

[18] For instance, a rare pilot study in this direction: Fleary et al. [9]. Also see the WHO program for school teachers aimed at the prevention of NCDs. https://www.who.int/publications/i/item/9789290227519

"Critical" health literacy[19] should be taught alongside interactive health literacy: it includes the ability to act critically on risk factors by modifying risk conditions and reducing their impact by better controlling behavior and life events. Better health conditions are sought by promoting critical health education, just as practical results to identify specific factors leading to chronic diseases and decrease the percentage of severe cases and hospitalizations.[20] Clearly, this form of education is strongly recommended in tertiary prevention programs too, especially in the case of chronic diseases with comorbidity risks and the potential onset of more complex metabolic syndromes. Finding one's way around the health prevention systems is one of the hardest skills to achieve. Access systems are normally developed for treatment, cure, and therapy such as the touch points (interface) of the health systems. As a result, treatment bias does not favor adequate motor perceptual and judgement automatisms for potential users of primary and secondary prevention.

Diagnostic uncertainty is a sign of this difficulty in orienting oneself, as health insurances well know. Faced with an uncertain vague and changing symptoms, the potential patient seeks an answer by undergoing a series of diagnostic tests that do not necessarily answer the requirements of a preventive validated and accredited protocol. *Overdiagnosis* is another reaction well known to doctors, which is the diagnosis of medical conditions that have little or no chance of turning into a problematic symptomatic clinical picture;[21] as is *overmedication*, which is the administration of drugs, preventive therapies, and treatments that can lead to iatrogenous diseases.[22] However, the strongest evidence is supplied by Type 2 diabetes, heart, respiratory, and kidney diseases, which cannot be effectively prevented if not diagnosed in time.[23] Such cases raise the dilemma for secondary prevention targeting early identification of at-risk patients: the psychological, social, and medical implications of medicalization due to preventive screening require a careful assessment and raise ethical issues on the boundaries and limitations of medical knowledge.[24] For instance, compulsory mass screening is indicated for etiological conditions with well-defined risk factors as is the case of breast and colon cancer prevention (early diagnosis). Early diagnosis of Type 1 diabetes is an opposite example: screening is not advised because of the uncertainty of the evolution of the disease and because of diagnostic anomalies that have been recorded. Many diagnostic anomalies do not lead to a full-blown version of the disease developing and a standard to know which anomalies are going to lead to a full-blown disease and which are not. In other words, precision medicine is a difficult challenge for prevention.

---

[19] Nutbeam, D., op cit.

[20] Nutbeam et al. [10].

[21] Welch et al. [11] and Brodersen et al. [12].

[22] Diamandis [13]; also Hofmann and Welch [14].

[23] According to the International Diabetes Federation, 44.7% of adults with Type 2 diabetes are undiagnosed. https://www.idf.org/news/240:diabetes-now-affects-one-in-10-adults-worldwide.html

[24] Kaczmarek [15].

Today's challenge is geared to the new opportunities decision-making technological supports offer, based on machine learning, artificial intelligence (AI), and wearables. The prevailing narrative is based on a strong belief in the evidence produced by the clinical data and by the new insights that the data bank can offer if shared and made available to the scientific, technological, and professional communities. Still, trust would be misplaced if data models were limited to the clinical and biological data of the prevention protocols.

According to the described ecosystemic approach, data models should be completed by a strong transdisciplinary contribution to establish the right connections between data models and data types. Barriers, mistrust, and subject as well as discipline-based biases have to be overcome to identify and prioritize at-risk profiles and the presence of risk groups and subgroups, including the complex intertwining between socioeconomic or structural, context or situational, and dispositional determinants (see Fig. 8.1). A transdisciplinary approach on primary prevention directly improves the cooperation among health communities and sets new frontiers for all, including precision medicine.

In terms of prevention, a transdisciplinary approach runs into an ecosystemic perspective, albeit lacking a ready data infrastructure. Communities of professionals, researchers, and market traders have the need for an infrastructure and many in fact are setting themselves up so that when it is available, they can use it. Researchers, sustainable innovation designers, and agents of change have a task to suggest strategies for an ecosystemic perspective, favoring cooperating, data sharing, and the progress of an experimental approach in real life. From this point of view, we might wonder which are the main necessary ingredients to create a data infrastructure according to an ecosystemic point of view. After over 30 years of experiments in so-called telemedicine (aka distance or remote medicine), we can avail ourselves of a vast set of digital technologies and wearables enabling us to gather and transfer precise data gathered from the individuals in their daily setting.

Currently, very high data transmission speeds (i.e., 5G) make it possible to gather data as it is generated. New services can be imagined and implemented, thanks to distance or remote monitoring during the trial and the secondary preventions aimed at people who have NCD risk factors. Technology could enable new services based on the data transfer gathered through *consumertek* (widely used technologies) that have the reliability and security of medical equipment. Precision medicine and prevention have an ambitious aim, that is, finding solutions tailored to individuals and their proximity social network: this means a future where prevention and research programs become part and parcel of real-life situations. Secondary prevention programs become experimental programs agreed on with individuals who decide to accept research protocols by making their data available. A transdisciplinary approach opens new possibilities to integrate behavior and context determinants in prevention programs. Since different behavior and social patterns (heterogeneity) are less understood and not easy to classify compared to molecular and biological classifications (taxonomies), it is reasonable to gather data on individual's experience and behavior in a structured manner. The aim is to increase the ability to consider a person as a whole while guaranteeing their privacy. This opportunity offers secondary and tertiary prevention great advantages and brings forward the opportunity to implement precision prevention programs.

11.2 New LifeStyle Programs

In 2010, a large team of US researchers from 17 centers of excellence at the *National Institute of Health* (NIH), part of the *U.S. Department of Health and Human Services*, began exploring the possibility of merging other areas into a program establishing the Science of Behavioral Change (SOBC).[25] One of its main aims is to include a study of the behavior change mechanisms in clinical research programs. This requires research to describe the mechanisms triggering behavior changes in real life, possibly during randomized controlled trials (RCTs): the protocol should include micro-trial design aimed at a single person to gain a better understanding of the evolution of complex health conditions.[26]

The inclusion of behavior and context determinants in clinical research aimed at precision medicine and prevention is a realistic cutting-edge aim, currently being widely used. Chapter 9 already described some of the user-centered designs (UCDs) or human-centered designs (HCDs), which have proved extremely useful in accelerating sustainable innovation programs, solutions favoring agentivity, and cooperation. They can play a key role in identifying the combination of risk factors for individuals, groups, and communities in a step-by-step approach, establishing how they can be dealt with in a secondary prevention program. Since most of the real-life methodologies and techniques are already widely used in marketing, we could see whether they are accredited and useable in programs to improve our medical knowledge and facilitate lifestyle and behavior modifications and evolutions. Techniques must also check for biases in the project structure to avoid undermining the significance of results. They must also offer practical and systematic answers to precise questions on how to implement and articulate solutions and health services, beyond the mere drug administration.

A 2000–2020 literature review using medical–scientific databases, such as PubMed, CINAHL, Embase, the Cochrane Library, Web of Science, PsycINFO, and Sociological Abstracts, analyzed how UCD, HCD, and design thinking used techniques and method standards in designing health innovation projects.[27] The review reached the conclusion that application and reporting standards have to be agreed upon (e.g., see Bazzano and colleagues[28]) if this research is to be incorporated into projects using biomedical research standards. The definition of reporting

---

[25] Nielsen et al. [16].

[26] Hekler et al. [17].

[27] Göttgens and Oertelt-Prigione [18].

[28] Bazzano et al. [19].

standards would help considerably to access highly standardized and regulated design environments, as is the case of innovation in health care.

There are two questionnaires known by their acronyms PROM (patient-reported outcome measure) and PREM (patient-reported experience measure)[29] that have proved to be reliable tools for the collection of measurable qualitative data in clinical trials and in service definition programs. Their use is prevalently aimed at assessing treatment quality and the support that the patient is receiving at a given moment of the research protocol. These data gathering tools prove especially valuable in qualitative research programs, such as ethnographic, netnographic, and digital ethnographic research. Medical anthropology techniques make it possible to gather emotional expressions, feelings, stories, assessments, as well as organized information gathered using cultural probes, such as diaries and mood boards. These are tools planned ad hoc to establish a conversation with the patient and collect the thoughts, values, and episodes that make it possible to appreciate the patient's life context.[30] The use of these tools is an advantage when coding results gathered and structurally organized throughout the research project, offering an interpretation key to the understanding of deep insights that the relationship with the patient makes it possible to develop. The main limitation of data gathering tools is their low predictive capacity: the limitation is shared by other similar tools and questionnaire to measure patients' quality of life (QoL).[31] Since behavior and context determinant data are gathered at a given time in the Patient's Journey, although they offer useful and necessary information, data are only referred to that precise moment and cannot be used to predict what the person's situation will be a few weeks later. As a result, the relative weight of the data has to be measured in relation to the aims they intend to pursue and to the practicality-usefulness of gathering new data sets at several moments of the Patient's Journey.

An NIH team (see above) developed a very interesting and advanced proposal on how to gather and process data on behavior and context determinants. ORBIT is a model that intends to overcome the lack of guidelines and protocols able to complete behavioral science knowledge in the standard protocol and clinical trial during Phase III.[32] The model was conceived and designed to deal with behavioral determinants in a large spectrum of NCDs: interventions may increase or decrease according to a path determined by the clinical context so as to generate the necessary evidence to test the treatment in a rigorous setting such as clinical trial Phase III. There are four phases in drug research, and the purpose of Phase III is to evaluate how the new medication works in comparison to existing medications for the same condition. The test is performed on a large sample of patients with the biological taxonomies identified in the previous two phases. If it is successful, then it is applied to a much large cohort in the same phase. According to the ORBIT model,

[29] Kingsley and Patel [20].

[30] Gaver et al. [21].

[31] https://www.who.int/tools/whoqol

[32] Czajkowski et al. [22].

the route to test behavior change is similar to the phases of clinical protocol to validate a new molecule or a new drug. Methods and techniques used during the treatment for risk prevention gather the data to depict life events, the patients' perceived experiences, and their proximity ecosystem. Furthermore, they make it possible to identify behavior risk factors, their combination, and the possible stratification of environmental, contextual, behavioral, social, and biological risk factors. According to precision medicine risk, risk stratification analysis is aimed at ranking risk factors on a personal basis and then possibly referring the individual case to homogenous clusters. However, it is a costly and long process, including the possibility of clustering individuals with similar risk factors. The possibility of designing secondary prevention programs for people with comparable risk factors and hierarchies cannot be ruled out. Precision medicine ought to develop practical solutions to identify common risk classes created by the incidence of various combinations of behavioral, environmental, and social context for each NCD. Admittedly, intervention models for specific clusters sharing behavior determinants are complex, especially when there are many possible combinations of risk factors. The aim is to identify clusters of individuals with homogenous characteristics measures risk factors that govern cluster variability. Risk factor measurement within homogenous groups can be validated using descriptive and inferential statistics. Cumulative risk assessment is a basic principle in the definition of intervention models: the greater the number of behavioral anomalies compared to the etiological models of NCDs, the greater is the risk to be managed with secondary prevention treatment.[33] A reduction of risk factors implies establishing risk factor hierarchies for each clinical situation. According to the intervention based on individual-centered approaches, one has to also consider the level of difficulty patients have in undertaking a corrective program for each behavior risk category.

One way to create subgroups—and therefore identify moderators—for a behavior risk treatment program is to group people according to their personal (subjective) ability to undertake a process within a preventive program. Subgroups contribute to determine the subjective ability of factors that concern the individual sphere, such as overall self-efficacy and agentivity (see Chap. 9). Furthermore, we have to consider context factors and the support the individual's proximity ecosystem can supply, such as a reliable relational network or belonging to associations, communities, or groups. Achieved ability is measured as the result of assessments by the patient and by program designers/implementers as part of admission to the secondary or tertiary prevention program. A case in point: two groups of patients with the same clinical picture for the risk factor of sedentary lifestyle are divided according to the degree of readiness in undergoing physical education programs and in adhering to organized physical exercise programs.[34] This makes it possible to judge the impact that a movement education program can have on the risk of devel-

[33] A similar criterion is used in algorithms to predict life expectancy.

[34] Resistance to following programs for moderators amounts to the patient judging that the risk factor is not "pliable" nor "modifiable."

oping cardiovascular disease. By clustering according to controllable moderator factors, it is very important to assess the effectiveness of intervention program in the early phases of the treatment. Randomized tests are not necessary for this purpose.[35] Readiness can easily be applied to other risk categories, such as the environmental and contextual determinants. For instance, if patients are grouped according to respiratory disease risk such as chronic obstructive pulmonary disease (COPD) and who live in very humid environments, and then compare them to those who live in environments with year-round well-controlled humidity, would make it possible to identify the weight of the environment program in the two groups.

Epigenetic studies also offer a great contribution to the definition of the principles used to build prevention models for behavior risk. Epigenomes are flexible, so if controlled and identified in time they can be reversed to the point they can be eliminated, as is the case of exposure of COPD patients to damp environments. Furthermore, patients may develop a specific expertise in avoiding damp environments. Epigenetic modifications become permanent if exposure is high or extended over time.[36] The aim of a secondary prevention program is therefore to identify modifiable risk factor target beforehand. These factors are likely to be the same that underlie the establishment of behavior phenotypes and identifiable clusters. The direction of any given risk factor depends on what risk factor it is.

Behavioral science has started to work on risk factor stratification (multifactorial risk) for clinical conditions that could become chronic: for example, positive results have been observed in risk reduction in obese patients for the prevention of Type 2 diabetes and breast cancer, by first treating some of the etiological behavioral risk factors. The ORBIT model was applied to obese insulin-resistant patients,[37] with a focus on lack of exercise (sedentariness), nutrition, and weight in this case. Likewise, in one of the pioneering research projects on diabetes prevention carried out in the United States, prediabetic treatment focused on weight loss, diet changes, and physical exercise.[38] Research included behavioral risk treatment by negotiated and agreed objectives, including possible modifications and adjustments in progress, the ways to manage fall in interest, and participation throughout the program. Participation reduced diabetes development by 58% compared to the placebo group, with a peak of 71% on over 60s. By comparison, the administration of metformin[39] reduced diabetes incidence by 31% and similar results were obtained in other countries. The Finnish results stand out where a 58% reduction of incidence with the

[35] According to this model, randomized controlled clinical trials are performed in Phase III of the intervention program on a large sample of participants. This differs from the ORBIT model, which does not include the use of "moderators" even in the early stages of a program. The proposal is consistent with the ORBIT model in conducting randomized trials in the later stages of the program.

[36] Lelièvre [23].

[37] Czajkowski et al., op. cit.

[38] Diabetes Prevention Program Research Group [24].

[39] Metformin is the drug of choice to treat Type 2 diabetes as it inhibits the formation of blood sugars and the absorption of diet sugars.

positive addition of fiber, fruit, and vegetables in nutrition, reduction of unsaturated fats, exercise, and a loss of body weight.[40] Results linked to lifestyle changes were considerably better than those obtained with metformin, as well as with prediabetic patients with impaired glucose tolerance (IGT). In this cluster of prediabetic patients, the annual conversion risk to diabetes dropped to 4.8% for those who were following preventive lifestyle change programs compared to 7.8% in patients who opted for the drug.[41]

The effectiveness of actions to improve lifestyle and prevent the conversion of risk factors into disease has been widely and repeatedly proven by scientific literature: nutrition control, exercise, body mass, alcohol and tobacco, the quality of sleep, and the quality of life play a key role in all NCD etiologies. Behavior and environment risk factors can be changed if appropriately dealt with in secondary prevention. Furthermore, opposition to prevention and the ways in which risk factors are identified and perceived are the result of their risk culture and of how they are identified and perceived by the person's proximity circle. There is also a degree of variability and difference for each risk factor due to the person's ability to self-regulate risk factors and follow programs in time. Normally, personalized approaches are sought when the risk target can be addressed in detail, as is the case of targeted screening. The limited understanding of behavior risk factors is also the result of the different combination of risk factors (heterogenesis) and of the early secondary prevention models.

Early onset and premenopausal breast cancer risk factors are an interesting case and maybe a point of reference in coming years also for other etiologies. The model is the result of a meta-analysis of research carried out on several cohorts of women over the past 25 years. A team of UK scientists conducted a comprehensive scientific literature review and developed an analysis for the categorization of risk factors.[42] The classification did not only focus on the relative contribution of each genetic risk factor or to their body-build in relation to behavior risk factors but also concerned the makeup of modifiable risk factors through behavior and choices. The review indicates that breast cancer in premenopausal women under 40s accounts for 12% of all cases. Unlike previously believed, when comparing women who exercise more than others, regular physical activity led to a significant 23% reduction in the onset of cancer. A regular quantity of physical activity had a significant preventive effect while apparently the intensity of the physical effort did not lead to an improvement. The relationship between the adiposity marker aka body mass index (BMI) and the onset of breast cancer was counterintuitive: the higher the BMI the lower is the risk. However, there are two counterbalancing effects: if the body mass increase is concentrated around the midriff, the risk of breast cancer increases. Overweight entails other risk factors and obesity adds cardiovascular risks to the breast cancer ones. A meta-analysis on alcohol use shows evidence of a strong association

[40] Tuomilehto et al. [25].

[41] Tuomilehto et al., op cit.

[42] Daly et al. [26].

between the use and breast cancer, which increases if associated to the use of tobacco. We should not be surprised that passive smoking has an even stronger impact than inhaling smoke directly. Lastly, it is interesting to observe the association between night work and the production of melatonin and the consequent reduction of its cancer suppressive function due to the regulatory function of estrogens. The model of the early onset breast cancer risk factors is a very good base for secondary prevention programs and can be used to establish a scalable approach to increase knowledge of the characterization of behavior risk factors to the point a targeted, adaptive action model can be attained as the NIH centers of excellence hope for.[43] Where risk factors are multidimensional and operate in more than one direction, the model must define the following for every NCD etiology: (a) priority ranking of changeable risk factor targets and (b) target moderators for each individual and homogenous group, so as to establish a feasibility program. These two methodological milestones can be achieved gradually following repeated the (iterative) cycles of the clinic test steps (see Table 11.1).[44]

Step 1 is the "program setup." This is where the necessary resources and the remit of the macro-program are defined. The first part (Cycle a) will benefit from the results of scientific research and, if possible, with the contribution of meta-analysis, epigenetics, and evidence factors available within the communities of patients or other local organized communities. The protocol of ethnographic research, participant selection screeners, and the criteria to involve associations of professionals, communities, and groups with potential risk factors are also listed in Cycle a of Step 1. The criteria for inclusion and exclusion of participant profiles in the pilot program are selected with the project stakeholders that will also have to consider the constraints of the acceleration project in relation to the health ecosystem characteristics.

The second part (Cycle b) sees the contribution of ethnographic research and the analysis of the health ecosystem. It is aimed at homing in on some hypotheses and assumptions that will be the criteria to establish priority ranking and moderators. Ethnographic research is the basis of the behavior model, the techniques and methods to use in the above-mentioned pilot project. The results of this phase converge into a model of behavioral and environmental risks, which in turn helps define action in Step 2. During this step (Step 2, Cycle c), initial tests will be carried out in parallel in several countries or locations in a country. The aim is to adapt the model of risk factors to the sample of participants and to locate the program with success indicators. Furthermore, local partners will be identified, and methods decided; data models for the establishment of the program data bank will also be set up as will success indicators for each risk factor included in the model.

[43] Czajkowski et al., op. cit.

[44] This model is made public for the first time in the present text. Design activities such as those described in the model have been carried out in multiple commercial projects. Funding proposals are currently underway to apply the model in a cardiovascular disease prevention and early detection program.

Table 11.1 Action programs by step and cycle to prevent behavioral and context risk

Cycles		Aims	Scope	Methods	Milestones and results
Step 1 Setup of the intervention program	a	Definition of resources and assessment of evidence for the etiological framework	Definition, scope, and targets/ ambitions of the program	Literature meta-analysis, epigenetic studies, and eliciting community knowledge	Ethnographic research protocol and ethical approval for inclusion/ exclusion criteria
	b	Analyzing the health ecosystem and the behavioral and environmental determinants	Defining assumptions and project hypothesis. Choice of digital technologies	Ethnographic research, qualitative research tools, and ethnographic probes	Risk factor priorities and moderators. Definition of the methods to adopt in the pilot program
Step 2 Launching the pilot program	c	Defining environmental risk models. Choosing the technological support	Tailoring and locating the pilot program in the selected countries. Identifying local partners and adapting the digital platform	Selecting, choosing, and preparing techniques to strengthen behavioral, contextual, and environmental determinants	Clustering logic and moderators. Implementation plan for the pilot project. Models for data and success indicators.
	d	Validating the stratified multifactorial risk model for the etiological frame	Validating the local risk model. Validating technologies and tools	Participatory workshop sessions	Validating clustering logics and moderators. Validating tools and technological equipment
	e	Gathering parts of evidence in the field	Selecting and onboarding participants, experts, and professionals	Completion of the Pilot Program and ongoing monitoring	Program results using success indicators. Recommendations for the subsequent steps and highlighting program limitations

(continued)

Table 11.1 (continued)

Cycles		Aims	Scope	Methods	Milestones and results
Step 3 Launching the large-scale program	f	Planning large scale data gathering	Selecting and onboarding participants and professions to complete clinical studies	Preparing randomized trials	Validating clinical studies and program efficiency over time on a scale
	g	Gathering data on a large scale	Publicize results and recommendation on program limitations	Implementation of study results using specific moderator sampling techniques	Publishing scientific results
Step 4 Ongoing monitoring of the action program	h	Monitoring program performance after the launch	Ongoing data collection as results come in	Using platforms for automatic data collection and targeted alert systems	Factoring the monitoring system and data bank for action and research programs

Participated workshops will be held to develop multifactorial risk models, contributing and validating the criteria whereby participants are distributed by risk factors and moderators chosen (Step 2, Cycle d). Professionals, patient association, local communities, and possible program funders will also have to be involved in the workshop sessions.

The third cycle (Step 2, Cycle e) is when the pilot study itself takes place, at the same time in more places and with several homogenous groups. The aim is to gather evidence in the field and compare samples of pilot program participants. This cycle is aimed at selecting participants for the program and expert professionals for the implementation of the pilot project. The central team of the program will avail itself of local teams of experts to monitor program execution and success indicators. The final report will include the pilot program results and the recommendations for the launch of the large-scale program stating program limitations.

The last two steps of the program for the prevention of context and behavior risks, and to contrast the growth in the number of chronic NCDs, respectively, concern the launch of large-scale programs (Step 3) and the ongoing monitoring of the program (Step 4). Step 3 tests specific research questions on combinations of risk factors. Exclusion criteria will also be defined in the course of Step 3 and expedients to manage swifter and more flexible routes and risk factors with a low impact on the success of the program. The choice of controlled randomized studies guarantees a more rigorous scientific method of the programs to improve lifestyles and strengthen good habits. It is currently possible to count on advanced techniques to manage multivariable programs according to a sequential and constructive logic.[45] Scalar

[45] Seewald et al. [27].

approaches, adaptable according to well-defined targets with the possibility of improving the action protocols in the course of the program itself, even on an individual basis, make the aim of transforming health-care systems with the help of behavior[46] science and design more realistic.

11.3 Participation, Data, and Automation

As will have become clear, the model we are proposing is based on a premise, i.e., that the acceleration of sustainable innovation for the transformation of health-care systems can be programmed and can be implemented on a global multicenter scale. These are the reasons why we need inclusive participatory models based on scientific premises and implemented by professionals used to and specialized in working in transdisciplinary teams. The design of IT aids, technological platforms, and wearables requires design skills even before software expertise: specific technologies require ongoing adjustments to guarantee consistency with programs, integration of technology in participants' daily lives, just as major technology product do. Participatory and inclusive models are the tenets of behavior design and sustainable innovation. Managing prevention programs based on behavior models in the community of health-care professionals (HCP) and families is a sine qua non for the development of sustainable health-care systems. Context can also increase the influence of patient associations. Organized communities and patient associations are now going beyond traditional advocacy and are becoming proactive: they play a key role in orienting health-care systems toward prevention, inclusion, and customizing. Within the patient communities, the variety of situations (heterogeneity) of chronic disease etiology can be better appreciated, thus giving it the appropriate consideration in identifying prevention solutions. New community-based approaches are also developing, the so-called Citizen Science with the participation of scientific communities of medical staff.[47]

Lastly, as for costs and who has to pay for the program, answers are country specific. Currently, in countries such as the United States, existing business models are prevalently built on disease treatment and care, while there is little or no offer of services to improve lifestyles and actively promote health.[48] All this is consistent with nonsustainable trends, especially if the United States want to lead research investments for many years to come. In Europe there appear to be a few serious intentions to systemically change course. The route has been marked and acceleration programs may play a key role.

In conclusion, the narrative that suggests we need masses of data to develop predictive models is misleading and misplaced. Currently available technologies to

---

[46] Hekler et al., op. cit.

[47] Palmer [28]. Also see: Marks et al. [29].

[48] https://www.christenseninstitute.org/publications/doh-business-models/

support programs are undoubtedly useful and favor participation and active awareness, support program remote monitoring, automate onboarding in prevention programs, allocate tasks in programs, and perform many other functions. The suggestion outlined in the present chapter is to build data models starting from ecosystemic perspectives and creates the conditions for a widespread prevention culture in the sphere of health supported by programs with the clear aim of gather data during program execution, with the participants' consent and participation, to promote individual, collective, and system advantages.

Highlights

- The lack of social integration and social status of people are precursors of the context strongly influencing behavioral options in everyday life.
- The traditional political tools is not enough to solve the problems of behavioral and biological risk among disadvantaged groups.
- Systemic prevention throughout life and in every interface between members of the public and the health service is highly necessary to reduce the social burden of all forms of chronic diseases.
- The ecosystemic perspective, favoring cooperating, data sharing, and the progress of an experimental approach in real life is the convergent model of addressing health prevention.
- The inclusion of behavior and context determinants in clinical research aimed at precision medicine and prevention is a realistic cutting-edge aim.
- Methods and techniques used during the treatment for risk prevention gather the data to depict life events, the patients' perceived experiences, and their proximity ecosystem.
- UCD methods make it possible to identify behavior risk factors, their combination, and the possible stratification of environmental, contextual, behavioral, social, and biological risk factors.
- Risk stratification analysis is aimed at ranking risk factors on a personal basis and then possibly referring the individual case to homogenous clusters.
- The possibility of designing secondary prevention programs for people with comparable risk factors and hierarchies cannot be ruled out.
- Cumulative risk assessment is a basic principle in the definition of intervention models: the greater the number of behavioral anomalies compared to the etiological models of NCDs, the greater is the risk to be managed with secondary prevention treatment.
- A reduction of risk factors implies establishing risk factor hierarchies for each clinical situation.
- The level of difficulty patients have in undertaking a corrective program for each behavior risk category is a key indicator for intervention programs.
- Context factors and the support the individual's proximity ecosystem can supply, such as a reliable relational network or belonging to associations, communities, or groups, should be assessed before the program implementation as part of admission to the secondary or tertiary prevention program.

- Clustering according to controllable moderator factors is very important to assess the effectiveness of intervention programs in the early phases of the treatment.
- Readiness can easily be applied to other risk categories, such as the environmental and contextual determinants.
- The aim of a secondary prevention program is to identify modifiable risk factor target beforehand.
- Behavioral science has started to work on risk factor stratification (multifactorial risk) for clinical conditions that could become chronic.
- Behavior and environment risk factors can be changed if appropriately dealt with in secondary prevention.
- Opposition to prevention and the ways in which risk factors are identified and perceived are the result of the risk culture and of how they are identified and perceived by the person's proximity circle.
- The degree of variability and difference for each risk factor is due to the person's ability to self-regulate risk factors and follow programs in time.
- The limited understanding of behavior risk factors is also the result of the different combination of risk factors (heterogenesis) and of the early secondary prevention models.
- Where risk factors are multidimensional and operate in more than one direction, the model must define (a) priority ranking of changeable risk factor targets and (b) target moderators for each individual and homogenous group, so as to establish a feasibility program.
- The methodological milestones of the intervention program can be achieved gradually following the (iterative) cycles of the clinic test steps.
- Scalar approaches, adaptable according to well-defined targets with the possibility of improving the action protocols in the course of the program itself, even on an individual basis, make the aim of transforming health-care systems with the help of behavior science and design more realistic.
- The acceleration of sustainable innovation for the transformation of health-care systems can be programmed and can be implemented on a global multi-center scale.
- Participatory and inclusive models are the tenets of behavior design and sustainable innovation.
- Managing prevention programs based on behavior models in the community of health-care professionals (HCP) and families is a sine qua non for the development of sustainable health-care systems.
- The narrative that suggests we need masses of data to develop predictive models is misleading and misplaced.
- Data models should be built starting from ecosystemic perspectives to create the conditions for a widespread prevention culture in the sphere of health supported by programs with the clear aim of gather data during program execution, with the participants' consent and participation, to promote individual, collective, and system advantages.

References

1. Govindaraju, D., Atzmon, G., & Barzilai, N. (2015, March). Genetics, lifestyle and longevity: Lessons from centenarians. *Applied & Translational Genomics, 4*, 23–32. https://doi.org/10.1016/J.ATG.2015.01.001
2. Vineis, P., Avendano-Pabon, M., Barros, H., Bartley, M., Carmeli, C., Carra, L., Chadeau-Hyam, M., Costa, G., Delpierre, C., D'Errico, A., Fraga, S., Giles, G., Goldberg, M., Kelly-Irving, M., Kivimaki, M., Lepage, B., Lang, T., Layte, R., MacGuire, F., Mackenbach, J. P., Marmot, M., McCrory, C., Milne, R. L., Muennig, P., Nusselder, W., Petrovic, D., Polidoro, S., Ricceri, F., Robinson, O., Stringhini, S., & Zins, M. (2020). Special report: The biology of inequalities in health: The Lifepath consortium. *Frontiers in Public Health, 8*, 118. https://doi.org/10.3389/fpubh.2020.00118
3. Snyder-Mackler, N., et al. (2020). *Science, 368*, eaax9553. https://doi.org/10.1126/science.aax9553
4. Loewenstein, G., Asch, D. A., Friedman, J. Y., Melichar, L. A., & Volpp, K. (2012). Can behavioural economics make us healthier? *BMJ, 344*, e3482.
5. Prainsack, B. (2020). The value of healthcare data: To nudge, or not? *Policy Studies, 41*(5), 547–562.
6. Loewenstein, G., Hagmann, D., Schwartz, J., Ericson, K., Kessler, J. B., Bhargava, S., & Zikmund-Fisher, B. J. (2017). A behavioral blueprint for improving health care policy. *Behavioral Science & Policy, 5*(1), 53–66.
7. Oliveira, M. C., Marcelin, G., Gautier, E. L., & Ferreira, A. V. M. (2022). Editorial: *Inflammation in obesity: From physiological to pathological aspects. Frontiers in Nutrition, 9*, 870131. https://doi.org/10.3389/fnut.2022.870131
8. Nutbeam, D. (2000). Health literacy as a public health goal: A challenge for contemporary health education and communication strategies into the 21st century. *Health Promotion International, 15*, 259–267.
9. Fleary, S., Heffer, R., Lisako McKyer, E., & Taylor, A. (2013). A parent-focused pilot intervention to increase parent health literacy and healthy lifestyle choices for young children and families. *International Scholarly Research Notices, 2013*, Article ID 619389. https://doi.org/10.5402/2013/619389
10. Nutbeam, D., McGill, B., & Premkumar, P. (2018, October 1). Improving health literacy in community populations: A review of progress. *Health Promotion International, 33*(5), 901–911. https://doi.org/10.1093/heapro/dax015. PMID: 28369557.
11. Welch, H. G., Schwartz, L., & Woloshin, S. (2011). *Overdiagnosed: Making people sick in the pursuit of health.* Beacon Press.
12. Brodersen, J., Schwartz, L. M., Heneghan, C., O'Sullivan, J. W., Aronson, J. K., & Woloshin, S. (2018). Overdiagnosis: What it is and what it isn't. *BMJ Evidence-Based Medicine, 23*, 1–3. https://doi.org/10.1136/ebmed-2017-110886. PMID: 29367314.
13. Diamandis, E. P. (2015). The hundred-person wellness project and Google's baseline study: Medical revolution or unnecessary and potentially harmful over-testing? *BMC Medicine, 13*, 5. https://doi.org/10.1186/s12916-014-0239-6. PMID:25575898.
14. Hofmann, B., & Welch, H. G. (2017). New diagnostic tests: More harm than good. *BMJ, 358*, j3314. https://doi.org/10.1136/bmj.j3314. PMID:28720607.
15. Kaczmarek, E. (2019, March). How to distinguish medicalization from over-medicalization? *Medicine, Health Care, and Philosophy, 22*(1), 119–128. https://doi.org/10.1007/s11019-018-9850-1. PMID: 29951940; PMCID: PMC6394498.
16. Nielsen, L., Riddle, M., King, J. W., NIH Science of Behavior Change Implementation Team, Aklin, W. M., Chen, W., Clark, D., Collier, E., Czajkowski, S., Esposito, L., Ferrer, R., Green, P., Hunter, C., Kehl, K., King, R., Onken, L., Simmons, J. M., Stoeckel, L., Stoney, C., Tully, L., & Weber, W. (2018, February). The NIH Science of Behavior Change Program: Transforming the science through a focus on mechanisms of change. *Behaviour Research and Therapy,*

101, 3–11. https://doi.org/10.1016/j.brat.2017.07.002. Epub 2017 July 6. PMID: 29110885; PMCID: PMC5756516.

17. Hekler, E., Tiro, J. A., Hunter, C. M., & Nebeker, C. (2020, November). Precision health: The role of the social and behavioral sciences in advancing the vision. *Annals of Behavioral Medicine, 54*(11), 805–826. https://doi.org/10.1093/abm/kaaa018
18. Göttgens, I., & Oertelt-Prigione, S. (2021, December 6). The application of human-centered design approaches in health research and innovation: A narrative review of current practices. *JMIR mHealth and uHealth, 9*(12), e28102. https://doi.org/10.2196/28102. PMID: 34874893; PMCID: PMC8691403.
19. Bazzano, A. N., Yan, S. D., Martin, J., et al. (2020). Improving the reporting of health research involving design: A proposed guideline. *BMJ Global Health, 5*, e002248. https://doi.org/10.1136/bmjgh-2019-002248
20. Kingsley, C., & Patel, S. (2017, April). Patient-reported outcome measures and patient-reported experience measures. *BJA Education, 17*(4), 137–144. https://doi.org/10.1093/bjaed/mkw060
21. Gaver, W., Dunne, A., & Pacenti, E. (1999, January/February). Design: Cultural probes. *Interactions, 6*, 1.
22. Czajkowski, S. M., Powell, L. H., Adler, N., Naar-King, S., Reynolds, K. D., Hunter, C. M., Laraia, B., Olster, D. H., Perna, F. M., Peterson, J. C., Epel, E., Boyington, J. E., & Charlson, M. E. (2015, October). From ideas to efficacy: The ORBIT model for developing behavioral treatments for chronic diseases. *Health Psychology, 34*(10), 971–982. https://doi.org/10.1037/hea0000161. Epub 2015 Feb 2. PMID: 25642841; PMCID: PMC4522392.
23. Lelièvre, S. A. (2021, November 1). Can the epigenome contribute to risk stratification for cancer onset? *NAR Cancer, 3*(4), zcab043. https://doi.org/10.1093/narcan/zcab043. PMID: 34734185; PMCID: PMC8559165.
24. Diabetes Prevention Program Research Group. (1999). The diabetes prevention program: Design and methods for a clinical trial in the prevention of type 2 diabetes. *Diabetes Care, 22*, 623–634.
25. Tuomilehto, J., Lindstrom, J., Eriksson, J. G., Valle, T. T., Hamalainen, H., Ilanne-Parikka, P., Keinanen-Kiukaanniemi, S., Laakso, M., Louheranta, A., Rastas, M., Salminen, V., & Uusitupa, M. (2001). Prevention of type 2 diabetes mellitus by changes in lifestyle among subjects with impaired glucose tolerance. *The New England Journal of Medicine, 344*, 1343–1350.
26. Daly, A. A., Rolph, R., Cutress, R. I., & Copson, E. R. (2021, April). A review of modifiable risk factors in young women for the prevention of breast cancer. *Breast Cancer (Dove Medical Press), 13*(13), 241–257. https://doi.org/10.2147/BCTT.S268401. PMID: 33883932; PMCID: PMC8053601.
27. Seewald, N. J., Hackworth, O., & Almirall, D. (2021). Sequential, multiple assignment, randomized trials (SMART). In S. Piantadosi & C. L. Meinert (Eds.), *Principles and practice of clinical trials*. Springer. https://doi.org/10.1007/978-3-319-52677-5_280-1
28. Palmer, V. J. (2020, January 10). The participatory zeitgeist in health care: It is time for a science of participation. *Journal of Participatory Medicine, 12*(1), e15101. https://doi.org/10.2196/15101. PMID: 33064092; PMCID: PMC7434075.
29. Marks, L., Laird, Y., Trevena, H., Smith, B. J., & Rowbotham, S. (2022). A scoping review of citizen science approaches in chronic disease prevention. *Frontiers in Public Health, 10*. https://www.frontiersin.org/articles/10.3389/fpubh.2022.743348

Chapter 12
Thinking as Behavior Scientists, Acting as Designers

In September 1975, I was an eager second year student at the University of Padua, a conservative Northern Italian town with a great university founded in the year 1222. My department was a fervent center of critical studies, open to the future of humanities and science. I had just completed my first year and my favorite professors had already given me the initial critical lesson that I still remember. Laboratory research—they said—is the most credible way we know to understand our cognitive and behavior processes, although we are not sure how to best use this knowledge and generalize it in real-life situations. That was the time when the ecological validity of experimental research was making inroads in the critical minds of Europe's research laboratories. Nowadays we can say that the ambitious aim to develop accurate generalizable knowledge to real-life contexts has been achieved and repeatedly proved beyond doubts, as this book describes. Humanistic, anthropologic, psychological, and sociological research can supply the scientific evidence, data, and behavior models to base intervention programs and facilitate behavior and culture modification favoring sustainable societies and lifestyles.

This book suggests that the alliance between humanities and design opens new key perspectives for change and innovation: shared challenges for sustainability and innovation. We can succeed if we leave behind us the innovation models that neither state nor document the intentions of the behavior and cultural changes they pursue. New challenges require considering the different levels of maturity, among cultures, favoring evolution and building reliable and sustainable reference models.

Innovative solutions must be premised by a clear statement and demonstrations of the value(s) they put forward on progress and advances in individual, group, and community well-being according to the Sustainable Innovation Readiness Ladder (SIRL). Thinking like behavior scientists and acting as designers indicates widespread experimental perspectives to accelerate our action in a fundamental moment of our evolution. It is up to us to do our part. The work that behavior and culture scientists can carry out in cooperation with designers concerns the undertaking of sustainable innovation over anonymous inventions for the consequences they entail.

M. Visciola, *Sustainable Innovation*,
https://doi.org/10.1007/978-3-031-18751-3_12

Innovation is sustainable only if it answers the primary goal of preventing and correcting the social consequences of bounded rationality, by promoting active awareness, widespread involvement, and collaboration as enabling factors for creative development.

This book is a crossroads that can be found at:

www.sustainableinnovationreadiness.org

Stay tuned!

MIX
Papier aus verantwortungsvollen Quellen
Paper from responsible sources
FSC® C105338

If you have any concerns about our products,
you can contact us on
ProductSafety@springernature.com

In case Publisher is established outside the EU,
the EU authorized representative is:
Springer Nature Customer Service Center GmbH
Europaplatz 3, 69115 Heidelberg, Germany

Printed by Libri Plureos GmbH
in Hamburg, Germany